I0826199

Praise for Decisionability

"Decisionability is a wonderful book ... not a cold, calculating method that would make you a decision-making automaton but rather a fully human approach that recognizes emotional and rational factors. What makes the book especially wonderful is that the intelligence comes with a large helping of humor that had me laughing out loud as well as taking notes."
Jonathan Peck MA, President and futurist: Institute of Alternative Futures, Washington DC

"As someone who spent and continues to spend his life trying to help individuals and companies come to optimal outcomes, what strikes me about the book is that it transforms the act of reaching a decision from a burden to an opportunity. Steve has created a framework that is not only intellectually rich but a framework that is fun to think about."
George M Milne PhD, Venture Partner, Radius Ventures, formerly Executive Vice President Pfizer

"From the complex decisions involved in biotech investing or developing new medicines, to the everyday "which lane should I drive in?" decision, we all can benefit from improving skills in decision-making. Steve's insightful and engaging book really does enable the reader to develop new decision-abilities that have immediate and practical application. The best decision you make today will be to read this book." **Liam Ratcliffe, MD PhD, New Leaf Venture Partners, formerly Senior Vice President, Pfizer**

"I wanted to respond and tell you how much I enjoyed Decisionability and learned from it. Also as a writer who has spent months at a time at a desk one of the things about your book is the apparent pleasure you got in writing it...that comes across..."
Bob Belinoff, President and Creative Director, Digital Workshop, Albuquerque

"This book is a must for leaders steering a course through the dynamic post recession minefield".
Damian McKinney, Chief Executive Officer: McKinney-Rogers, Barbados, former Lieutenant-Colonel, Royal Marines

"My agency, US Army Corps of Engineers, is using decision-analytical tools for complex engineering systems. The Decisionability approach will allow readers to structure information and improve decision in everyday life"
Igor Linkov, PhD, Army Corps of Engineers.

DECISION*ABILITY*®

The Skill to Make Your Decisions Productive, Practical and Painless

Stephen Alaric Williams MD PhD

With a foreword and contributions by
Declan P Doogan MD

Published by Decisionability LLC, 4817 6th Street, Boulder CO

ISBN 978-0-615-38589-1

First edition, 2010

If you have any comments or experiences to share after reading this book I would be interested to hear about them. Please email correspondence to: Decisionability@hotmail.com

Dedicated to the memory of my father, Michael Williams, a lifelong maximizer.

Acknowledgements

I am not claiming to have been born intuitively gifted at decisions. Perhaps if I had been, I wouldn't have seen the need for this book and would not have known how to write it down for other people. But no, I don't count myself as a in that category. What I am good at is taking things apart, dismantling and analyzing them, creating the stepwise logic that I need – for myself to understand how they work. And then I put them back together – and sometimes I don't even have any bits left over. Because of this de-convoluting journey of learning there have been many people who helped me along the way, too numerous to mention. Sorry to all the people I left out. There are a few who I have singled out as being especially influential in the creation of this manuscript.

First thanks go to Declan Doogan MD, not only for writing the foreword but for inventing the name – Decisionability, and especially the Decisionability triangle concept. Perhaps most importantly Declan believed in me and continually encouraged me to generate new ideas. When faced with particularly difficult problems he would say "what would Decisionability do?" and we found it an inspiring and creative challenge. We also worked together when developing many of the ideas in the book and on the practical testing of them. I am proud to have been able to call him my business partner.

Secondly, I would never have written this book without inspiration from David Slavin MD who introduced me to many important concepts such as tolerability of risk and mission leadership. His experience in nuclear regulation was invaluable – the "how safe is safe enough" saying led to my "how good is good enough" concept, and "knowing where you are not" was incorporated into the satisficing section.

Another important group I'd like to recognize is the people who taught me mission leadership which I adapted for every day decisions in the format of the purpose statement: Damian McKinney and his consultancy at McKinney Rogers and Stephen Bungay of Ashridge Strategic Management Center.

I am also indebted to Tim Rohde who made many helpful editorial comments and who was the first person to make me think that this book could actually be something special when he didn't want to give back the proofs.

Thanks to the anonymized donors of the examples in the book from my personal and business life.

Finally, thanks to Elizabeth, my wife who supported me throughout the writing process and tolerated my mind being constantly focused on this obsession.

Stephen Alaric Williams
July 2010

Foreword
Declan P Doogan MD

This is a book for professionals, students and Everyman. If you think about it, we make hundreds of decisions per day. Many are at a sub conscious level, but for the rest where we make a conscious decision this book helps to explain different approaches to reaching the best decision in the circumstances.

We are assaulted by information in such a way that we often find it difficult to know how to weigh the importance of different factors. This book will help you, the decision maker, work out when a decision approach is "good enough" - a powerful method to help you manage the information needed and avoid unnecessary analysis. It can also guide when <u>more</u> analysis is needed. Importantly this system is flexible and can be influenced by your personality. It can provide insights as to your default mode such as gut feeling or systematic analysis and when either approach is appropriate. The net effect is that when the system is used much of the anxiety of the uncertainty around decision making can be mitigated. It also enables a better dialogue between affected parties - this is equally true in business as in daily life.

Steve Williams, a friend and colleague and I developed the approach since leaving our employment in a large pharmaceutical company. We were struck by the different forces operating in such an environment and how many sub optimal decisions were made. We concluded that many decisions can be informed by three types of factors, Technical Human and Economic and that a new system of cost, risk value optimization could be developed. The ideas were further developed and simplified for improving daily life decisions.

Although this is not a reference manual, we hope that you will re-use sections repeatedly as you find your decision quality has improved and those affected are more satisfied. We would also be pleased to receive real examples of where the system helped make better decisions – or where you find that it didn't.

Steve read the literature on decision theory and has done a lot of the heavy lifting for the reader. This book is not biased by the desire of the author to select only certain evidence as the Decisionability method is made even more powerful in the face of all historical evidence. There are fascinating insights which can make you question your own bias. For example Steve unpacks the evidence on the OJ Simpson case and how each of the factors contributes to probability of guilt or innocence. We draw on our medical experience to provide examples where parents can come to a position on whether a child should be vaccinated or when there is enough information to make certain health related decisions. There is also guidance on decisions at a macroeconomic level over which you have no control but you can begin to understand whether or not the political judgments have merit. The reader will find these and the other examples intriguing and humorous.

It is also worth pausing for a moment to ask yourself why you are reading this foreword. In particular you are already using your Decisionability if you are reflecting if this investment of time was worth it and it helped you decide whether or not to read on!

Declan Doogan is CEO of Amarin Pharmaceuticals Inc, visiting professor at Harvard School of Public Health, professor at Glasgow University and he also spent 20 years at Pfizer Inc, latterly as Worldwide Head of Development

Contents

Chapter 1

How Decisionability can help you every day.

Regret.
Guilt.
Overload.
Failure.
Blame.
Anxiety.
Exasperation.
Frustration.

These feelings are often caused by a need for improved Decisionability. If you feel some of them and want to do something about it, or if you simply want to make decisions more productively, then this straightforward and systematic guide to improving your skills is for you.

The fundamental problem

Making decisions is inevitably part of your life. Some of your abilities are hard-wired: humans have evolved pretty-good inbuilt "heuristics", mental short-cuts to efficient decisions. These improve as you grow, expand your logical reasoning abilities and develop your personal experience of what decisions did or did not succeed. The problem is that your inbuilt methods are indeed quick and familiar, but they have inherent biases: "now" beats "later", anecdotes beat data, the perceived likelihood of rare but serious events is over-amplified by dread, and personal trust of an individual beats statistics. Credit card debt, failure to vaccinate children against measles and spurious breast-implant litigation are some examples of the adverse results of such bias. Perhaps this weakness reflects the environment millions of years ago in which these mental tools evolved and became genetically hard-wired for the purpose of protecting and growing small tribes of early humans. Perhaps it is simply a limitation of our brains' computational power if the complexity exceeds our capability to process multi-dimensional data.

Whatever the cause of the bias, in the modern world where there is data and knowledge overload, if you rely on instinctive approaches and personal logic you won't feel that you are effectively responding to the opportunities and threats you face. Yet if you routinely try to utilize all the knowledge available, every task can become over-complex and frustrating. Either way, the outcome is personal anguish, stress and guilt.

Fortunately it doesn't have to be so. You can balance the scorecard and solve these issues with a variety of simple and sophisticated decision-making tools. But do you know what they are and how to use them? Do you know anyone who does? If you don't know them do you feel guilty or stressed about decisions? If you do use them, do you know when they are better or worse than your inbuilt instincts and heuristics? Perhaps most importantly do you know when <u>not</u> to use an intensive method because a simple method is "good enough?"

Decisionability is the skill to make your decisions productive, practical and painless

The fundamental thesis of this book is that you can improve the productivity of your every-day decision-making by learning simple disciplines, principles, shortcuts, tricks and arithmetic: methods that don't require a computer model. This is not simply requiring you to increase your effort or to make things more rigorous and complicated. In fact it is just as often the opposite – making less effort with less complexity – because productivity by definition implies getting the most out of your decision for the least input. In other words you will learn when less is less, when more is more, when less is more and when more is less. Phew!

Decisionability enables you to assess:

- **When less is less**
- **When less is more**
- **When more is less**
- **When more is more**

Fortunately, Decisionability is easy to learn and you will find that it reduces the wasted effort of over-engineering a decision, eliminates the stress of attempting to find unnecessary information and attenuates the guilt that accompanies failure. The Decisionability system is flexible enough to compliment your personality; as Dan Ariely points out in "Predictably Irrational" you might be a habitual "maximizer" – that is, you seek the best for every decision. Unfortunately you are unlikely to be happy about this: the stress of dedication to complexity and always seeking perfection when it is not possible can cause you to put off decisions or be miserable about making them. Alternatively you might be a habitual "satisficer" – making "good enough" and quick decisions using your instinctive heuristics without seeking the best outcome. While you are likely to be happier as a satisficer, this reliance on the simplest decision methods is inappropriate when information is abundant and the decision is of high value if successful, or high harm if unsuccessful. Whichever your personality type, this book will help you know when to depend on the strength of your instinct and when to substitute something more appropriate to the situation you face.

I am not going to pretend that you will find this to be a lighthearted narrative, although some of it is. This is not "mental popcorn" and I am not Malcolm Gladwell so you will not be able to "blink" your way out of this task. Developing and practicing these decision making skills and disciplines is an investment of time and effort, but it is not difficult and you might even find it fun and interesting. Even if I am delusional about the fun factor, this work is an appropriate response to the quote below from Michael LeGault's "Think":

"As our intellectual framework for perceiving and assessing the world becomes more stunted and fragile, we rely more on ideology, perceived knowledge, conventional wisdom and blind faith to make our way through life".

Take the quote as a challenge: do you want this to be you?
Is this you already? Do you want to own the weapons to fight back?

Take the simple quiz on the next page to assess your need.

Decisionability quiz: answer "yes" or "no"; count the number of your "yes" answers

1. I always seek the best decision by carefully considering every possible alternative
2. My life is dominated by rules and others' decisions so I have very little need to decide for myself
3. I often feel overwhelmed by the choices I have to make
4. I feel guilty or regretful about many past decisions
5. I put off making key decisions because the information is incomplete and I dread being wrong
6. I hate committees because their decisions are often the lowest common denominator
7. I pride myself on always being fast and decisive
8. I only need my brain to decide, calculations and models aren't necessary
9. If things didn't turn out the way I wanted it is a clear signal to me that my decision was wrong
10. I don't know what a heuristic really is and I don't care

The correct answer for each question should be "no". For some questions that is obvious, but probably not for many of them. The rationale is explained in Appendix 1 on page 309 at the end of the book.

- If you scored 0-3 "yes" answers, you either cheated or you already have terrific Decisionability; put the book down and take a nap.
- If you scored 3-6 "yes" answers, you would benefit significantly from the book
- If you have more than 6 "yes" answers, don't put the book down until you have finished!

Why is this book different?

You may well ask: surely this is a well-trodden path with many self-help and business books already available that will similarly help anyone make better decisions? Indeed there are plenty of existing books on decision making and they range from entertaining rubbish, through wonderful philosophy to academic texts. Unfortunately, the only common message is that contradictions abound; for every book that makes an assertion in one direction, there is another that makes the opposite.

For example, one common assertion is that your brain is a "giant computer" that subconsciously reaches the right decision effortlessly: Malcolm Gladwell in "Blink" promises you "the power of thinking without thinking" and Jonah Lehrer makes the same assertion in "How We Decide", proposing that you should leave complex decisions entirely to your emotional [subconscious] brain. Well I'm sorry but aside from the application of heuristics to very specific situations I just don't buy this theory that the "unconscious brain is a reliable and validated technology that beats everything else for making complex decisions". I've spent my career testing new technologies and fantastic though the brain is, the data presented just don't support the assertion. For example, when art experts spot a "fake" work of art within a few seconds, you are told in Gladwell's "Blink" that it is evidence of such instant computation. But these experts took years to develop their expertise and you don't know how many fake works of art they miss, or how many true relics they falsely identify as fake because – astoundingly – they weren't actually tested scientifically to support the assertion being made in the book. Similarly in Lehrer's "How We Decide" heroic airline pilots who quickly found a new method of controlling a plane with failed hydraulics and an intuitive radar operator who instantly identified a missile in the gulf war are put forward as success stories for unconscious decision making, but once again the book does not assess the number of cases where the pilots failed and died, or where the radar operators were responsible for losing friendly aircraft. The authors have not sought the opposing evidence to their attractive narrative hypotheses. Don't get me wrong – I do think the brain's computational power is phenomenal and it really can make fabulous decisions; I'm even ready to accept it has a major contribution to make to every decision. I'm just not ready to accept the brain autopilot theory. And I'm not the only skeptic; as a direct response to "Blink" Michael LeGault in "Think" spends a whole book telling us the opposite: why crucial decisions can't be made in the blink of an eye, and calls Gladwell's approach part of our "trash culture".

The next conflicting message you get from other books is that you can learn decision-making from narratives – stories about how other people made good or bad decisions. Narratives are clearly popular: Michael Useem in "The Go Point" uses them from interviews with decision makers to educate you about what he thinks works and what does not, and "Blink" and "How to Decide" are both full of entertaining narratives. However, I agree with Nassim Taleb in "The Black Swan" when he warns us to beware; he claims that narratives about prior decisions are almost worthless because humans tend to assign causality and factual explanations within them that are not actually real. The narrative is chosen and only supporting data sought for it. The bottom line appears to be that narratives are attractive to read because they are entertaining. They are useful when you make them because you can condense information in a memorable way and you can build a story that protects your interests, but they cannot be trusted as convincing evidence of support or refutation for a particular hypothesis. Why? - because they aren't entirely truthful, they often depend on being more open to supportive evidence than the opposite, and they are always made with the benefit of hindsight.

At least books like Levitt and Dubner's "Freakonomics" and Dan Ariely's "Predictably Irrational" not only include interesting narratives, but these are backed-up by quantitative data analyses and behavioral economic calculations to explain why we behave in the ways that we do – although Taleb would again tell us to be highly suspicious of the generalizability of their calculations. Unfortunately even if the behavioral economic calculation process is more generalizable than expected by Taleb, it doesn't help us much as individuals when we make our own decisions because we don't have the data and/or can't do those complex behavioral economic computations ourselves for every-day decisions.

Another confusing issue is whether humans are inherently good or bad at decision making. Hammond's "Smart Choices" is a great book on practical decision making but states in the first chapter "we don't know how to make decisions well" whereas Gerd Gigerenzer's "Simple Heuristics that Make us Smart" shows through results of rigorous academic testing of models of instinctive heuristics that indeed they are great decision-making tools, outperforming statistical models in some cases – as long as they are applied only in situations where they are fit for their purpose. What is fascinating about Gigenzerer's discoveries is that for years our instinctive heuristics were thought to be vastly inferior to statistical models, because every time a heuristic was compared with statistics it fared worse. Well it turns out that researchers in the past weren't being fair; they defined the statistics as the truth, and because heuristics gave different answers they were defined as worse. What Gigenzerer's team did that was different was to use an external "truth standard". This means that they tested both heuristics and statistics against one another in situations where the real truth was actually known – with the result that in some situations heuristics were better than statistics. The secret is to know when to apply them!

The final paradox is that groups or crowds seem to be both delusional and wise: "Extraordinary Popular Delusions and the Madness of Crowds" was published in 1841 and about 150 years later was opposed by Surowiecki's "The Wisdom of Crowds". I am sure you can bring to mind examples of scary delusions of crowds from history such as cult suicides, final solutions and witch trials. This is countered by stories of good crowd-based decisions in Surowiecki's book. However, much of the crowds' "wisdom" seems to depend on post-hoc statistical analysis rather than the expectation of collective or "group" wisdom – it is mathematical analysis and averaging of the result that provides the wisdom, which is really a greater degree of precision in the estimate. That's not what I call wisdom, it's statistics.

What, therefore, are you to make of this literature "tennis game" where every stroke of understanding seems to be returned by a counter-stroke of apparent contradiction? Although I have presented all of these books in apparently contradictory pairs, I don't believe that half of them are wrong: there is usually a plausible explanation as to when and why both apparently contradictory positions can be correct in different situations.

And that's the point: this book is different. It is different because it is agnostic to a particular approach or method. It is different because it doesn't simply advocate greater complexity, or indeed the opposite; it is an integrated system for making either of those strategic choices when they are best in different situations. Finally it is different because it also contains a number of fundamentally new concepts that you won't find anywhere else!

*Improving your Decisionability is **not** complex and boring!*

The overall approach is very simple and only requires you to know 6 steps and 5 key decision-making methods. I use real examples throughout the text and surely they can't all be boring? The steps are outlined below:

1. Determine whether you can avoid a new decision through using a rule or principle.
2. Define the purpose of the decision: what is the intended effect and why is it important?
3. Use the purpose to define what resources are appropriate for this type of decision and "how good is good enough?"
4. Define the appropriate decision-making strategy: "good enough" [satisficing] vs. "the best" [maximizing].

5. Define the alternatives available for the decision and their differentiating features.
6. Use one of 5 key methods to make the decision:
    a. A heuristic
    b. Even swaps
    c. Dawes' rule
    d. Decisionability tradeoff
    e. Call in an expert

I also use an analogy as part of a recurring process framework throughout the book: that making a decision is like mailing a letter. Consider how much you can deduce by examining the outside of a mailing envelope, whether you are sending it or receiving it. Does it have "urgent" written in large red writing? Who sent it and where from? Where did it go? Is it for me or for more people than me? Was it mailed "express" with a costly stamp or is the stamp inadequate, and the letter delayed with postage due? Is it ripped or battered by a hostile environment or was it well prepared to withstand the expected conditions? Are the contents insured against risk of loss or damage because they are valuable or because the risks are high?

So it is with decisions; if you are the decision maker you will have to go to the trouble of creating a metaphorical envelope that addresses all of the issues that a real one has, an envelope that ensures that the decision goes from where the envelope is today – its current state - to its desired future destination. You will ensure that you don't attempt to stuff too much in a small envelope with a low priced stamp, or alternatively that you don't put enough in the envelope to justify the expensive stamp that you used. Perhaps most importantly you want the recipient – whether that's you or others – to open it and use the contents once it arrives. Each of these issues will be covered in depth in the following chapters.

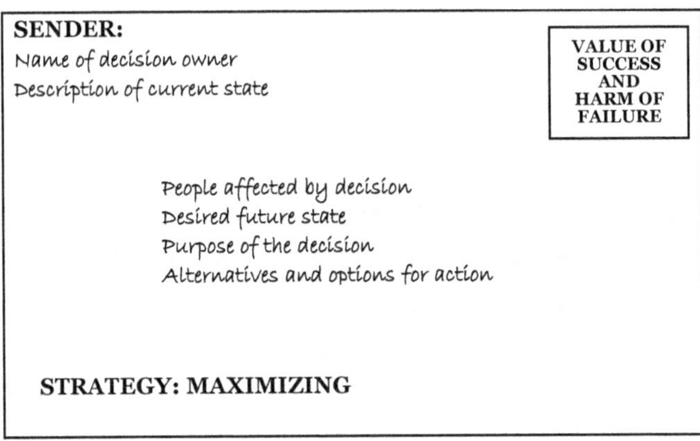

The "Decision Envelope"

How these methods will help you in common situations at work and at home.

On the following pages I briefly describe some examples of the type of questions that I will help you ask and answer as you go thought the book, and some illustrative examples that show you the type of knowledge that you will attain.

Can I avoid making a new decision by using an existing rule or principle?

Q: I manage a department and I supervise 10 people. I have been told by management that I need to let one person go; Jennifer is clearly the least productive person but she is my friend. What do I do? I feel so guilty.

A: At work the principle "maintain the good health of the company" has a higher currency value than "be good to my friends". Fire Jennifer. Tell yourself that this will prevent the entire business collapsing or losing productivity due to favoritism. [Chapter 2]

Should I make a new rule?

Q: I am a principal in a middle school and several board members have suggested that I propose a "zero tolerance" rule that immediately suspends any student using any word or gesture that another person perceives as threatening to them. What do I do?

A: Don't make the rule; show the board that it violates several of the "METRIC" good practices for rules, but advocate for creating workshops around supporting the principle of treating others with respect. [Chapter 2]

How do I decide strategically what my decision is really about?

Q: I am on the board of a nonprofit organization and we keep focusing on fundraising because we haven't been able to pay for all of our existing obligations. We keep going back to the same people for more money but they are reaching their limits and are telling us that they will only contribute if we find other people too. How do we get more money from other people?

A: You have jumped ahead too quickly and defined the problem as "get more money" and only one alternative for the solution "get more money from other people". Step back and describe the current situation: that the organization has obligations and desired actions that it cannot pay for by the current fundraising methods. The desired future state is that it can meet its obligations and move in new directions. There are a number of different possible alternatives that should be assessed: reduce the cost of one or more current obligations, choose new activities that cost less money or find new methods of raising funds. [Chapter 3]

What is the purpose of this decision?

Q: "I don't need any help; I already know what the purpose of my decision is – to find the best house to move into!"
A: That isn't a good enough description of the purpose to help you make the right choice for your family. What does "best" mean - what is the desired effect of moving house – what are you trying to achieve? Can any of your desires be achieved without moving? What are your freedoms and constraints? All of these will shape your search, and will change the alternatives open to you. It is important to have a clear "what" statement about the intended effect of your decision and a "why" statement that shows why it is important to you. [Ch. 3]

Is this decision going to send me into decision debt?

Q: "I always get frustrated during my hour-long commute to work – I've had to start taking antacids before I drive. The traffic is so bad, and I always seem to choose the wrong lane to be in – even if I change lanes. If the other lane goes faster I'm sure people are smirking at me as they go past me for having made the wrong decision – I feel like ramming them!"
A: You are in decision debt! Making the perfect lane-changing decision would require information that you don't actually have, and constantly sampling the traffic flows, monitoring your position against other cars and changing lanes when you detect a

difference is more expensive in terms of effort than the benefits [unless your wife is having a baby on the seat next to you]. What's more, even if you get it right somewhat more than 50% of the time, when you get it wrong the intensity of the negative emotion more than counterbalances the positives of getting it right. Avoid this decision – a low value decision where the benefits exceed the costs; be a lemming, stick in the same lane and listen to the radio or book-tapes. [Chapter 3]

What do I do if there is extreme time pressure to make the decision?

Q: In May 2003, with no water and as little hope of survival, Aspen mountaineer Aron Ralston, 27, used a pocket-knife to amputate his own arm and free himself from a boulder weighing 800-1,000 pounds that fell and trapped him for five days in a remote desert canyon in eastern Utah. Ralston told rescuers that he realized he would not survive unless he took drastic action. Was he just lucky or was this the right thing to do? How would you decide what to do this in his place?

A: Ralston correctly put off a decision, hoping for rescue until his water had run out and he had to make the decision urgently to act or to stay put before he lost the choice through becoming too weak and dehydrated. He did not know the probability of rescue, but he did know the two types of decision error. The worst error would be to fail to cut his arm off if it was the only means of escape, causing him to die under a rock. The lesser error would be to cut off his arm when it was not necessary, if rescuers were to arrive before he otherwise would have died. He used the "safe side" heuristic and chose the action associated with a less serious error if he was wrong, and cut off his arm. [Chapter 4]

What is my appropriate decision-making strategy, should I be making a "good enough" decision [satisficing] or seeking the best [maximizing]?

Q: "My car lease is up and I've got to get something with lower payments than my current BMW. I've looked at decision making books and online information and they often use the example of buying a car to illustrate the methods. I think I get it – I need to identify which factors are important in a car, such as crash test rating, reliability, number of seats, price, fuel economy, number of airbags, performance etc. Then I need to weight each factor for how important it is to me, score each car that I am interested in and then add up the total and buy the one with the highest score. Is that right?"
A: That's probably the wrong answer. The method you describe is an unbounded "maximizing" strategy – to try and select the very best combination of options using near- perfect knowledge. It is expensive in terms of time and effort, which is fine if you like getting detailed information about cars, but most people don't. It also requires considerable knowledge and expertise which you probably don't have. For example you may be interested in safety as an important factor to you but do you actually know what the number of airbags or the number of stars in the crash-test rating does to the true outcome - the number of fatalities or injuries? Can you find and interpret those statistics from the Internet? If not, then what good is your rating of safety other than a resource intensive "self-opinion poll"? There are several simpler and better alternatives to becoming an expert yourself and applying an approach that has statistical assumptions that you don't know are true. Firstly you could choose a "satisficing" strategy [seeking a solution that is "good enough"] – to deliberately not bother comparing any of the features amongst the cars that fit your price range that exceed a "good enough" thre-

shold, and eliminate any vehicle that has any features that are not "good enough". Then use your subjective feelings to choose the car you like the best that has all "good enough" features. Alternatively, if you want to "maximize" – to seek only the best - and are prepared to ignore your own feelings and subjective opinions about a vehicle, consult an expert on maximization of the features such as Consumer Reports and simply buy their "Best Buy" make and model for your price. [Chapters 3 and 4]. And by the way, the "weight and rate" method you propose using – while commonly used - is seriously flawed and not recommended here [Chapter 6].

How can I use a simple heuristic to narrow down overwhelming choices?

Q: "Tastings" is a chain of wine bars that have a novel feature – you buy a "debit card" that fits into electronic wine dispensers, and you can select from a 1oz "tasting" through a half a glass or a full glass of wine from over 70 choices, and your card gets debited. Some of the wines are $20 a bottle and some are $300 a bottle. The point is that you can sample expensive wines that you couldn't necessarily afford to buy in a restaurant, and because you are only buying a small taste, you can experience a wider variety of wines without spending a fortune. Everyone wins, right? Wrong! Since one opened in our neighborhood I've been there 3 times with different groups of friends and each time about a third of the people just ask for a glass of "house red" or "house white". In other words, when faced with a wider opportunity for choice than usual, they've moved in the opposite direction, avoided all choice except for color of wine. I've asked them why and the general answer is having too many choices and too little time to make a "good" choice. Although I didn't do Myers-Briggs personality testing, I also think it goes with

personality type – people who like to "maximize", to make the best possible choices are overwhelmed when they have to choose quickly among so many alternatives. They'd rather make no choice than feel regrets that they didn't choose right. How can good choices be made quickly with limited information?
A: My wife chose the most rapidly without reading dozens of labels and was happy with her choice, so I asked her what she did, and it turned out that she used what is called by heuristics experts the "take the best" heuristic. As I mentioned above, this approach under some circumstances outperforms computational mathematics so – unexpectedly – it isn't necessarily a compromise for compulsive maximizers even though they wouldn't normally choose the method. She decided that the most important feature was wine color, and she used that first to eliminate all the white wines, as she wanted red. Second she had determined that grape variety was the second most important feature and she eliminated everything except Pinot Noir. Third she decided that geography was the next most important feature and eliminated everything that wasn't from the North West USA. She was left with a manageable number of about 4 wines to choose from, and she sampled the most expensive and the least expensive! This simple heuristic [a mental short cut that is a mathematical approximation] - choosing what factors to apply in the right order in order to narrow down the choices - enabled her to enjoy the opportunity without putting her into "decision debt". [Chapter 4]

How do I manage uncertainty?

Q: "I have arthritis pain and I've been taking a drug called diclofenac, but I've been getting indigestion and my doctor is worried that it is causing a stomach ulcer. He wants me to switch to a drug that he says is more selective or something, but it has prominent warnings on the label that it can cause heart attacks. Heart attacks are worse than stomach ulcers right? So why would I switch? Is my doctor getting a free gift from the drug company to try and prescribe me this drug?"

A: When neither type of side effect is certain, the harm of each type of side effect needs to be compared in terms of seriousness and likelihood. While it is true that heart attacks appear more serious, and most people would dread them more than an ulcer, in fact many people do die of serious bleeding from stomach and duodenal ulcers that occur with a key type of pain medication called non-steroidal anti-inflammatory drugs. In one major study, serious stomach effects occurred in 150 people out of every thousand [15%] for diclofenac, but the heart attack effect for the newer more selective drug was only 2 people out of every thousand [0.2%]. Physicians rated the seriousness [in terms of life threatening effect] of heart attacks at 60% and serious GI effects at 20%. Multiplying the probability by the seriousness to get a harm score, the harm of diclofenac is about 3% of a life [15% of 20%] whereas the harm of the selective agent is about 0.1% of a life [60% of 0.2%], about 30 times less. Given that you already have indigestion, your chance of a serious ulcer is even higher than shown in the study population; if you don't have any particular risk factors for heart disease, you should switch [Chapter 7]. The drug labeling doesn't reflect the harm calculated in this way, but rather the level of human concern in the scientific community – which in contrast to the calculation, is currently greater for heart-attack risk and for a new drug.

Integration of these processes in practice

The Decisionability process diagram below shows how the phases of the process fit together:

(1) Gather Decision Inputs

Purpose: What and Why?	Value of Success	Harm of Failure	Limits of Resource and Time	Type and Amount of Data

(2) Address Decisionability Questions

How Good is Good Enough?	What Methods Fit Constraints?	Maximize or Satisfice?

(3) Choose and Use the Right Method

Rule or Principle	Simple Heuristics	Dawes' Rule or Even Swaps	Decisionability Tradeoff	Call an Expert

How decision quality depends on resourcing

A key aspect of Decisionability which I haven't discussed yet is how you can narrow down the range of methods that you could possibly use to address the decision. The most important driver of this narrowing process is the interaction between the performance of the different approaches – the decision quality – and the amount of resource, time or knowledge applied.

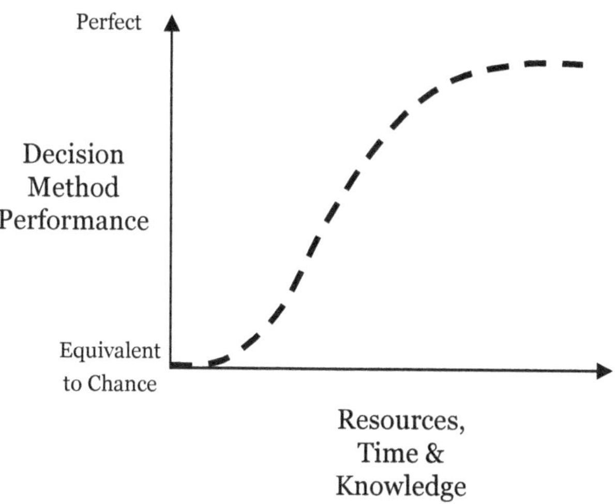

In the diagram above, start by looking at the axis labels. The label on the left shows "decision method performance", which can be viewed as: how often will the decision be correct? The bottom of this scale is not zero but the equivalent of a random choice like a coin flip, which could be correct 50% of the time. Obviously you'd like your methods to be perfect with a 100% score but you know they can't always be so. The label on the bottom axis is "resources, time and knowledge", in other words, the amount of personal effort, data seeking, knowhow and possibly actual resourcing costs that you will have to put in to make a decision. Now look at the curved dashed line which shows an idea of what the relationship between the two is; generally as you put more effort in to a decision, and as you have more access to knowledge, you move up the line as your decision error rate can get lower and your decision method gets closer to perfect, closer to a zero error rate. The shape of the line isn't terribly important, but I drew it the shape of a curve with a plateau at the top because it is easy to imagine that putting more and more resources on a decision will at some point stop having a meaningful effect on the outcome. The upward bulge in the middle of the curve is there because some methods, such as heuristics, which only require middling amounts of resources and knowledge appear to perform nearly as well as those which require extensive computation. Below I have taken the same diagram as on the previous page but I but added 2 "no go" areas to it: these effectively block off the availability of parts of the line.

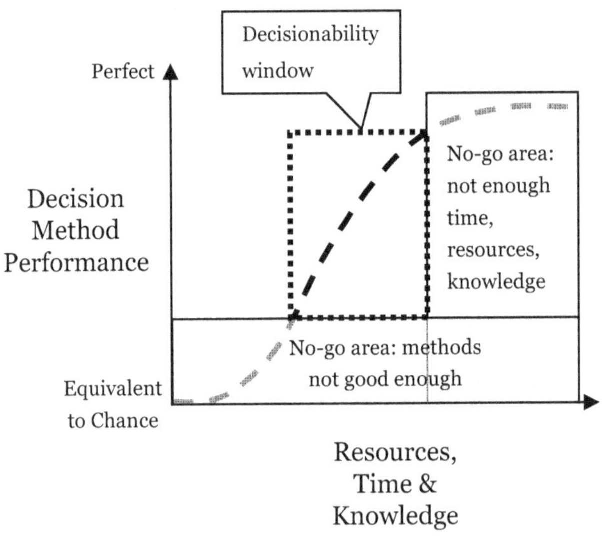

The "no go" areas prevent us from using decision-making methods that might otherwise be on that line. The horizontal box is an imaginary "no go" area where for a particular decision the performance is "not good enough", where the error rate is not tolerable for that type of decision. The height of that box would increase for decisions of high value if successful, and high harm if they failed, because the need for better performance is driven by the value of success and harm of failure. Similarly the height of the box would decrease for low value low harm decisions, to the ultimate extreme for a very trivial decision where a coin flip might actually be "good enough". The vertical box on the right represents the "no go" area for a particular decision where you do not have sufficient resources or knowledge to go. Its width would change depending on your access to resources. If your knowledge was very limited the box would get wider, extending to the left and blocking off some decision methods that would need greater knowledge than you have. You might also choose to impose your own limits on resourcing because even though knowledge might be available, the decision is not be worth spending time, effort and money on – so the box can be imposed voluntarily by you or involuntarily by external circumstances.

Importantly though, the area of the available line not covered by either "no go" box is the "Decisionability window". Deciding where to be on this line is explored more fully in Chapter 4: "How Good is Good Enough" starting on page 91.

The "Decisionability Window" bounds the region of the performance vs. resources line where performance is at least "good enough" and where knowledge and resourcing is adequate.

Benefits of improved Decisionability

By matching the right method to your specific need and resource, the approaches in this book will keep you from using methods that are unnecessarily complex when you don't need them, and will encourage you to use more sophisticated methods when you do. This will improve the results of your decisions and will also make you more efficient at doing them. It won't mean that you will always be right, but your decisions will be less likely to fail because of use of the wrong method.

Using the methods in this book will also change what you **feel** about the very process of decision making. My definition of "painless" decisions might be an exaggeration [please forgive the alliterative indulgence] and you still might not look forward to difficult decisions, but hopefully you will not dread them or avoid them. Decision dread is surprisingly common: I was recently discussing school choices with a friend; she currently drives her son James to and from an expensive private high-school an hour away from her home in Providence. They had just been to see a new and less expensive school about 15 minutes away from their house. "We wanted to hate that school" she said, surprisingly vehemently. "Why?" I asked – surprised because a closer, cheaper school would seem to be ideal. "Because then the decision would have been easy; we'd have said "no" to the new school and there would be no risk of it being our fault if James was unhappy later." Just think of the logic, instead of being happy with the existence of a real – and apparently superior – alternative to their current option, she would rather have not had the option at all, mainly because of the dread of making the wrong decision, hurting her son and fearing the guilt that would accompany it. The reason that this book can change dread and guilt is that it changes the expectations of making decisions. When pursuing the many "satisficing" – "good enough" approaches, you do not expect to optimize every feature of the decision. You are less disappointed when they aren't all perfect; in fact you expect it and failing to achieve perfection doesn't mean you were wrong to make that choice. Even with "maximizing" methods such as the Decisionability tradeoff method, you actually get an estimate of the probability of achieving every part of your decision, and it will **always** be less than 100%. This will help you manage any unrealistic expectations of perfection. We all tend to think that if only we try hard enough our decision will be right, and if it doesn't turn out that way that's convincing evidence that we've made a mistake. These methods will show that both of those assertions are wrong. You don't have to be religious to appreciate the deep human needs expressed by the prayer:

"Oh God, give us courage to change what must be altered, serenity to accept what cannot be helped, and insight to know the one from the other" [Mildred Pinkerton, 1936].

This is a fitting framework for Decisionability: facing up to decisions with the confidence and courage that is built upon a foundation of insights and knowledge. Insights that enable us to identify risks and issues that could be changed, skills for deciding which ones should be changed or left alone and knowledge of how it should be done. And yes, in the end it is about serenity, because when you have the confidence that you have the best chance of achieving the intended effect of your decision, you have managed your risks well, you used a decision-making method that you know is fit for the purpose and have realistic expectations about how much of your desired outcome is likely to be achieved, you can be serene. At least until something changes!

Part 1: Preparing for your decision

Chapter 2

Avoiding decisions by using rules or principles.

Rules and principles are discussed here because a rule may enable you to avoid a new decision. The methods in the following chapters in the book could be unnecessarily complicated if a rule will do! The advantage of a good rule is that it repeatedly enables you (or whoever the target of the rule is) to efficiently avoid making new decisions and therefore avoid the effort and costs of making them each time. Taking away the decisions also reduces the number of "temptations" to succumb to opposing personal desires. Finally, the existence of a rule can increase compliance with what is known to be a correct decision because the consequence for rule breaking can be made greater than for making one wrong individual decision in the absence of a rule. Paying $5 for swearing – the "swear box" penalty – is greater than the offense caused by any one swearword. The personal disappointment or guilt from breaking your vegetarianism pledge which you have held for 6 months is much greater than the benefit of eating a single juicy steak. The combination of the last two issues – reducing the number of temptations and increasing the leverage for compliance – means that one of the key advantages of a rule is that it performs best where there is little or no trust, whether that is trust of yourself or of others.

However there are a number of disadvantages of rules and you should consider these next.

Failure to manage complex situations

If the situation is very complex your rule would have to be more like a computer model, and would be too difficult to understand or explain to another person. For example, some school "dress codes" which define which types of clothing are or are not acceptable can get so complicated that they are exploited shamelessly; I was once on a school board that had to consider whether "Saran Wrap" would be specifically disallowed as a dress item because of the clever manipulations of a student. If you have such a complex situation then compliance with a rule becomes difficult to measure and policing it becomes impossible.

Restriction of innovation

It is also impossible to make a rule that delivers the intended benefits in every new context that did not necessarily exist at the time the rule was made, so rules don't adapt to innovation – indeed they can restrict it because there is no benefit to a new process. For example, if you make a rule that everyone in the workplace must have their time card punched from 9 to 5 you prevent flexible working or remote working options.

Exceptions exist

Given that rules always have exceptions, it is important that you look at the consequences of the rule being wrong, and assess how often that is likely to happen. If exceptions are too commonly tolerated because the rule doesn't fit the circumstances very well, the rule gets devalued and becomes worthless. It becomes less transparent whether a rule is being really broken or whether the exception is being used. Alternatively, over-rigid application of a rule without allowing exceptions can defy common sense, such as requiring fire-engines to keep to speed limits.

Rules require policing

Finally, there is a resource burden to having too many rules that require policing and enforcing, and humans often willfully resist.

Rules for rules – the rule "METRIC"

For all these reasons rules are often replaced by principles – general guidance statements that require a judgment to be made, or they may be avoided by making entirely new decisions on each occasion. However, for situations that are likely to be repeated a number of times, the efficiency of a rule can be highly appealing, so I will take a look at the specific situations when creating a rule is most likely to deliver more benefits than disbenefits.

The list of requirements below is intended to build on the advantages of rules but to avoid the key shortcomings I discussed earlier. A mnemonic for remembering the requirements by using the first letter of each attribute is "**M.E.T.R.I.C.**".

Rule "METRIC" – Requirements for Valid Rules

1. **Measurable simply**. Measurability is important because rules are worthless if they can be broken without detection. This also pushes rule-making away from complex situations.
2. **Exceptions are rare.** Common exceptions devalue a rule and lead to its' being widely ignored.
3. **Trust is lacking**. In the absence of a rule people cannot be trusted to do the right thing because:
    a. They are incompetent
    b. They aren't trusted because they have behaved badly in the past
    c. They aren't trusted because they don't share the value system of the rules' originators
    d. The reward for doing the wrong thing is likely to exceed the strength of character of the target audience
4. **Repetitive situation.** The value of a rule is its efficiency in repetitive situations.
5. **Innovation is unnecessary.** Rules don't allow creativity, flexibility, adaptability or innovation, so they should be restricted to areas where these attributes are unnecessary.
6. **Correlation with an outcome.** Forbidden actions should be directly correlated with a bad outcome and required actions with a good outcome. Rules that are only weakly associated with outcomes have unpredictable unintended consequences and might be harmful.

Note that it is only worthwhile for you to accept the rigidity of a rule and the obligations to police its adherence if the "wrong" thing is consequential and will occur without a rule. People who are trustworthy, competent and have strength of character will be more creative and productive without a rule. It is also possible to create personal rules; some rules I've created for myself are:

- No dessert or sodas – because I have a long term objective not to put on weight but don't trust myself to refuse in individual situations.
- Do some exercise every day even if it is only stretching – because I don't trust myself not to find a reason why I can't do it today.
- Drive at less than 75mph on the highway even if the traffic is going faster – because I have a long term safety objective and yet it's easy and fun to go fast.

These rules all comply with the "**Rule-METRIC**" and save me from making about 20 decisions a week, that's 1040 decisions a year from just 3 simple rules. Of course the only penalty for rule-breaking is my guilt, but the guilt and self-recrimination [i.e. the punishment] for breaking a rule that I have complied with for some time – and building a precious personal track-record – is greater than for any single individual decision, so it becomes a deterrent. Thinking now about a business environment, let's examine some common rules:

- No dating amongst managers and subordinates
- No cheating on petty expenses
- Work hours must equal 40
- No downloading of external files onto company computers

All are potentially repetitive situations that save many individual decisions – the intended benefit. However, not all of them are fully compliant with rule METRIC. Although dating between managers and subordinates is sometimes associated with a "bad" outcome, bringing an unwanted new meaning to "performance appraisal" there is also a positive outcome to it: 60% of single people meet their spouses though work. Thus the correlation requirement – that the rule purely prevents a bad outcome is violated. Cheating on expenses probably used to fail on difficulty of measurement, but with electronic receipts and payments it likely now meets the requirements. Work hours used to be easy to measure but recently with flexible workspaces this has become more difficult to monitor and might challenge the measurability requirement. Similarly its correlation with outcome isn't always clear; people allowed greater flexibility in work-time and work-place may work less than the allocated time, but this could be compensated for by greater productivity when they are working and by their increased loyalty to the company. Downloading of external files is easy for the Information Technology department to police but is not well correlated with a "bad" outcome, as some of those files are useful to the company, and therefore exceptions where the rule is not useful are common. This may explain why – perhaps aside from the pentagon and homeland security – enforcement in corporations is lax.

If you do have a recurring situation in your life or work that fits this framework, then make a rule – but use rule METRIC to test whether it will be worth it in advance. I would wager that not many of the politically popular "zero tolerance of ...." rules would comply with this system, and perhaps if "New Year's Resolutions" were made to fit this specification then fewer would be made but more would be kept. However, in general I don't like many rules because they aren't adaptable to innovation or changes in context and because I like to think of myself as competent and trustworthy – and so do most employees, who therefore perceive rules as a negative judgment on themselves.

"It's a matter of principle"- when can you use principles to make a decision?

The phrase "It's a matter of principle" is both useful and routinely abused as a decision-making tool. As used typically – as a veto to some proposed course of action - it appears to close down debate and pre-empt a decision based on any other factors. It is a "**non-compensatory**" position – that no amount of other "good" can compensate for a failure to meet a standard in the principle not being met, and it's therefore indistinguishable from a rule. Non-compensatory principles can also be viewed as "rights" – for example opponents in opposition to research into the cost-effectiveness of medicines have opined that this will interfere with a physician and a patients "right" to have whatever medicine they wish. In my view, non-compensatory principles should be called rules, and the word "principle" reserved for positions that are "**compensatory**." This term means that it is permissible to violate one principle as long as this can reasonably be compensated for by some "greater good" elsewhere. I was having an argument the other day with a friend of mine who asserted that George Bush had principles but Barack Obama did not. I countered with the assertion that they both had principles, but George Bush treated his as non-compensatory whereas Barack Obama's are compensatory, reversing some of his predecessors positions for his perception of the "greater good". For example, on reversing the ban on federal funding for stem-cell research, President Obama said that our obligations were "to care for each other" and to "ease human suffering", so justifying the use of embryos that would otherwise be destroyed.

Meanwhile Pope Benedict XVI condemned this action as immoral because it involved the destruction of human embryos - "non compensatory" language. Clearly some of us are more programmed by our genetics or influenced by an environment such as politics and some religions to be relative "non compensators" or "compensators". Unquestioning adherence to non-compensatory principles leads to quick decisions that are consistent with the principles but which are not targeted at causing the least harm or the greatest good in general, only the specific harm or good from that principle without regard to off-target consequences. People who are non-compensators, or who are in an environment or culture that promotes principles as rights, can become very unhappy when they actually do make choices that are compensatory, feeling very guilty at having "betrayed" their principles. Therefore, if you have a personal choice as to which way to operate at work or at home, and you are confident in your own abilities to make the evaluations about the "good" or "harm" of applying one principle or another then I recommend that you choose to be a compensator! Have consistent principles and regard them as a currency to be valued, even prized - but don't make the price of any of them infinitely high [wouldn't you kill somebody to protect your children?]. Be reluctant, but when it is necessary, be prepared to trade one principle vs. another to find the path of least harm or greatest good. If you maintain that clarity of purpose for the trading of principles, you are not obliged to feel guilty.

However, in the spirit of even-handed debate I can acknowledge that there are also reasons for being or becoming a non-compensator depending on your personality. Firstly, it will make your decisions on any subject involving such principles very quick and efficient. Secondly, because a non-compensatory principle leads to fewer evaluations – you don't need to compare the currency value of one principle with another – they work like rules and create an environment with fewer temptations to err on the side of weakness or self-indulgence. If you have consciously decided to become a non-compensator in order to reduce temptations because you know and understand your own weaknesses then this can be a beneficial approach for you. It is no coincidence that Pope Benedict provides us with another convenient example, advocating against condom use even in Africa where AIDS is rampant because "it increases the problem". The "problem" condom-use increases is the temptation to have extra-marital sex, or non-procreatory sex – two important rules [or non compensatory principles] of the Roman Catholic Church. Clearly, even the benefits of reduced HIV transmission and fewer AIDS deaths from condom use are not viewed as compensatory. Whether you agree with his approach or not, this is nonetheless supporting evidence that avoiding temptation is one purpose for creation of a non-compensatory principle. You just might feel guilty more frequently if you can't always adhere to the non-compensatory ideal that you demand of yourself.

Even for "compensators", quick decisions can be made when there are few or no other competing principles, or where the currency value of the competing principle that is violated is far lower than the value of the one being pursued. However, if there are other competing principles of near similar value, or if there is a harm-harm tradeoff or a risk-benefit tradeoff to be made, compensators will want to make that assessment rather than simply following a single principle.

A couple of years ago, the National Cancer Institute [NCI], one of the respected National Institutes of Health approached the Food and Drug Administration to discuss an idea about accelerating cancer drug development with an "institutional review board" - an ethics committee. The proposal was that some of the standard safety testing required before drugs reach humans could be relaxed a bit, as long as the human subjects were terminally ill and all prior treatments had failed. The argument was that this would enable more rapid testing of new cancer therapies in humans at lower cost, so the NCI could test more of them, with the result that more new medicines would be found that work. They proposed that the patients would be fully informed and completely free to refuse without any consequence for their refusal. It would be made quite clear to them that there would be no possible benefit to them, and the risks of side effects would be higher than had been previously allowed; they would be doing it purely to benefit other patients by screening these drugs more cost-effectively, to find more cures. The NCI asked the committee for an ethical opinion as to whether it would be tolerable. The response from the review board may not have literally been "no way Jose" but was equally plain: this was ethically unacceptable because it risks exploiting seriously ill patients who are vulnerable to suggestions from their caregivers, and because the increased risks were not acceptable where there was no direct benefit to the patients exposed to the risks. The principles used to make the decision and close the debate were undeclared but are plausibly:

1. Do not exploit the goodwill of patients who are in a vulnerable situation
2. Do not reduce safety requirements in one individual to benefit another individual

That seems perfectly straightforward and ethical; perhaps it is after all a "matter of principle" where more serious decision-making tools are unnecessary? But wait a minute: what if I am a dying cancer patient and I want to help other people even at some risk to myself? Does anyone have the right to say I am not competent to make that decision? Would they stop me changing my will to benefit the hospital or a cancer charity for the same reason? And there is contrary evidence to the second principle above that shows it to be weak or invalid: terminally ill patients that are highly unlikely to get any benefit of a new drug are already routinely used in initial cancer trials - with a higher tolerance for nasty side effects than in other clinical trials in other diseases. In different clinical trials, healthy volunteers that receive new drugs also have no possibility of benefit to themselves. Soldiers [bullets] miners [being buried alive] deep-sea fishermen [drowning] and radiologists [cancer induced by exposure to radiation] also tolerate increased occupational risks for others to benefit.

Principles that could therefore be viewed as competing to counterbalance the ones above are:

1. Right to self determination
2. Right to self-sacrifice for the benefit of others

So, when <u>can</u> a principle be used as a decision short-cut? Well I would rule out cases like the one above where there is a competition between different principles of similar perceived value – that would require a more sophisticated analysis that looked at the outcomes of violating each kind of principle, in particular how serious and how frequent they would be, such as the Decisionability tradeoff analysis in chapter 7. Perhaps the clearest case is where there is only one principle being violated, or where the currency value of a principle is clearly higher than any of the other principles or benefits that are competing with it. Here are some examples where a principle does deliver a decision short-cut:

- A church vestry [the board of directors] rejects the notion of using credit card payments for donations because the principle of not encouraging consumer debt outweighed any of the benefits of potentially increased donations.
- A climber halfway up Everest stops to help an injured climber and returns to base-camp with him; the principle of helping an injured person outweighed the benefits of making the top himself.
- When evaluating competing opportunities at work, a manager selects the one that has the most merit rather than the one presented by his closest friend because of the principle of doing the best for the business rather than rewarding one's friends [the "business is business" principle].

Decision making using a principle

Principles can be used to make a decision when:

- There are no competing principles, or
- There are other principles which would be violated but they are clearly of lower importance, and
- All principles used to make the decisions are valid

Creating a personal Decisionability culture

Before we leave principles as decision-making tools, I invite you to think briefly about what personal principles you should have, and why you should have them to improve your Decisionability.

I am not talking about principles against murder or contraception but those which are relevant to daily life at home or in business. I've made a table of my human traits in the table below. This is not meant to be a full list of all possible human traits, but they are the ones that I will admit to and which if unchecked would lead directly to an imbalance in my daily decision-making that would favor my own interests and which would harm productivity of the organization I am a part of. As well as identifying my traits, I created counterbalancing principles that I need to reduce the harm of my traits:

Negative Human Traits	**Counter-balancing principle**	**Effect of counter-balancing principle**
I like my own ideas and I like to tell other people what I think	I make extra effort to listen to others	I hear more about different alternatives, risks or approaches
I want to preserve my own position, budget and organization	I do what is best for the company	I prevent decisions in self-interest in conflict with company interest
I get annoyed if others aren't cooperating	I focus on understanding why people are resisting	If I understand resistance early I can change the approach
I am friends with some people in my group and I want to favor them	I judge proposals only on technical merits	A meritocracy is preserved – company value is enhanced
I like it when people agree with me	I encourage diversity and disagreement	I expose risks and value that I haven't thought of
I want to hide things I did wrong	I admit my mistakes publicly	This helps me make the next decision better
I want everyone to like me	I say what I think even if unpopular	The right thing to do may not be popular
I am an optimist	I value pessimists and include them in decisions	I use pessimists to identify risks and to challenge assumptions

For example, if I failed to recognize and balance the "I like my own ideas and to tell people what I think" trait in my current environment it would lead to the following adverse consequences:

- I would dictate what my organization works on, so people with their own ideas would be stifled and might leave the company
- All of my ideas cannot possibly be the best, so productivity would be harmed
- I would be perceived as an arrogant pig - which would be entirely true and the attitude would adversely compete with my "I want everyone to like me" trait.

This is not intended to be a list of all kinds of virtuous acts; the purpose of the counterbalancing principles is to focus specifically on improving Decisionability so the concept is to focus on only a few of the most important potentially destructive tendencies that you know that you have. These are the traits that bias you or that get in the way of balanced decision making. Only you can know what might help you live by the principles you create; however as Thaler and Sunstein argue in "Nudge" you can "nudge" yourself in the right direction by creating targets or rewards for yourself, get a friend to give you feedback, create situations where you are likely to do it well, or avoid situations where you might succumb to negative traits. If you do go wrong, you can often go back and do it right in the cold light of day. Although it is much harder to measure how these principles are affecting decision making than for rules, they can have an incredibly broad environmental effect – in actuality they can redefine your **personal Decisionability culture**. They are not meant to overcome the natural human trait completely because these traits are not always negative, rather they are intended to give you the choice of how to act rather than being a slave to instinct. There are also personal traits that you are blind to, which you can't control, or where you are in denial about the downside – that's OK, the point of this approach is merely to evolve in the right direction, to improve on where you were – you don't have to become a perfect being. If you like this concept, then list your top 5-10 personal traits, create counterbalancing principles for yourself, say what effect you want each one to have on your decision-making and what your "nudge" will be to help you live your intent. Perhaps this is as simple as writing down the ones you already have; hide it in your desk drawer where you can read it from time to time and check whether you have been successful.

Personal Decisionability Culture

Your personal Decisionability is improved when:

- You identify what human traits you have that often lead to biased or bad decisions
- You construct counterbalancing principles and live by them
- You create "nudges" or rewards to help yourself to behave well

A workplace example where rules and principles are tested.

Brian is a senior manager at a medium-sized contract-research organization called CR Engineering. He has worked there for over 20 years and is within a few years of retirement. He doesn't aspire towards ascending any higher in the organization, but has significant loyalty to his company and wants to do the best for them. CR Engineering performs engineering research and pilot manufacturing work for private companies and on occasional military contracts on a fee-for-service basis – they don't have their own products but fix the problems that other people have with making theirs. The profit margins have been good and they have been doing well for over a decade. Until 2 years ago they had revenues of about $30M a year. However, last year their revenues fell by 10% and this year have fallen by another 20% as the companies giving them the 2 biggest contracts have run into financial difficulties. They were also disappointed as they were expecting to get royalty payments for one of the products they had helped to commercialize, but the company they developed it for abandoned the project.

As a response to the economic crisis, the company has decided to cut routine expenses, lay off 10% of the workforce, aggressively seek new "fee for service" clients, and to investigate developing its own novel products that it would license to big companies for marketing and distribution. Brian is responsible for the latter initiative; he has already held two "idea generation" sessions with leaders in the company, and everyone in the company has been invited to make suggestions. As a result, there are 15 possibilities for "innovation projects" and the company has set aside a budget of $500k to investigate them.

Brian is held accountable by his manager for deciding what to spend the $500k budget on. He has already had one rather chaotic discussion with the executive team of the company, where everyone was competing to get some of the new budget in a time of otherwise shrinking expenditures, but the overall strategy people were trying appeared to be "force of personality". Brian decides to try again and before the next meeting he pre-specifies some rules that each project has to meet, and the proposers of the projects have provided information on how well their project meets the specifications.

Brian's proposed rules:

1. No project budget should be more than $100k
2. Any project proposed must be ready to launch within 3 months
3. Any project must lead directly to a go/no go decision without further funding
4. All projects must have a probability of technical success of at least 50%

The rules reflected Brian's long experience with similar projects and of company politics. The first rule reflected a desire to spread the risks for innovative projects - at least 5 projects would be launched under his budget of $500k. He thinks that would be better than spending it on one or two expensive projects that might fail so he would have nothing to show for his spending. The second rule's intent was to avoid long ramp-up times that would mean that the project wouldn't spend its budget allocation in this calendar year. In the past Brian has been exasperated when teams grabbed the budgets but then didn't spend all of it in the financial year it was allocated in because they were too slow to get going. The third rule – requiring that funded projects would lead to a go/no-go decision also reflected Brian's past experience of "sneaky" project proposals that were in reality over a pre-specified budget maximum, but the proposers had split them into pieces to get the first piece funded even though it would not lead to a valid scientific or business conclusion without substantially more money. Finally, Brian wanted a high probability of technical success, because even though his budget was branded as a for "innovation" projects, he was concerned that the organization wouldn't tolerate the majority of them failing.

Brian also added a principle that any project must be relevant to the past experience of CR Engineering

Unfortunately Brian has already started hearing conflicting and negative feedback from various parts of the organization. The 4 department heads are saying that Brian's committee is unnecessary, that the money should just be divided equally between them and they should be allowed to spend it how they wish, innovating within their own departments. One department is saying that the $100k limit for innovation projects should be increased because they have a great innovative project proposal that costs $300k. They say it is "not fair" to departments that are based on expensive technologies to limit the individual project budget, when the benefits of these projects might be greater than "cheap" projects. The CEO has been overheard telling the CSO that he doesn't want any of the new projects, that the company should be focusing back on its existing core business, the only reason he is going along is because this is what the board wants to see. With the intent of being helpful, one of Brian's direct reports proposes that they use a weighted scoring system for compliance with each of the rules and simply choose the projects with the biggest score as a way of overcoming the interdepartmental rivalry.

Brian really wants to do the best for the company but he is beginning to get anxious, feeling overwhelmed by the conflicting inputs, fearing that others may take this as an opportunity to criticize his efforts and further their own agendas. He also sees his personal status being potentially undermined by some of the possibilities and his bonus under threat.

Should he do any of the options he is hearing about or something else? I will use the rule METRIC evaluation and see whether his rules should just be kept in place.

Brian's rules	**Measurable**	**Exceptions rare**	**Trust low**	**Repetitive**	**Innovation - no**	**Correlated**
No more than $100k per project	OK	Violation – there are a number of good projects >$200k	OK – teams have failed to spend bigger budgets in the past	OK	Violation – innovation is necessary	Violation – unknown relation to outcomes
Ready to go in 3 months	OK	Violation – calendar does not predict success	OK – poor estimates of time	OK	Violation – innovation is necessary	OK – ability to spend budget
Leads directly to a go/no go decision	OK	Violation – unexpected new findings are common	OK – people cheat and split up projects	OK	Violation – innovation is necessary	OK
Probability of technical success >50%	Violation – difficult to measure	Violation – low probability is common	OK – difficult to estimate	OK	Violation – innovation is necessary	Violation – low % high value projects are good

The table shows that all of Brian's rules violate at least two rule METRIC factors. This is a strong indication that they are unlikely to work without unintended negative consequences in practice and should not be retained. Now Brian knows that he shouldn't use his rules although they might still be useable as contributing factors in a different decision making process and he must use another decision making method. "But what about the principle of alignment with what the company has done in the past" he says, desperately trying to avoid a method that might involve incomprehensible mathematics or statistics. Can that be used as a driving force for decision making? Should his principle that new projects should be aligned with the past experience of the company be retained? Well it's not a bad principle, presumably it was designed to improve the odds of success, but in order for it to work when used alone as a "matter of principle", we would have to be sure that there aren't any other competing principles and that the principle itself is valid. Unfortunately neither of those requirements is met. Firstly, by restricting the scope of projects, value may be limited so a competing and equally worthwhile principle of "maximizing value for the company" could be violated. Secondly, although it is a plausible idea that past experience is useful, there isn't any statistical evidence that the principle is valid. The company isn't necessarily less successful when doing new projects where it has no past experience, nobody has collected the information – it is just a gut feeling. Although the principle looked good, it was not valid. For these reasons, Brian reluctantly lets go of the principle too. We'll find out what he can do in later chapters.

Key learnings from Chapter 2:

- You may be able to bypass complex or repetitive decisions by using a rule.
- If you apply a rule it should meet **METRIC** standards: the action must be **M**easurable, **E**xceptions must be rare, **T**rust or competence must be lacking, they must govern **R**epetitive situations, **I**nnovation must be unnecessary and rules must **C**orrelate with an outcome.
- If you can't use a rule it may be possible to make a decision "as a matter of principle" if a principle is valid and of higher currency value than any competing principles or benefits
- You may apply principles in a "non-compensatory" way where they eliminate all other options. This reduces the number of temptations but does not maximize good or minimize unintended harm.
- You may also apply principles in a "compensatory" way where each has a currency value and competes with other principles for the "greatest overall good". This is my recommended approach.
- Your natural negative traits can be countered with principles that improve your Decisionability – your personal Decisionability culture.
- The decision tree on the following page shows how you can conduct your thought process.

Decision tree for rules and principles

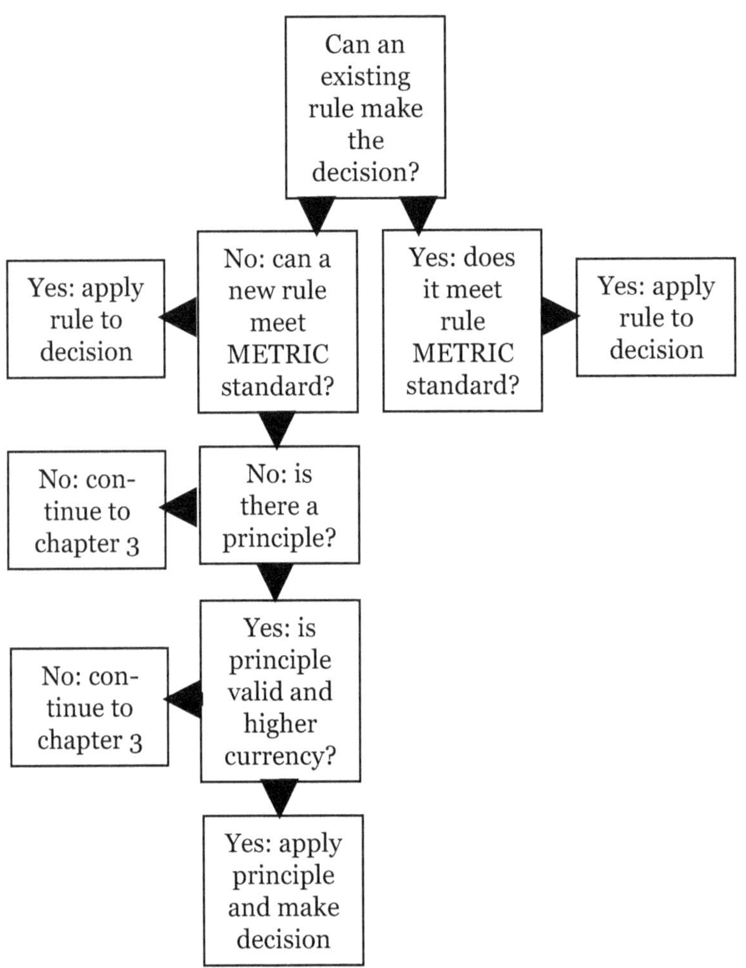

Chapter 3

What are you trying to achieve and why?

Defining the "decision purpose"

In order to define the purpose of a decision you will have to define the difference between what you want and what you have got. Some authors recommend that you should go directly to defining a decision problem. I do want to get to an understanding of the problem but it is often too much of a jump to go straight there so I am proposing smaller steps.

The first step before launching into this process is to think about just how much resource, time and effort is it worth putting into it. I consider this extensively in Chapter 4; I deliberately discussed it later – after defining a purpose in this chapter, because only then is there enough understanding of the decision to do a proper job of it. Nonetheless I am going to give you a heads' up now, because when approaching the definition of the decision purpose, it is already obvious that some decisions don't deserve much effort in this regard and others should receive every ounce of attention that you can give. The simple guidance here is that you should not make much effort defining a purpose for decisions with a low value of success and a low consequence of failure. The opposite is true for decisions with a high value of success and/or a high cost of failure. And if you are under extreme time pressure – seconds or minutes – I don't think you are going to examine the purpose of your decision much, you will be jumping straight to the next chapter and using a heuristic!

Assuming that you have determined that your decision is worth spending time and effort on, the subsequent steps are to define what you have got, your "current state" [analogous to the sender's address on a letter] and most importantly the good and bad effects it has on you, your work or your families. Then consider what you want: the "desired future state" and the effects it will have – analogous to the destination address on the envelope. The difference between the two helps to define the purpose of the decision – to take the letter from its current state to the future destination.

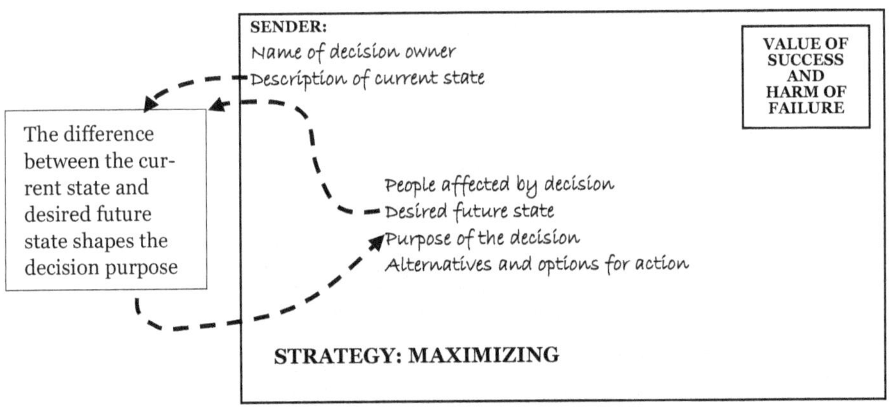

What is the current state?

What you need to achieve is a comprehensive description of the current state that is causing your dissatisfaction or which is driving your wish to make a decision. There is a trick to making your assessment truly comprehensive. The trick is that you assess the relevant status of a triad of issues that we might call "technical", "human" and "economic" or that you have at least looked at each of these domains – you can use T.H.E. as a mnemonic for this breadth of approach, and it forms “T.H.E. Decisionability triangle” for assessing issues. This is a recurring theme: the same triad is used later in the book for categorizing risks and solutions – and you can use it any time that a holistic view of issues is an advantage.

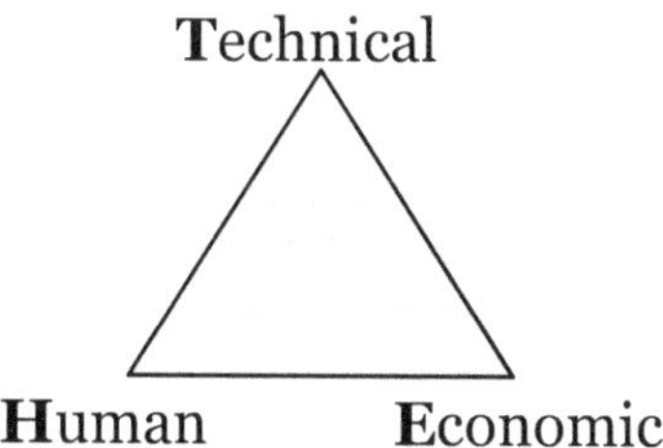

T.H.E. Decisionability Triangle

A table that shows the general kinds of issue that you should include in each of the three categories in the triangle is shown below. Actually it doesn't matter much which category you allocate an issue to, so don't get obsessive about it, the purpose of having them is simply to encourage a holistic viewpoint.

Technical, Human and Economic Categories		
Technical	**Human**	**Economic**
Performance	Political	Money
Measurements	Emotional	Patents
Practical actions	Ethical	Competition
Size, distance, time	Self protection	Time to revenues

Your “current state” description may be quite simple, or alternatively it may require some research – of yourself and others that would either own or be affected by the decision. There may be a temptation to only find supportive opinions of your own perceptions but you should resist them and focus on speaking to people who need to feel that they own the decision alongside you, and/or who would be affected by it. The process may be emotionally sterile, or may involve feelings such as anger, fear, dread or sadness. If these emotions limit your abilities and yet there is nobody else who can do the job, then simply do your best. Just as a lack of resources or knowledge can limit a decision, so can the existence of emotional constraints. You can only do what you are capable of and don't need to feel any more shame or guilt about this type of constraint than you would about the lack of resourcing or knowledge.

What is an ideal but realistic new state after the decision?

You will need to make the same kind of evaluation as you did for the current state using the triad of technical, human and economic categories in T.H.E. Decisionability triangle to ensure a holistic assessment. Each issue that you identified in the current state should be reproduced in the future state with a response – often that the issue has been resolved or improved in the future state, but some issues will simply stay the same, and some could be worse. This inclusion of even things that don't change is not necessarily a waste of time; listing important factors that don't change guards against them being made invisibly worse by some alternative routes to the future state. There may also be some new issues that you'd like in the future state that are not simply resolution of negative issues in the current state, so these should also be added to your table. Having done both, you will be in a position to describe the overall purpose of your decision.

Example - what is the purpose of a new car?

Don is a 25 year-old graduate working in a bank, and he is looking to buy a new car. He already has a 3 year old Ford Focus that has done 36,000 miles and he is just about to finish paying off his car-loan on it. When that is done, he is considering trading in the car in for a new one. He has already seen a nice Scion tC that looks sportier than the Focus, is significantly more economical on fuel, and he could get it for the same payment as he makes already. The Ford might start to become unreliable and the warranty is expiring, so he might save money on future repairs too. Also, he blames his unexciting car for contributing to his lack of a girlfriend - and colleagues at work have made fun of his apparently modest transport. They keep telling him to "Focus" on getting a new girlfriend and "not to lose his Focus" on work. When asked directly what the purpose of his decision is Don responds that he is "deciding whether to get a new car in order to save on overall costs". What do you think? In order to reach a best answer, I will go through the process as outlined above.

Category	Current state	Effect
Technical	Means of transport for himself and occasional passengers, Ford Focus	No problem exists
Human	Don doesn't have a girlfriend	Don is lonely and doesn't have sex
	Don suffers from disparaging comments by friends at work	Don is sad and angry
	Don views his current vehicle as boring to drive	Don doesn't feel good when driving around
Economic	Car payments on Focus are about to expire	Don will have more money if he keeps this car
	Future maintenance may increase as Focus ages	Don <u>may</u> have less money if he keeps this car

Now here's the table of what Don wants:

Category	**Future realistic ideal state**	**Desired effect vs. current state**
Technical	Reliable means of transport	No effect, Don already has a reliable means of transport
Human	Don will get a girlfriend	Don won't be lonely and will have sex often
	Friends at work won't make disparaging comments	Don won't be sad and will have more friends
	The car will be interesting to drive	Don will feel good when driving around
Economic	Total costs no higher than current	No effect, Don will have the same amount of money

So when we look at the difference in the two tables, we see that technical and economic issues are the same [or worse] before and after the decision. The real purpose of his decision is therefore entirely based on human factors:

"To choose a new car in order to feel less sad and lonely and to get more sex".

Let's not deride this purpose statement too readily, although I don't think Don would show it to his so-called friends. Decisions that are intended to benefit emotional factors are just as important as any other. The problem is that Don has deceived us and himself, or at least created a smokescreen, with his original declared purpose of the decision. Any effort he puts into decision making for the incorrect purpose could have been wasted. If he had correctly identified the purpose that he had fixed on subconsciously above, he might have asked himself why a new car would be expected to deliver the outcome. If he had doubts about whether a car could actually be the best route to what he wants he could have broadened the purpose to identify any other alternatives that might deliver his hoped-for benefits – for example seeing a therapist, getting plastic surgery, changing his deodorant, subscribing to e-Harmony, visiting a prostitute or taking antidepressants! Alternatively, he would have been able, using the techniques I describe later, to identify how much of his intended purpose could be delivered by the new car option – and let's face it, many people do buy new cars hoping for an increased appeal to potential partners and much of the advertising is intended to support exactly those fantasies.

Why "objectives" for your decision are premature – stick to a simple purpose statement

What you are not seeing here is a requirement to list all the objectives of your decision in great detail. In contrast to many texts on decision making I don't recommend this right now. Although you should create a table like the one above for Don's future state, please don't call it a list of objectives. There are several reasons why you should not think of your "desired future state" as a list of objectives at this stage:

- You might still decide to abandon the decision [see next chapter] so not listing objectives now saves you work
- You expect things called "objectives" to actually be achieved in practice. Because most decisions are based on some uncertainties – good or bad things that might or might not happen – the issues in your list may be only partially achieved by your decision. So you are doomed to fail, or will at least be disappointed if you think you will

achieve all of desired future state as your objectives all of the time.

- If you lock in your "objectives" now it starts to force your decision making process into methods that weigh all the objectives; these are not necessarily bad, but there are some simpler methods that might not need such complexity because they only use a few components not all of them.
- When you actually start looking at the alternatives available for fulfilling your decision you will likely get some new ideas that should be added to your list and some might fall off the list. If you called them objectives now then that might be a barrier to changing them later.

Structuring a purpose statement with a "what" and a "why"

In 1806, the Prussian Army was resoundingly defeated by Napoleon at Jena, now a part of Germany – they lost 25,000 men to the French loss of only 5000. It is difficult to overstate the devastating effect this had on the morale of the Prussians; until that point they had been renowned for their ability to strictly execute central plans. But this all fell apart in the battle with Napoleon. In the aftermath of defeat, they began to develop a strategy that is the antidote to the rigidity of "command and control" that had failed them. Instead of telling people exactly what action to take and how to take it down to the smallest detail – a strategy that falls apart the instant something unexpected happens that isn't on the list of orders – it would be more effective to define the outcome that they were trying to achieve and why it was important. They developed a system where these "missions" were communicated down the ranks in a linked-up way, but where specific tasks weren't controlled or micro-managed and junior officers had the freedom to be creative in the way that they achieved their missions and adapt to changes. Stephen Bungay, a military historian and exponent of "Mission Leadership" or "Mission Command" has shown that this type of leadership, having been implemented for 130 years in the German Army was instrumental in Rommel's initial success in the Second World War at El-Alamein, and that the Allies under Montgomery only became successful when they adopted a similar tactic. The process is rather more complex than simply defining the purpose and the reason it is important [see box on P61], but that is the first step; it is now standard practice for NATO forces, and has been applied to civilian corporations such as Diageo and Wal-Mart by consultants in this specialty such as McKinney-Rogers. At Pfizer we tested the ability of this type of training to accelerate R&D timelines and hold fewer meetings. Several teams received the training, and their ability to deliver to timelines and the number of meetings held were compared with similar but untrained "control" teams. The number of meetings fell, and the delivery improved. Clearly the training process is beyond the scope of this book, but that does not stop us from routinely using some simple principles of this type of training to define the purpose of a decision like fulfilling a "mission". For specific decisions, as opposed to broader "missions" we can simply adopt the good practice of defining the "what", as "what is the intended effect of the decision" and the "why" as the reason why it is important.

Returning to the car purchasing example I discussed earlier, you can see that Don's ultimate decision purpose statement has 2 parts, part 1 is an <u>honest</u> and sometimes self-analytical description of the purpose – **the intended effect** - of the decision, in Don's case this is "To buy a new car". Part 2 is **the reason why it is important** and that is "in order to avoid being sad and lonely and to get more sex”. Honesty and specificity can be encouraged through using tables like the ones above. Defining the decision’s purpose and the reason why will take a bit of practice, because often you have in mind multiple possible reasons and many possible purposes. When you do this yourself, examine whether you really do have one decision or a related series of decisions [see next section]. If you are sure there really is only one decision, force yourself to define the “main effect” of your decision as one particular outcome [which becomes the “what” in your purpose statement] and keep all the others as factors you can use in your evaluation of alternatives. If you use the tables in the same way that I did for Don, you will eliminate possible purposes that are important but which won’t actually change during the decision – such as Don’s cost-saving purpose which was really just a smokescreen. If they still seem like multiple purposes, can you merge some of them into a more general category of effect so that you don’t get a long list of purposes? Remember that this can all be done before you look at what options are available for achieving the objectives, and you should resist the temptation to dive into evaluating solutions – often irresistible to committees discussing such issues. It is silly to think of solutions until you are satisfied that your purpose is correctly described because you can’t be sure that they are aligned to the purpose. In other words: don’t put your solution-finding hat on until you have succinctly described the purpose of the decision.

Best practices in defining the purpose of a decision:

Essential:

1. Define the intended "what" as a desired outcome or effect of the decision, not just the activities or options available
2. Add to the "what" the reason why you want the decision purpose to succeed

Optional but desirable for important decisions:

3. Freedoms: define what actions you are free to do or resources you can use in order to make your decision
4. Constraints: define what constraints such as time you have to observe when making your decision
5. Metrics: define how success will be measured: not in terms of activities completed but in terms of outcomes or predictors of outcomes

Freedoms, constraints and metrics

Aside from a well defined purpose – or mission – mission leadership or mission command teaches that the freedoms, constraints and metrics should also be defined. This isn't necessary for trivial decisions but for important decisions this is highly desirable because it is difficult to make a good decision without them. For example, knowing how much time and effort you have available, and how much knowledge exists is are both key inputs to your choice of decision method – remember the graphs showing how resources and error rates interacted [pages 20 and 21]? If you choose a method that is data-hungry but you don't have the data, or which takes more time than you have, that is a recipe for frustration and worse decision performance than a simpler method.

In the choosing a car example Don doesn't have any constraints on the make of vehicle or on time he might take to decide, but he is financially constrained to spend no more than his current payment. He is theoretically free to take as long as he likes to decide, but he gets bored easily and imposes another constraint that he isn't prepared to spend more than 9 hours seeking and looking at information to make a decision about a car.

If constraints are obvious, perhaps it is less obvious why you should define upfront the metrics – why can't you leave those until later when your decision has been made? The reason for including them at the beginning at least for important decisions, is that the discipline of defining measurable success is often helpful during the decision making process; if you base your decision entirely on changing things that can't be measured then it will be difficult for you to know whether your decision was ultimately successful. So Don might have defined metrics such as: reduction in derogatory comments about his vehicle, number of girlfriends willing to have sex with him and total costs including fuel and maintenance. At least if none of these improved over the next couple of years, he would perhaps realize his self-deception at that point. He could then take corrective action, such as making other choices than buying another new car. But if he didn't measure anything he might duplicate the error unwittingly.

This is true even for experts. Philip Tetlock in "Nudge" showed that when people – even famous experts – know that their forecasts will be monitored, they take more care over making them and are less likely to take an extreme position of certainty that is not supported by evidence. So the inclusion of metrics will also improve the quality inputs you get from other people as they feel more accountable.

Related decisions – creating a decision purpose cascade.

Sometimes you will find there really is more than one decision to be made, but that it is related to others in a hierarchy or flow. In that case the purpose statements can be used to clearly and specifically relate and integrate all the layers of decisions. For each new decision layer that is below the one above, the "why" statement of the lower layer is the same as the "what" statement of the upper layer. For example, let's say you were the Secretary of State for the US and you want to get a peace agreement in the Middle East:

Primary Purpose. To decide how to achieve a joint peace agreement between Israel and the Palestinians in order to achieve peace and prosperity in the Middle-East.

See how the structure is the same as before: the "what" is the intended outcome, a peace agreement. The "why" it is important is for peace and prosperity in the region. But of course this decision is at the top of a pyramid and I will now consider what is below it.

Secondary purpose 1. Determine how to get the Israeli people to agree to a peace agreement in order to achieve a joint agreement between Israel and the Palestinians.

Secondary purpose 2. Determine how to get the Palestinian people as a whole to agree to a peace agreement in order to achieve a joint agreement between Israel and the Palestinians.

Once again the purposes of the secondary decisions have the same structure, but see how the "what" statements are different from the upper layer but the "why" is the same as the "what" for the next layer up. This is the way that the decisions are connected, and even if there are many layers they can all be connected. As the NASA janitor said when asked what he was doing: "I am helping send a man to the moon".

Tertiary purpose 1. Enable an elected Israeli government to feel sufficiently secure in order to agree to a peace agreement.
Tertiary purpose 2. Solve the problem of Israeli settlers that occupy land apparently owned by Palestinians in order to get the Israeli people to agree to a peace agreement.

These purposes are of course linked to the first secondary purpose, while the ones below are linked to the second secondary purpose:

Tertiary purpose 3. Incentivize Fatah, the official government of the Palestinian people to agree or acquiesce to a peace agreement.
Tertiary purpose 4. Obtain agreement or acquiescence from Hamas, the governing party of the Gaza Strip in order to get the agreement of the Palestinian people.

I wish that peace in the Middle East was as easy as describing the relationship between such decisions and splitting them into manageable pieces and dealing with them individually from the bottom up. Obviously those decisions are still going to be terribly difficult, but the purpose of the example is to show that even for very important decisions, describing the relationship between sub-decisions can be essential if the actions to solve them are to be an integrated whole. Obviously the example above may not fit your decision series; you may have more layers or fewer layers, and more or fewer sub-decisions. It is also quite hard to do in practice and can need expert facilitation, but it is included here because even if you don't do this perfectly, if you think it is better than your current approach [which might be nothing!] then there is no loss to trying it.

Example purpose statements

Here are some more decision purpose statements that meet the requirements from the above and I also offer some explanations as to why they are better than a competing alternative:

1. A family deciding whether to move house:

To decide how to change our accommodation in order to improve our family's quality of life. This is better than "to move to a new house to get more space and be nearer to work, because moving house is not the only way to get more space [the family could build an addition] and the intended effects – the outcome - of "more space" or being "nearer to work" aren't defined. Failing to include the outcome in a statement increases the risk of unintended consequences. For example if the family had used the inferior definition, they might have bought a more expensive house with more space nearer to work. But in order to pay for it, the family breadwinners have to work longer hours and the family doesn't go on vacation to save money. The family's quality of life is reduced – and this might have been prevented by including the overall intended outcome in my recommended statement, even though the decision would have been apparently successful in the second statement.

2. A manager at work:

To select a new employee with the best blend of skills to resolve the backlog of unfinished projects and to improve productivity. Although the skills aren't specified individually, the intended purpose and likely process is clear – that the necessary skills must be identified and the candidates evaluated against them. This is an example of merging multiple possible purposes into one; if you instead listed the skills such as: interpersonal, work ethic, technical knowledge, managerial, etc., it would add little to the efficiency of communication and perhaps would remove flexibility to weight them differently or to use only some of them to select the candidate [chapter 5]. This doesn't have to be done yet as you haven't selected the decision-making method. Two beneficial outcomes are listed: resolving the backlog and improving productivity. This isn't quite as ideal as just one outcome but in this case they are justified as being equally important and covering 2 time horizons, a short-term resolution of a backlog and a long-term improvement in productivity. Productivity is – like "skills"- also a general category with a number of potential levers within it, but as a general outcome, improved productivity is not a bad objective.

3. A physician in a hospital:

To decide how or whether to treat Mrs. Johnson in order to have the greatest potential benefit to her disease with the least risk. In this case the purpose is very specific. As stated it is better than an alternative "to decide which drug to give" because that would exclude viable alternatives such as surgery or other therapies, or even no treatment at all. The outcome is also well specified; the alternative of "achieve the greatest potential benefit" would have favored treatments with high risk.

Getting to the true outcome statement

A trick to getting to the true outcome for a decision purpose statement is to keep asking two questions: "why?" and "what is the intended effect of this?" until it no longer makes sense. Often our decision-making process starts when we spontaneously identify a potential action, not its intended effect. Asking "why?" – as in "why should I take that action?" helps drive this towards the identification of the intended effect of a purpose. For the example of the physician treating a patient, if she had started with a draft purpose of "to decide which drug to give" and asked herself "why?" then she might have answered her own question that she needed to decide how to treat Mrs. Johnson. Asking "why?" again might have revealed that maybe one option should be not to treat her at all, so the word "whether" should be substituted for or added to "how". Similarly, if the family in the first example had asked why they wanted more space and to be nearer to work might have come up with "to improve our family life". Because some of these nuances might be missed at this early stage, it is good to keep reviewing the purpose as you go through the process later in this book; feel free to keep refining it as you go.

Why oh why is "why" so important?

I mentioned above that including a "why?" statement that describes why the intended effect is important helps guard against unintended consequences. There is another reason why the "why?" is important: because it specifies the nature of the harm that arises when a decision is incorrect. This is a key piece of information that helps drive what degree of diligence should be performed, how sophisticated a decision-making process should be used, how much knowledge should be sought and how much resource can be justified when making a decision. For those reasons, a decision purpose without a "why is it important" is dreadfully incomplete, and the appropriate subsequent process cannot be defined without it.

As an illustration of just how important this is, the table on the next page shows how changing the "why?" but keeping the "what" unchanged, can completely change the perceived harm from an incorrect decision. The example used is a decision with the purpose of advancing or terminating the development of a new medicine based on the current state of knowledge. For this to make sense, I have imagined different stakeholders in a decision using different "why" statements even though the "what" statement is the same.

As well as showing the importance of the "why" statement, the table shows that if you need other stakeholders than yourself to accept the purpose of your decision, it would be wise to discuss it with them before you make it. If they have a significantly different "why" statement, then their perceived harm from an erroneous decision is inevitably different to yours. They might not accept your purpose, or if you have failed to declare a purpose they will substitute their own and declare that you have failed! It is better to find out earlier rather than later if there is a major clash in the perceived rationale for a decision.

"What" statement for all stakeholders: To decide whether to advance or terminate a new drug program		
Stakeholder name and their different "Why?" statements	**Harm from decision error to advance an ineffective drug**	**Harm from decision error to stop an effective drug**
Oncologist In order to provide the first potentially effective therapy in a terminal disease	**Low** – there is no effective therapy anyway and the disease is already fatal	**High** - patients die unnecessarily because an effective treatment is falsely terminated
Food and Drug Administration In order to protect the public from harm	**High** – if a drug is advanced that is not safe or effective then this represents a failure to protect the public and FDA will be criticized	**Low** – such errors are usually invisible, there is forgiveness of good intentions, and stakeholders that judge the effectiveness of FDA's work are not likely to criticize over-toughness
Pharmaceutical company In order to maximize revenues	**Low** – if the drug is marketed but not very effective it might still make money unless litigation ensues	**High** – unnecessary loss of all the revenues that would have been earned and all the benefit to patients
Health insurance company In order to minimize costs for my company	**High** – paying a high price for a drug that is not effective	**Low** – if the drug isn't developed nobody will criticize insurers; benefits will never be known

No "why" = no benefit?

Failing to include a "why?" statement at all increases the risk that there will be no benefit at all from a decision that has consumed substantial resources. As an example of this, I recently attended a meeting where a software company presented a beautiful computer model that connected several thousand employees with the amount and nature of work they were doing. The model had taken thousands of hours of input from all departments in the organization, and had cost a seven figure sum to create. The model showed that almost all of their departments were at least 10% overworked. I asked if they were going to hire 10% more staff and the answer was a surprising "no". Was the model in error because people had included a safety margin when telling the model creators how hard they worked? Did the company think the model was true but over-working everyone by 10% was beneficial? Or did they recognize the harm of overwork but thought that overwork was viewed as less harmful to the organization than under-working? The answer was that they "didn't know what to do with the data". Why was the model created? Nobody could say, other than "to learn about their resourcing patterns".

I suggest to you that if the purpose of creating the model had been explicitly defined upfront: "to adjust departmental resources to the requirements predicted by a model in order to maximize operating efficiency" then the missing pieces such as policies, research and actions to turn the pretty graphs and bar charts into actual changes would have been included in the plan as related decisions. Instead, the "build a resourcing model" was viewed as a task or an activity to be completed on its own, without a reason why. As a result it had very little value.

How the environment can limit the purpose of a decision

Returning to the example of Brian's dilemma at CR Engineering introduced in the previous chapter, recall that Brian was supposed to choose between competing innovation projects for his struggling company. Bearing in mind the best practice we've just seen above, and recalling that Brian knows he can't just use the rules he proposed earlier, let's imagine that I got him to write down several possible purposes for the decision so he could choose which was the most appropriate. Here are the three purpose statements:

1. To launch the most popular innovation projects in order to meet management's requirements
2. To assist the innovation committee with a credible scoring system so that they can decide on the best projects
3. To launch cost-effective new projects with the greatest risk-adjusted impact in order to improve the future revenues of CR engineering

Which one do you think is the most appropriate? Of course it is a trick question because most of the options could be appropriate for a particular environment, but let's go through them and pick holes in them – and let's also look at what environments would successfully support each decision purpose.

1. To launch the most popular innovation projects in order to meet management's requirements

For this purpose the phrasing is weak because the intended effect of the decision, to find the "most popular" projects doesn't necessarily have a positive effect on the business. Popularity is rarely the best way of running a business and making decisions

– unless perhaps the committee believes in Surowiecki's "Wisdom of Crowds" more than I do. Although the purpose is honestly described here, in actuality nobody would write it down like this, especially in a low trust environment. It would be more likely that even if popularity is the real objective, it would not be admitted, this purpose would be "latent" – hidden from public view while one of the other purposes was the declared one. Continuing with discussion of purpose 1, the stated reason why: "to meet management requirements" is potentially a "cop-out" or at least a deliberately weak rationale, perhaps to avoid responsibility and to avoid the perception of failure. Unfortunately a failure to define the outcome means that it can be creatively redefined post-hoc by opponents of the project to show that it has failed even if it didn't. It is difficult to see this ever being the most appropriate selection, but perhaps could be viewed as the least bad option in some environments. Perhaps Brian knows that the CEO is intending to attack the program and he can't escape and is going to be the "fall guy", this modest purpose with other stakeholders involved might minimize the adverse effect on him and spread the blame to others.

2. To assist the committee with a credible scoring system so that they can decide on the best innovation projects

This is the most modest purpose – the "what" is merely to assist the committee and the "why" is to decide on the best innovation projects. The phrasing isn't particularly good because the "why?" – so that they can decide on the best innovation projects – is merely an activity; it isn't outcome-related at all and we don't know what the effect of the best innovation projects on the organization is intended to be. Recall that I proposed that you should keep asking "why" until you get to the ultimate outcome? Well here would be a good place to ask "Why is the committee deciding on the best projects?" That would lead to a productivity statement which would be better. We also need a word more specific than "best". Nonetheless, let's consider: could purpose 2. ever be the most appropriate option or is it routinely inferior to the other options? Well, if the phrasing was improved it could still be the best option in a low-trust environment. If the data on the projects is viewed as biased, not trusted or corrupt, or if the people who provided it are regarded as untrustworthy, then having a committee that is comprised of independent and trusted people could be the best option.

3. To launch cost-effective new projects with the greatest risk-adjusted impact in order to improve the future revenues of CR engineering

This is my favorite because it does have a "what" that is an intended effect – to launch the most cost-effective projects with the greatest risk-adjusted impact and a "why?" that is important and relevant to the business: to improve the future revenues of the company. If you picked that option, or wrote one like it yourself then you are already intuitively operating "Mission Command" or have picked up the best-practice above rapidly. This means that projects with the biggest "bang for the buck" when adjusted for risk will be selected, so the key elements of utility, cost and risk are included, and I like the economic responsibility. I will go through a simple method of doing this without having to use statistics or computation in chapter 7. In some respects this is a "gutsy" option because it recognizes that some departments may get nothing, and that could indeed be good business even if they are upset. The problem in this option is that it requires that projects costs, risks and benefits be predicted or at least estimated – and sometimes they can't be.

To my chagrin, Brian doesn't choose purpose c) but chooses b) – to assist the committee with a credible scoring system so that they can decide on the best innovation projects. He tells me that he actually likes purpose c) the best but he is not confident that cost-effectiveness and risk can be discerned from the project proposals because he hasn't yet read chapter 7 in this book. He also knows that several members of the management team view cost-effectiveness as a threat to their independence, undermining their "right to choose". Perhaps most importantly they don't trust the veracity of one another's data – and they'd have to do that in order to accept this option. In choosing the apparently inferior purpose declaration, he leaves open his option to incorporate the methods in subsequent chapters, and avoids raising objections at this stage.

Deliberately declaring a less than ideal purpose:

Advocate for the choice of the ideal purpose statement for your decision, but if you can't get it or if it won't survive the environment, then select the purpose that is the least bad but which will advance the organization towards the ideal.

The arguments and examples so far in this chapter have shown that the stated purpose of the decision is incredibly important, that it may not be possible to declare an ideal purpose if the environment will not support it, and that some purposes are hidden or "latent" because nobody declared them or because they deliberately declared the wrong purpose.

I do not like hidden or less than ideal purposes for decisions, because the effectiveness of communication that arises from a "good" purpose statement has been compromised and people can't efficiently and creatively have ideas that will deliver it. A complicated latent environment is therefore a sign of an inefficient organization. It also introduces new risks of failure that can't overtly be managed because they are hidden and won't be listed as relevant to the ideal purpose. Nonetheless, if the alternative was declaring an ideal purpose that would be unacceptable to management, this would represent the pragmatic best that we could do in that environment.

I got Brian to create a table that showed CR Engineering's declarations about its own environment, along with his observations and conclusions about the "latent" [hidden] environment that will actually receive the decision – and the latent environment was substantially different from that which the company overtly declared.

Declared environment	**Observations**	**Conclusions on "Latent" environment**
Supportive of innovation	Provision of budget for innovation projects Reluctance of CEO to accept program	Brian needs the appearance of innovation but the projects may be judged harshly and prematurely
Collegiate, honest, high integrity	Different teams compete fiercely for the same budget Information provided by the teams is often wildly optimistic and inaccurate	Dishonesty is tolerated if it has the intention of securing budget for a department Once the project is funded nobody tracks the veracity of initial information
Financially careful	At the beginning good practice is valued. Near calendar year end it is usually "spend, spend, spend" to meet annual targets	The appearance of financial responsibility is important for some of the year but meeting an annual target is more important than financial efficiency

Deducing a purpose when it isn't declared – becoming a purpose "detective"

It is not just Brian who accidentally or by design did not want to declare an ideal purpose in advance – it just isn't a common discipline to do so, and is sometimes deliberately avoided to leave flexibility for "spin" about declaring success. As a result, critics of decisions can get great mileage out of creating their own version of the intended purpose after the event, and showing the decision clearly failed for that purpose. Advocates can perform the same magic, on the same outcome but changing the apparently intended purpose of a decision to show that it did succeed for something different. In fact it is human nature for us to become "purpose detectives", and ironically we can become more annoyed about the motives for a purpose that we perceive to be wrong than the actions that occurred as a result of it.

The danger is that if your "natural conclusion" about somebody else's intended purpose is wrong then all that righteous indignation you may feel is wasted [and potentially harmful] and the solutions you would propose to correct the situation are likely to be incorrect. A comprehensive evaluation of an undeclared purpose is very like real detective work – it requires seeking evidence in a comprehensive and fair manner.

Example: publication bias, the dog that didn't bark

In order to demonstrate good practice for how to "track down" an undeclared purpose, I have chosen an important example in the scientific and medical literature of the well known effect called "publication bias". Although this sounds utterly boring it has potentially quite profoundly important effects – because medical practice is established and improved based on what is published. Physicians, nurses and health insurance companies all base their practices on what they read in independent journals: our medicines, our surgeries, our diagnostics and indeed our individual survival may depend on the quality of this published evidence. The problem called "publication bias" arose when some statisticians studied the entire landscape of clinical trials of new treatments and therapies, including all that were actually published in scientific journals. They looked at how "positive" the studies were and they found something equivalent to "the curious incident of the dog in the night time"

As Sherlock Holmes put it in Conan-Doyle's story "Silver Blaze" written in 1892:

Gregory (Scotland Yard detective): "Is there any other point to which you would wish to draw my attention?"
Sherlock Holmes: "To the curious incident of the dog in the night-time."
Gregory: "The dog did nothing in the night-time."
Sherlock Holmes: "That was the curious incident."

Our analogous "curious incident" with medical publications is that when studies and clinical trials were negative, when they showed that the treatment did not work or was no different to the existing therapy, they were much less likely to be published.

They were silent – like Sherlock Holmes' dog.

This means that the medical literature on which practice is based is incomplete. There has been a substantial outcry against this: key opinion leaders have stated that it "...distorts the body of evidence available for clinical decision-making", that it represents "a severe impediment to combining the statistical results of studies collected from the literature" and it is "one of the most vexing and chronic problems facing medicine today".

This statistical evidence of wrongdoing in an environment where there is little respect or trust for drug companies has been viewed as a "smoking-gun" that shows unethical decision-making practice by drug companies and academics funded by industry. Even though nobody has admitted it, the undeclared purpose of this bias is assumed by journal editors and some outspoken academics to be:

"To publish results that are beneficial to new medical products and suppress ones that are not, in order to maximize revenues for drug companies and the academics they support."

Aside from a large dollop of righteous indignation, a solution has been served up: academic investigators are told that they "have an ethical obligation to submit the results of their research for publication" and any funding of academics by industry is regarded as a conflict as it is causative of bias. Harvard has been accused of ethics violations simply for accepting funding for research projects from the drug industry. Huge effort has been taken to eliminate industry support for any academics at the National Institutes of Health, to prevent academics supported by industry from giving advice on some important advisory committees to the Food and Drug Administration, and to track the completion and publication of all clinical trials.

But what if this is wrong? The purpose statement above is simply plausible but imagined. If the purpose has been misconstrued then all of this effort is misplaced and the sense of scandal and indignation is erroneous. Perhaps worst of all, the proposed solutions may be unnecessary, costly and harmful. I therefore examined whether other purposes than the one above might explain what is seen in the publication of medical research.

For this I make the analogy that the publication system is like a diagnostic test for "scientific truth". A traditional diagnostic test can be "tuned" to reveal the most important "truth" for a particular medical or scientific purpose by changing its decision threshold. For example, there is published guidance from the American Heart Association for what degree of difference from "normal" defines whether your cholesterol or high blood pressure should be treated. These are called decision thresholds and creating them for yourself is discussed in Chapter 9. Changing the position of the threshold changes the performance of the test: if I set a threshold where even tiny changes are counted as being positive, the test will be very sensitive to real positive changes, but natural variation or "noise" in the test or in the patient will also cause small positive changes which are not actually true but nonetheless these will be counted as positive – so-called "false positives". For example if the threshold for high blood pressure was set at 80mmHg diastolic, everyone who is simply nervous of their doctor would be treated unnecessarily. If I try and fix that problem by setting a very large threshold so that only big changes are counted as positive, bigger than most random variation, say 95 millimeters of mercury [mmHg] diastolic, nearly all of my positive tests [higher than 95] will be in people who truly do have high blood pressure because simple nervousness of the doctor doesn't usually cause increases in blood pressure above that level. Unfortunately, the downside of increasing the threshold is that a number of "real" but mild cases of high blood pressure will falsely be called negative and won't be treated because they were under my threshold – so-called "false negatives". This shows how changes in the decision threshold will vary the true and false positive and true and false negative rates of the test. In practice the decision thresholds are adjusted for a particular population depending on the likelihood and the effect of a false positive or false negative result. A test where the decision-threshold is "tuned" for one purpose in one population is not likely to perform so well for other purposes in other populations: normal diastolic blood pressure in a giraffe is 160mmHg!

I hypothesized that the observed bias – that the current decision thresholds for medical publications that appear to favor positive studies over negative studies – could simply represent good "tuning" for purposes that the critics have not considered. Even though nobody had consciously or overtly defined such a tuning process and nobody created specific decision thresholds, it is not difficult to hypothesize that the publications could behave like a free market. In that case the publication [or not] of an article is like the price of a share, responsive to hidden value perceived by the human "buyers" – the journal editors and reviewers. In other words, it might be the "right thing" that the publication system has a decision threshold that appears to count even small positive changes as true, but which tends to disbelieve and not publish negative studies. If that were true, the effect would persist not because of the "smoking gun" reasons of poor ethics by industry, but because these other purposes are important and useful, and this translates unconsciously into a persistent effect to support those purposes.

Being a decision purpose detective, I therefore wrote down all the names of the suspects – all the possible purposes of a journal publication system that I could think of. I've used the style for purposes recommended earlier in the chapter:

a. Entertainment for scientific readership in order to maximize sales of medical journals
b. An accurate and complete record of scientific research in order to create a basis for statistical analyses across many studies to improve clinical decision making
c. Sensitive detection of new scientific signals in order to guide directions for new research
d. Advertising of scientific skills, academic experience or therapeutic or diagnostic products in order to maximize revenues or enhance academic status
e. Providing scientific information with the greatest benefit/risk to the readership in order to have the greatest beneficial impact on medical practice and the least harm

Each purpose would lead to a different prioritization of particular kinds of content for the journals. Prioritization is another word for "bias". So I am really identifying what type of bias would be needed to optimize the publication system for each kind of purpose. As I mentioned before, prior assertions by journal editors and academics have been that that purpose d) advertising to maximize revenues has created the bias that undermines purpose b) an accurate and complete record of research. Because that was rather conveniently aligned with some editors' known political agendas, I was curious to see whether any other possibilities are equally likely – and indeed that turned out to be the case.

The first point of note is that the journal editors have advocated as a principle that purpose b), the creation of an accurate and complete scientific record is an ethical direction for their journals. I agree with them; however, thinking back to our principles chapter, it is worth seeking other alternative purposes that might be equally [or indeed more] ethically principled.

Interestingly, I find that there are 2 other candidates that have equal or higher ethical "principle currency value": purpose c) the sensitive detection of early scientific signals and purpose e) maximizing the benefit/risk of scientific information. So these other purposes cannot be trumped on principle.

Here is a summary of the effects that each undeclared purpose would have on the contents of the journal if the content responded to the market forces driving that purpose:

- Purpose a) entertainment would drive the publication of controversial or interesting results; positive studies are generally more interesting than negative ones.
- Purpose b) an accurate and complete scientific record would have no bias, all studies would be published independent of their result.
- Purpose c) the sensitive detection of new scientific signals would drive the publication of preliminary positive studies so that more research could be directed in that direction. It would also set a higher hurdle for the publication of negative studies lest resources be falsely removed from an area that should continue to be researched.
- Purpose d) advertizing would lead to the preferred publication of positive studies of benefit to a product but the under-publication of positive studies of harm.
- Purpose e) greatest benefit-risk would lead to publication of positive studies if the benefit is high but the harm of error is low, and similar principles in negative studies.

The summary shows that three of the five purposes: a), c) and d) can each drive the bias towards what is actually observed: the observed over-reporting of positive studies and under-reporting of negative studies. However the explanation usually offered: d), advertizing is not a straightforward driver of this bias. That would lead to over-reporting of benefits to products such as positive results of benefits and negative results of adverse effects combined with under-reporting of issues that undermine products such as positive results of adverse effects and negative effects of benefits. That is a type of context-dependent bias that might possibly exist but which has not typically examined through the statistical methods that are used to support the overall conclusions of bias.

The purpose that is simplest and most consistent with the bias actually seen in the literature is therefore b) sensitive detection of new scientific signals in order to guide directions for new research, as this drives a pure emphasis on reporting of any positive study, and under-reporting of any negative study so that sensitivity, which drives new resources to interesting areas is maximized and false negative reporting that would lead to a false reduction in research resourcing to existing areas is minimized. Not only is this more consistent with the evidence than the purposes offered by the journals and academic politicians, it is also a very worthy and ethical approach for journals to take.

Why did the journal editors jump to a specific conclusion about the purpose of the bias that might be wrong and isn't the best fit for what is actually seen? We don't know of course, but surely the lack of trust of the drug industry was a contributing factor and let's face it, being an even-handed purpose detective isn't the first response that comes to mind when an interesting and juicy scandal surfaces. What is more important though is that if the definition of the problem is wrong, the proposed solution that is being executed by journals and academic institutions is probably wrong too: they advocate for severing or exposing links between the drug industry and academia, and requiring publication of all studies whether positive or negative. Action has already been taken in this direction with the required registration of all clinical trials so that a count can be made and publication of all studies ensured as we go forward. Unfortunately, if the optimal purpose of the journal system really is to identify promising new findings as I suggest, then that purpose would be made substantially less efficient by the so-called solution that changes the decision threshold back to neutral. Some of the limited attention span of readers will be soaked up by the publication of falsely negative studies that were poorly designed or which had unexpectedly high variability or just simply went wrong in their execution. The real purpose of the journals: sensitivity to new findings will be compromised. Requiring severance of links between academics and industry will at best be irrelevant and at worst will reduce commercial support for important and excellent academic research. Now of course I can't prove that my deduced purpose is the real one any more than the journal editors can, but it is disappointing that there has been no real debate about the unintended consequences of the actions.

This exercise reveals that imputing a purpose, for good or ill, for somebody else's decision is not to be undertaken lightly. Although declaring mal-intent is a well-recognized tool of the trade in politics and in those interested in scandal-creation, the risk to the decision-maker can be mitigated by declaring clearly the intended purpose in advance.

Involving others when defining a decision mission

In the examples above we have assumed that you or a small number of close associates, colleagues or family members can adequately view the current state, the desired future state and the environment to define an adequate decision mission with its constraints and freedoms. For many decisions this is reasonable, but as Paul Nutt shows in his analysis of "Why Decisions Fail", failure to involve key stakeholders from the beginning can lead to the definition of an incorrect purpose, or of missing some constraints that the left-out stakeholders would require. For example he cites the decision of Shell to dispose of the Brent Spar oil platform at sea, where the management was focused on the most cost-effective disposal method. Had they involved the environmentalists earlier, they would perhaps have realized some of the potential constraints, in particular an opposition to deep-sea disposal that ultimately forced them to reverse their decision.

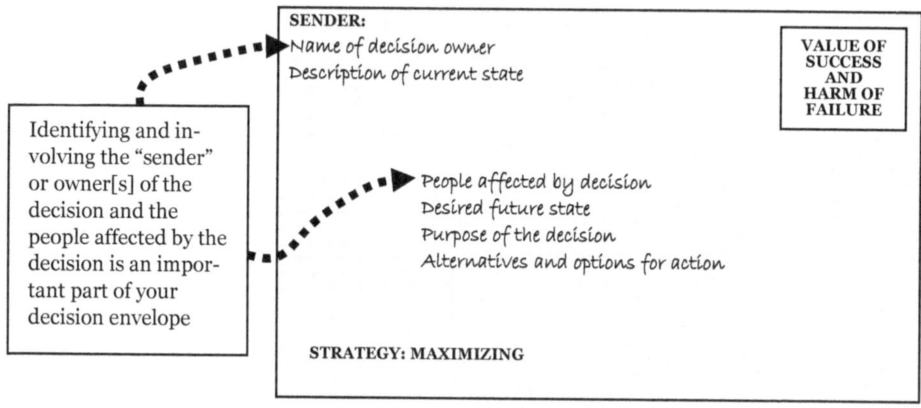

It is also worth you asking "who owns this decision?"or "who thinks they own this decision?" If it is not you, or if it is not clear and you are unilaterally trying to impose an approach to decision-making on the owner or somebody who perceives that they are the owner then you'd better backtrack and address that issue now. Even if you are not the owner, you can still run the decision-making process – you can be the "decision architect" as named by Thaler and Sunstein in "Nudge" as long as the owner[s] or stakeholder[s] have agreed that you can do so, or at least that they will look at your result. Your process could be perfect but will almost certainly be rejected if somebody doesn't think it is your decision to make and you've gone off and done it on your own. Have a look at the diagram below which describes key issues you need to remember:

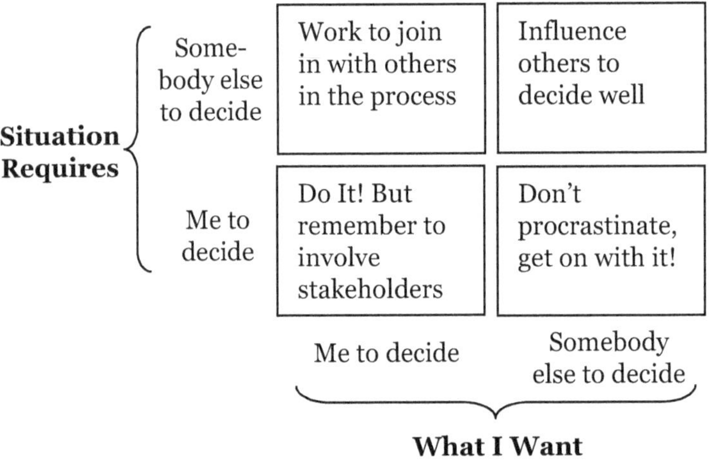

Because of my drive towards simplicity, and because I haven't yet defined the value of this decision or the harm it might cause, I recommend only involving key stakeholders at this stage; there will be another opportunity to broaden stakeholder input when discussing the consequences of the alternatives.

Decision Purpose Checklist

- Are you sure your decision is important enough to spend the effort of defining a purpose? Is it at least of moderate value if successful and moderate harm if it fails?
  - Don't get into decision debt!
- Did you evaluate the current state and desired future state?
- Did you describe your freedoms and constraints?
- Did you get input from key stakeholders?
- Have you defined a purpose statement with a "what" is the intended effect and a "why" is it important?
- Is your statement completely honest?
- Is the purpose realistically achievable?
- Do you know how you will measure the extent to which it has been achieved?
- Will the overt and the latent environments accept your purpose or do you need to pragmatically adjust it?

Key learnings from chapter 3:

- When you are defining the purpose of a decision, the process starts with an honest appraisal of the current state and the ideal but realistic state after a successful decision - with input from key stakeholders.
- If the decision is important you should include a view of technical, economic and human factors: T.H.E. Decisionability triangle in your appraisals of the current and future state.
- Your decision purpose statement should contain: a "what" is the intended effect and a reason: a "why?" this is important.
- Your reason "why" is important because it can completely change the perceived harm from decision errors.
- Remember, if the decision is important, to add your freedoms, constraints and how you will assess the success of the decision.
- If you understand the overt and latent parts of the environment you face, you will understand whether your ideal purpose may pragmatically have to be changed – but be very reluctant to do this!
- If you or others do not specify a purpose, it is difficult to judge whether a decision is wrong or right – but politicians make much mileage out of this; a decision that appears "wrong" may be "right" for a different purpose that has not been identified, and a decision that appears "right" may be "wrong."

- If you need to "reverse engineer" a purpose – when it was not declared, or where somebody else has imputed a purpose for good or ill requires the following steps:
    - List the currently observed actions/effects of a decision
    - Identify all the possible purposes that might be behind the decision
    - Identify the likely observations that would be associated with each different purpose
    - Determine whether the actual observed effects for one option are a "best match" for a given purpose

Chapter 4: How good is "good enough?"

Identifying the motive force for your decision – what value stamp is on your envelope?

The chart below shows how the driving force for your decision can be estimated, and is represented as a postage stamp:

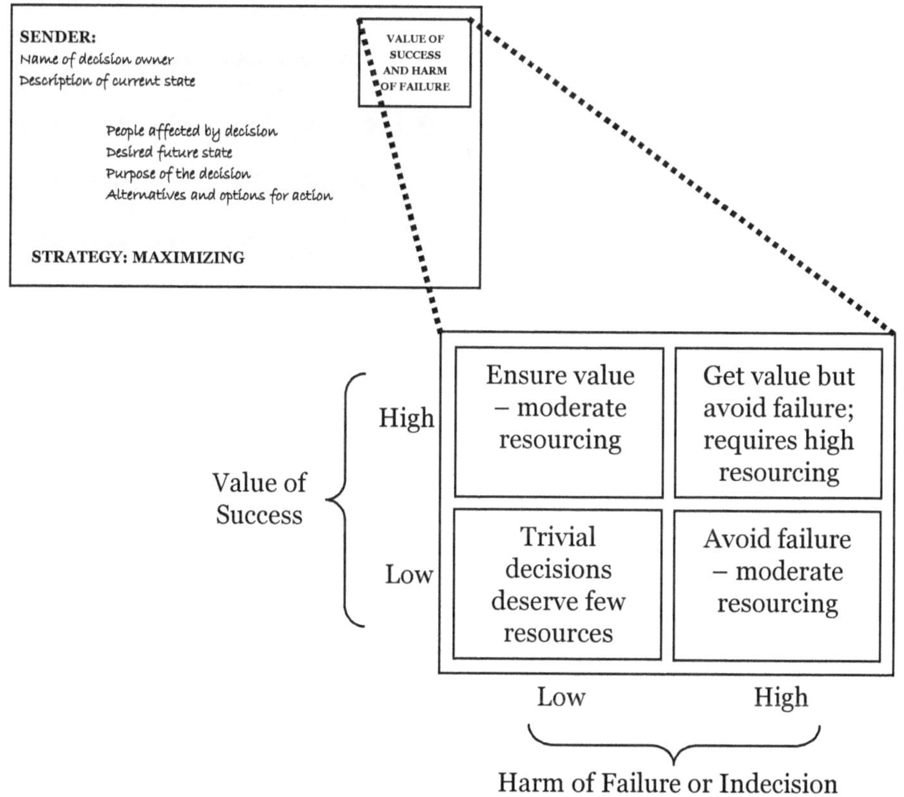

The postage-stamp chart has 2 inputs: the expected value of successfully achieving the decision purpose, and the harm of an unsuccessful decision or of failing to make a decision. The output of the chart is a limit on the degree of effort that would be supported by such a decision, or the "motive-force" for your decision. Thus, a high value of success and a high harm of failure or indecision is analogous to a high value stamp. Just as an expensive stamp would pay for a large, heavy envelope stuffed with documents, a high value high harm motive pays for a large, heavy decision stuffed with care, thought and information! Conversely, an envelope with a high value stamp with very little inside it represents inefficiency and waste, as does a decision of trivial value or harm which has received a thorough and obsessive evaluation. Decisionability requires you to proceed with decisions where the effort of making them is at worst equal to - but ideally much less than the value achieved, or the harm avoided: where the stamp pays for the weight of the contents.

I have already proposed that you get specific about the value of your successful decision when you construct your purpose, but what of evaluating the harm of failure? The original Hippocratic oath for physicians contained the phrase "to abstain from doing harm" and more controversially perhaps to prevent harm the oath also contained the phrase: "I will not use the knife for the stone" – which effectively banned surgery for kidney stones. For obvious reasons the last phrase was dropped from the oath in modern times. Can't a decision just avoid harm altogether?

Unfortunately, as it is not possible to perform surgery without the harm of a wound, it is rarely possible to take an action as part of a decision that has no possible harm. The harm can arise from some unintended consequences of a decision that were not predicted, from known and expected consequences that are indelibly associated with some of the alternatives analogous to military "collateral damage" and from indecision: failing to take action can often be harmful in itself.

Don't worry about trying to be quantitative with this; the point of the postage stamp chart is simply to explain the driving principles. For most decisions your subjective opinion is all that is required: which of the 4 quadrants do you think you are in?

What comes after characterizing your purpose?

The formation of a purpose will have taken time, sometimes only a few seconds, other times a few days or even weeks. Having done so, there are at least 4 choices of what to do right now:

- **Abandon**: Don't expend any further effort, the decision purpose isn't worth the effort of proceeding, abandon the process right here and go make a cup of tea.
- **Defer**: When you are not sure of a purpose or when some important new information will become available and there is no adverse consequence of delaying the process.
- **Jump**: Under extreme time pressure jump straight to a heuristic and act without spending the time to identify all alternatives and their features.
- **Proceed carefully**: When the decision is likely to be worth the effort, where there is sufficient time to get it right and to make sure the decision is "good enough."

Most of this chapter will be spent discussing the actions that result from the "proceed" choice, but first let's briefly discuss the legitimate and illegitimate uses of the other choices at this stage.

Abandoning a decision is sometimes "good enough" - a legitimate option; it is the best option if your decision is worth less than costs or effort of making it. When you are a Decisionability expert this will become a simple assessment because you will be able to look forwards, predict the right method and estimate the time and effort needed. However, right now you may or may not be that expert in how much effort each method will take, but you can still take some simple "abandon" decisions. Almost all of the methods in this book will be too costly in time and effort for decisions in the very lower left quadrant of the chart – those of low value and low harm. It is still OK to make those decisions simply but the key is to avoid "decision debt". This is where the effort of making the decision is greater than the benefit of having made it. This is an odd case of a decision not being "good enough"; it is not that the decision was taken and failed, but that the decision was taken when it should not have been.

Causes of "decision debt"

- You made a decision where the perceived effort or cost of making it was already as high as [or higher than] the perceived value of success.
- You had to expend the effort of monitoring whether you made the right decision.
- You were sometimes wrong and had to add even more cost: the cost of self-blame or guilt.

Examples of decisions with a low value and low harm where the benefit of deciding is less than the cost of the decision include:

- I am in slow-moving traffic; do I change lanes repeatedly to go faster?

- Which checkout line do I stand in at Wal-Mart?
- My wife sent me to the supermarket for bread - what brand do I buy? [Note: if your wife is bigger and stronger than you this may not be a low harm decision!]
- Which of my favorite dishes do I choose from the Chinese restaurant menu?
- Do I answer all the emails in my inbox?

Given that these decisions often cause considerable anguish, annoyance and frustration, not to mention road-rage, it seems strange that we devote so much wasted emotion to them. It is partly that making the effort to take a decision in a low value low harm situation is annoying because the cost of the decision has already exceeded the value. Then if the decision turns out to have been unsuccessful – the traffic in your original lane is now moving faster, the line in the other aisle that you left has now accelerated – the annoyance rises because not only did you "pay" too much in terms of effort for the decision, but now you are stuck with the negative feelings from the personal responsibility of being wrong. Additionally, if you did decide to make the decision, you probably specified a metric – you picked a "marker" car in the other lane, or you picked a person in another aisle, and you expended effort on looking to see if you beat them or not. You just went into "Decision Debt" – you mailed a decision envelope where the stamp isn't sufficient to support the weight and size of the envelope! Postage due: return to sender!

Deciding not to decide

Abandoning your decision once you have identified the above dangers avoids a lot of frustration – but you will have to keep reminding yourself not to decide and not to monitor others' progress as you drive in the slow lane in traffic, or not to count the people in each supermarket aisle. Just turn up the radio or just think about something useful like writing a book on decision making. For executives bombarded with trivial email, either you or a delegate should screen the mails and make the calculations – is reading this email worth the cost, is making a decision and giving an answer worth the cost? If no, then the emails should be deleted without a reply – and more importantly without the effort of making the decision. Annoyingly this is hard to do in practice, because the very act of reading carries a cost that is often higher than the value of the email, and then it is hard not to start making the decision.

When you decide not to decide, you should still keep an eye open for changes in value or harm – if the fundamental value or harm of the decision changes as you go forward then re-evaluate. If they close the cashier in front of you, or if there is a crashed car or lane closure sign, then the cost/benefit of making the decision has changed with new information, and you can change your mind.

If you have decided not to decide but a choice needs to be made because there isn't a "do nothing" option then you can employ a coin-flip or close your eyes and stick a pin into the choices. Alternatively, if there is someone available who will get pleasure out of making the choice, or where there is some value to be had from the appearance of asking others, then ask them to decide. But don't just try and pass on your decision burden to somebody else if they don't want it or if it would not be a positive experience for them, that's not fair.

The cost of decision making in low value low harm situations may also explain the apparent distortion of "free" gifts on the behavioral economics of decision making. In "Predictably Irrational" Dan Ariely explains how making an object "free" distorts the economics vs. another choice. A great example of this was an experiment he conducted when people were offered a Hershey's Kiss for one cent or a Lindt Truffle for 15 cents, where 27% chose the Kiss and 73% the truffle. Then the researchers dropped the price of each item by one cent – the Hershey's Kiss became free and the truffle was 14 cents but the price difference between them was still 14 cents. Surprisingly, with only a one-cent change, the number choosing the Kiss increased from 27% to 69% and the number choosing the truffle fell from 73% to 31%. Ariely's explanation is that the concept of "free" gives us such an emotional charge that it helps us overlook the downside of it. The downside in this case was that people who chose the "free" Hershey's kiss denied themselves the opportunity of a "bargain" truffle. My alternate explanation for at least a part of the free effect is that it represents relief from the mental cost of having to make a decision. If something is free, you don't have to create a decision envelope and evaluate whether the stamp on it supports the weight of the contents. In other words, if the mental effort of making the cost-benefit decision between a Kiss and the truffle was more than the value of the truffle, then abandoning the decision and just taking the free item makes sense without having to consider the existence of an emotional charge of a "free" item.

Avoiding self-blame or blame from others is a legitimate reason for abandonment of a decision ONLY if the value is low and the harm of indecision is low. This is not legitimate if the value of harm is high. In that case it is a reason for continuing despite the risk, but expending more care on the decision, even if you don't want to. When you realize that making a decision is going to require considerable effort, perhaps more effort than you realized, you must avoid the temptation to abandon it if the benefits are significant or if the harm of failing to act is significant.

An Example of Wrongful Abandonment

My old neighbor Tim has a very nice BMW 550 and he ordered it with 19-inch wheels and high performance tires which grip wonderfully well on warm roads in the summer. Unfortunately snow was on the ground in Connecticut while I was writing this part of the book, and his car was sliding so much on the highway the week before that a Police officer had to escort him off at the next ramp, much to his embarrassment. Drivers of BMWs don't like such indignities!

So he borrowed his wife's minivan and left his car in the garage. I and others convinced him that winter tires would make a huge difference to this problem, and so he went online and reviewed the different makes, sizes and prices. Then there were online review comments to read from people who had already bought different tires, some of them scathing and some of them glowing with praise – but how do you know whether to believe them? Nonetheless, he made an evaluation of the opinions he read. Then he had to decide whether to pay extra for tire pressure monitors and he anguished over the style and price of wheel that the tires came on. Finally, when he came to hit the order button, the brand he chose was out of stock. So what did he do? You probably already guessed it, he was already frustrated with the unexpected complexity of the process and he abandoned, or unnecessarily deferred the decision.

This is not a low value situation – the tires could save his – and his children's- lives. It is not a low harm of indecision/delay situation, he has to use his wife's van and when she is using it, he uses his car and risks sliding or getting stuck. The stamp on the decision envelope was a big one, but nonetheless the temptation to abandon arose principally because the decision was more complex than expected and budgeted for.

When you find yourself in such a situation it is a good idea to focus back on the value-harm equation and to stick it out and complete the process as planned. Another idea is to use simpler, less frustrating decision strategy of which we will hear more later, but the hint given here is that for Tim, any winter tire is substantially safer than what he has on his car, so he doesn't need a complex decision procedure to maximize the tire price and performance, just choosing something "good enough" that fits his car and is in-stock should be acceptable.

When is deferring the decision process "good enough"?

You can legitimately defer a decision if there is a low harm from deferral or delay, and where there is some potential value to delay such as the availability of new information. Do not confuse this with procrastination, which is the illegitimate delay of a decision or process. If you are in doubt and you know you are a procrastinator then you should not defer – your doubts probably come from your natural tendencies to delay and you should decide now. If you are a "doer" and you are in doubt, then you should probably defer, your natural tendencies to do things first and ask questions later are probably biasing the assessment of whether to defer.

Keeping your options open like this does carry a cost. You need to keep an eye on your deferred decision like managing a small project: timelines have to be remembered, information relevant to the decision acquired and cataloged so you can make regular evaluations whether it is the right time to actually make the decision. If you are not good at tracking information the danger is that you might forget. The decision value is then lost, and the consequences of indecision acquired accidentally. The costs of carrying many open options may be small for each decision, but if you or your organization is carrying a lot of them it can add up to be a significant burden. It can also turn into an inefficient and unproductive cultural routine, where excuses are made for not making decisions. The antidote to this is for you to ask: "what would it take for us to be able to reach a decision on this option" and to list the information required at the time of deferral. Then you can make a plan to acquire the information, and check regularly on it so that options are closed out as quickly as possible.

Defer your decision if:

- There is low harm from delay.
- There is value to be gained from delay, such as availability of more information.
- You can define the information you are waiting for at the time of deferral.
- You are prepared to track the information you are waiting for.
- You don't have so many open options or deferred decisions that the overall burden of carrying them is large.

<u>Deciding to decide vs. deciding not to decide</u>

Your comfort level in deciding when to decide and deciding when not to make a decision is tied up with your personality type and experience. This can be represented on a chart called a "receiver operating characteristic" or ROC curve usually used to represent how good a medical test is, but I have borrowed it for subjective decision making here. The reason that this chart is special and worth taking a minute on, even though a little complicated, is that it is the best way to show the tradeoff between deciding and not deciding that we are all forced to make.

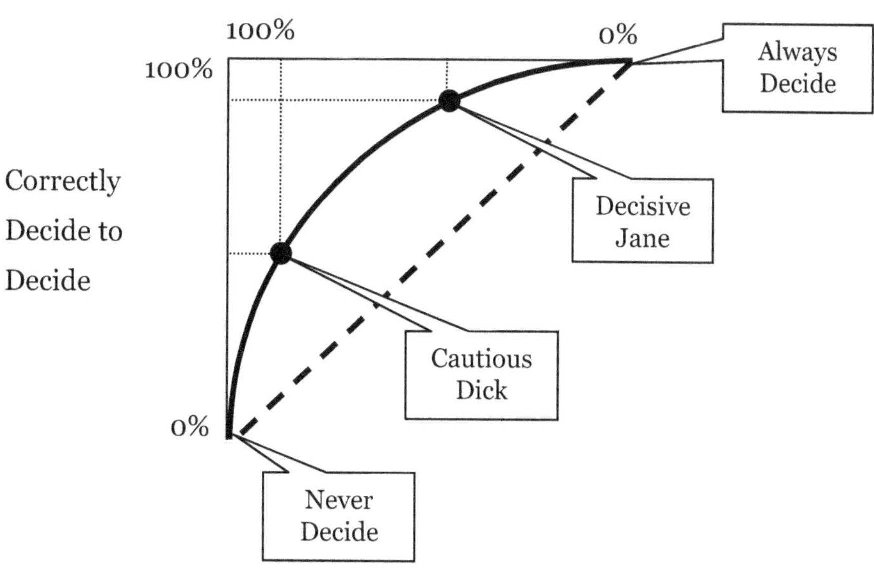

The simplest way to be sure that you are correctly deciding <u>not</u> to decide is to never decide anything; in that case you are in the bottom left hand corner of the chart: you score 100% on the correctly not deciding but 0% on the deciding to decide.

Conversely, the simplest way to ensure that you always decide when you should is to always decide; in that case you are in the top right hand corner of the graph and you score 100% on the correctly deciding to decide but 0% on the correctly deciding not to decide. Unfortunately you are not adding real value to the process at all if you choose one of these extremes; the value of a coin flip is shown on the dashed diagonal line and both of the above selections are on it!

Where you and I both should wish that we are is in the top left hand corner of the box with 100% scores on each but that would require perfect Decisionability. More realistically, I have drawn a curved line for a modest degree of expertise in this area – better than the coin flip but not perfect. On this line I show two people of the same degree of expertise [because they are both on the same curve] but considerably different personalities, both of whom I am sure you have met, perhaps staring at you in the mirror.

"Cautious Dick" likes to make perfect decisions, He doesn't like to decide until he is really sure he is going to be right, and he demands lots of information before deciding. He sees himself as a bastion against poor quality decisions. As a result he scores very highly on correctly avoiding a decision – about 80%, but he only scores 30% on correctly deciding to decide because he often procrastinates or simply refuses to make decisions where he can't maximize, even in situations that don't demand it.

On the other hand, "Decisive Jane" loves being decisive, she sees herself as "just getting on with it"; she advances without delay. She doesn't often wait to get more data because she values speed the most. She scores more than 80% on the correctly deciding to decide but she doesn't do so well on correctly avoiding a decision, again about 30%. I have seen situations at work where these 2 experts sometimes despise one another – Dick sees Jane as making poor quality decisions whereas Jane sees Dick as unnecessarily delaying things. I have also seen – in my own parents – "Dick" married to "Jane", where the combination of the two skill sets symbiotically enabled the couple to have access to both types of skill.

In this story both Dick and Jane have the same degree of Decisionability, just in different flavors. As your Decisionability improves using the principles in this chapter the line you are on in the chart a couple of pages ago will bulge more towards the top left hand corner - your scores for correctly deciding to decide and correctly deciding not to decide will improve. For a specific situation you will be also be able to choose to be Dick or Jane, or in fact anywhere on the same expertise line. This doesn't involve any cross-dressing, but rather that you will be able to make a conscious choice about your decision threshold, whether to just do it or whether to get more information. This will depend on what the worse error will be for a given situation: is it worse to fail to act or to act when it is not necessary? If the failure to act has a higher cost then you will be Jane. If the acting spuriously has a higher cost then you will be Dick!

<u>When to seek the best and when to seek what is "good enough"</u>

Having eliminated all the ways of avoiding decisions, you have arrived at the "proceed" part of the decision making process. Now I need to introduce two important concepts that impact the decision making strategy: **satisficing** and **maximizing** [I'd abbreviate this to S and M but that one's taken by something else equally painful].

Satisficing is a term that was apparently a local word from Northumberland UK, but first brought into use in decision theory by Herbert Simon, a Nobel-prize winning economist and psychologist and advanced by Gigerenzer [Simple Heuristics that Make us Smart] and further in "The paradox of Choice" by Barry Schwartz.

> **Satisficing is**: *"to settle for something that is good enough and not to worry about the possibility of something better".*

Having lived in Northumberland for a while, I couldn't resist theorizing that the word originated there because it is a satisficing place – it is pretty, but not as pretty as the neighboring Cumbria or Yorkshire, the weather is better than Scotland but worse than southern England, the cost of living is reasonable but not the lowest – and so on, so that it is at least "good enough" in every important factor but winner in none – and most importantly it doesn't lose badly in any category either. As a result it is a nice place to live. In the previous example, "Decisive Jane" was a habitual satisficer in her search for getting things done quickly.

I like to think of satisficing as "knowing where you are not" – as in navigating away from the rocks or other harmful situations – but not needing to know exactly where you are. In contrast:

> ***Maximizing*** *is "to seek and accept only the best".*

Maximizing is a much more familiar concept; in navigation terms, this is analogous to knowing as precisely as possible where you are on the map. In decision-making it means that you should examine all possible options and do the best possible characterization of them in order to make the best decision. In the previous example, "Cautious Dick" was a habitual maximizer, seeking the best quality decisions and procrastinating or refusing to make decisions where maximization wasn't possible.

In general, habitual maximizers do not necessarily plan to limit their resources, understand the boundaries of knowledge or limit the expectation of performance to anything other than perfection. However, maximizers in Decisionability do all of those things. Recall the graph I used in Chapter 1 to illustrate the available and acceptable part of the line relating decision performance to knowledge, time and resources.

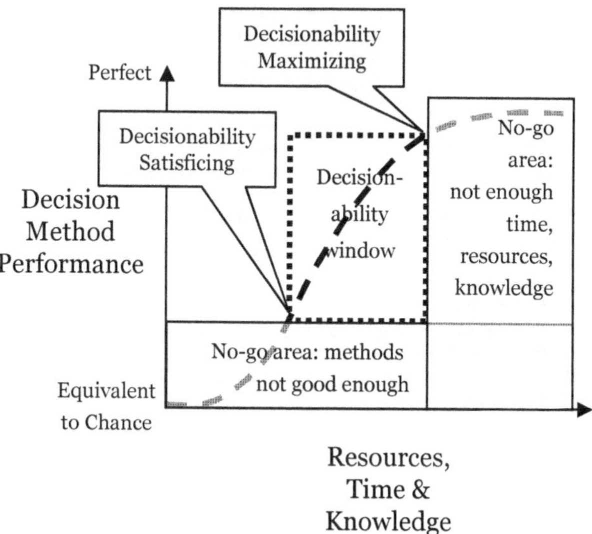

I have now added Decisionability satisficing and Decisionability maximizing labels to the chart. As a reminder, the dashed line shows an imagined relationship between resourcing/knowledge and the performance of decision making methods. The bottom left origin of the dashed line is unavailable – covered by the "not good enough" box. The "not good enough" box is a different size in different situations: it grows as the value of a decision or the harm of indecision is higher and shrinks in situations where value and harm are lower. The upper right of the dashed line is close to perfection but it is obscured by the "not enough resources" box, resource limits which can be imposed externally by the lack of availability of data, or by you because you don't want to go into decision debt by expending more effort than the decision is worth. Again, in a given situation your "not enough resources" box can be large or small. In the case shown on this graph there is quite a bit of the useable line that is not obscured by the "no-go" areas.

The difference between what I am recommending and prior uses of these words is that I have defined acceptable boundaries. In contrast I do not support unbounded maximizing or unbounded satisficing. Unbounded maximizing leads to seeking the best beyond the appropriate or available resources. In "The Paradox of Choice" Schwartz shows that maximization as a strategy is associated with much misery and regret – even when people do make objectively better decisions because of their maximization, they do not appear to be subjectively happier because they are still disappointed that some elements of their decision weren't perfect. The intent of my "Decisionability maximization" approach is to have less cause for regret by eliminating the expectation of perfection and of piercing the illusion of unlimited resources. In contrast, Decisionability satisficing prevents the making of decisions with an unacceptable decision failure rate.

The "least bad" decision

The next graph shows the unpleasant situation where the entire Decisionability line is obscured, because the resourcing "no go" box has extended to the left (you have very few resources available) and the "methods not good enough" box has grown upwards because your decision is high value and high harm. In that case you are stuck with the least bad choice: select the best approach that you can up to the limit in time, resources or knowledge even if it is not "good enough" it is still better than random chance.

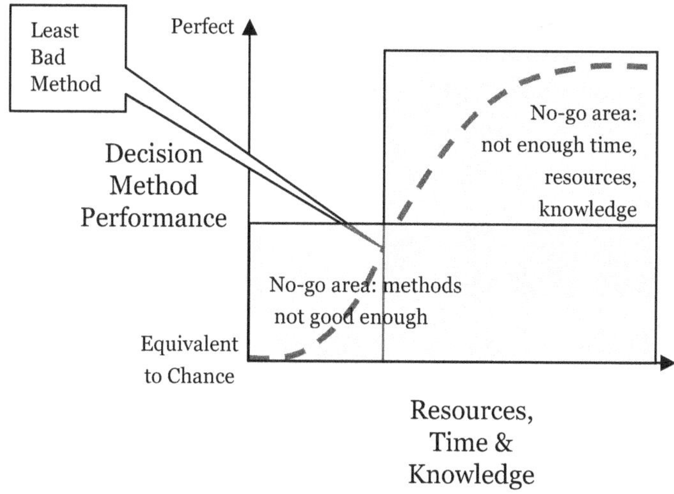

A decision making method is good enough when:

- The likelihood and value of a correct decision exceeds the likelihood and seriousness of an incorrect decision
- When maximizing: its performance is unlikely to be exceeded within current resources and knowledge
  When satisficing: better performance is possible but the benefits aren't worth the extra effort

Putting principles into practice

The purpose of these charts is to illustrate the principles so that you can understand what you are aiming for. In practice this is just a concept; you aren't really able to quantify "good enough" in terms of any meaningful units but there are some simple things that you can do to follow the principles. What I want you do to is to imagine that you are looking at your decision situation and you can see the Decisionability line through a "window". The window frame is simply the boundaries of the "not enough resources" box on the right and the "not good enough" box below. Through the window you should see the "available" area of the line which is not obscured by boxes. The window is the smallest rectangle through which you can see your line. I have illustrated 4 examples of imaginary "windows" on the line that would be bounded by various sized no-go boxes below:

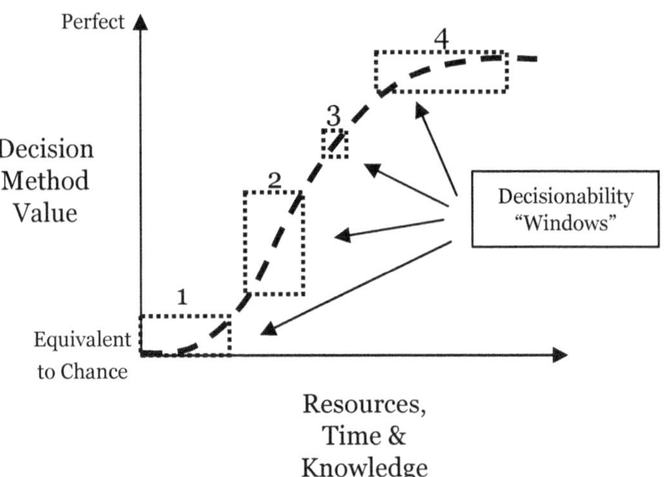

Note how I have subtly changed the scale on the left from the previously-used generic "performance" to "value" – I am now asking you to think about the relative value of the decision, not performance in terms of percentage errors, and how it might or might not change with increased resourcing.

Bear with me, this might not look easy yet but it could be easier than you think. You don't need to know what the real Decisionability line as a whole looks like, or to be able to quantify the performance you need, you only need to be able to imagine what you see in your window, and what region of the curve it would be looking upon.

Referring back to the numbered boxes on the curve on the previous page, I will explain how you can do this quite simply:

Window #1 and Window #4:

When you think that increasing the amount of resourcing on this decision won't have a great effect on the value of it to you, then the window is wide and the slope of the line is shallow. This is telling you that **you should satisfice** within the bounds of your window; the extra value of maximizing isn't worth much in terms of increased value. However the placement of the window is also important. Window #1 is in the "cheap seats" – so the satisficing method should be simple such as the recognition heuristic or you will be in decision debt. Window #4 is at the high end of the curve so even though you are satisficing within the window, the minimally acceptable method should be something of high performance such as the "take the best" heuristic or if probabilities are involved the "Decisionability tradeoff method".

Window #2

When a modest amount more effort significantly increases the value of the decision to you [or reduces the harm of a wrong decision] the window is tall and the line slopes upwards steeply. This type of window demands that **you should maximize**, because the reward for the extra effort is worthwhile. If the window is positioned at the low end of the curve because of modest decision value this will mean trading up from [say] the "safe side" heuristic to the "even swaps" method. If the window is positioned at the high value end of the curve it will mean trading up from "even swaps" to the "Decisionability tradeoff" method.

Window #3

In this situation the window is very small and you can't really determine the slope of the line within it. This is really a symptom of lack of choices, usually because of a limit of resourcing. In that case you can't really determine whether the method is good enough or not, you can only do what you have the resources to do. **This is a satisficing situation**, where you use the best method you can for the resources you have available.

Once you have chosen the most appropriate strategy, you can even revisit the wording for your decision purpose and add the relevant approach as shown in the following examples:
"To choose the best treatment for my cancer in order to have the best chance of recovery" becomes: "To maximize the likelihood

of choosing the best treatment for my cancer in order to have the best chance of recovery".

"To choose the most appropriate dishwasher in order to replace my broken one" becomes "To satisfice dishwasher selection so that I replace my broken one with one that is good enough while avoiding the frustration of looking at too many appliances in too many stores."

Evidentiary standards: when to satisfice

The choice of decisionability windows has involved only two key dimensions to your satisficing vs. maximizing strategy: knowledge and quality and that is most often the case. But sometimes there is a third dimension: the harm of delay [or its flipside, the benefit of a rapid decision]. When the harm from delaying the decision by collecting more or better quality information is much greater than the value of actually acquiring the knowledge or data, then you should satisfice, even if you are looking through window #2 and it is a high value high consequence decision. The following examples illustrate this issue.

Currently, over 150,000 people a year die of lung cancer. It kills more people than any other cancer. The good news is that it is almost completely curable: 90% of people who go to the doctor when the tumor is small [stage I] can be cured by a relatively simple surgery. The bad news is that only about 1 in 7 people go to the doctor when the cancer is curable because symptoms don't occur early. Imaging tests such as computerized tomography can find some tumors, but they have a lot of false results and they give people a dose of radiation which causes cancer, so their cost-effectiveness is controversial, and imaging is not recommended for screening people at-risk on a large scale.

Several diagnostics companies [including my own, SomaLogic] are working on simple blood tests which will detect the cancer early, and could be used for screening. The question is: how much evidence of what quality is needed to launch such a test? For such an important test with a high value of success and a high consequence of failure, surely we are looking through window #2 and we should maximize? Indeed, the conventional view is that a lot of evidence would be needed.

Take a different example of a test: mammography for breast cancer detection. Digital software which enhances the performance of the human radiologist is already accepted and approved by the FDA. If I develop a slightly different type of software that I claim improves the diagnosis a bit more than the last generation of software, then the conventional view would be that not much evidence would be needed for acceptance of the new software because it is similar to the existing product.

The conventional view in both cases above is too simplistic. In the lung cancer test, the value of a true result to an individual is indeed high – they are correctly informed that they do not have cancer or if they do have cancer it is detected early and their life is saved. In the population, thousands of lives would be saved. The consequence of a false negative result is that a cancer would be missed. That is a "bad" consequence; but "bad" compared to what? If the at-risk patients are currently getting no test at all, then the consequence of missing a cancer with the new test in some of those people is nothing. Yes zero. It just mimics the status quo without the new test. So that puts it into a "high value low consequence" category.

That is important, because when the value of a true result is far higher than the consequence of a false result I can tolerate a higher failure rate because each success "pays" for many failures. That's the first reason why I can satisfice the evidentiary standard. The second reason is that the harm of delaying patients' access to the test if it works is very high: 10,000 people are dying every month, so if I deferred the decision to do more studies and get better data I am causing serious consequences far worse than simply accepting a test which might sometimes be wrong. This is analogous to creating a "decision debt" described in the last chapter. The third reason I can satisfice the evidence is that I don't need a very precise estimate of the numbers of true results vs. false results if the true ones are much more consequential than the errors.

In contrast, the apparently improved mammography test is going to displace a known effective product. If the new test is wrong, then the consequence is serious: a cancer missed in somebody who would have had their cancer detected with the old software. The existence of a good available alternative that would be replaced by the new product makes the consequence of a false result with a new test much more serious. Additionally, the value of success is low: the test is only a little bit better than the old one. And even though it looks similar to the old test, if they share no source-code then it is actually a completely different calculation and the risk of failure is the same as for a completely new test. The combination of high consequence of error and low value of success makes my tolerance for failure quite low; I need to be strict because any one failure would need a large number of successes to "pay" its cost in a cost-benefit equation. The harm of delay while more evidence is collected is also modest – just use the old test which is not much worse! So that's a second reason why there is no particular drive to satisfice on the evidentiary standard for the mammography test. The relationship between evidentiary standards and consequence/value when delays from acquiring more or better knowledge are seriously harmful is shown below:

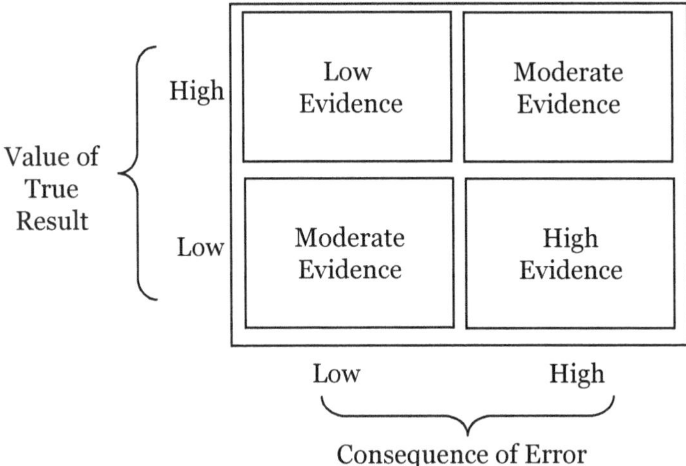

Satisficing on evidentiary standards is appropriate when:

- The consequences of failure/errors are low
- The value of the truth/success is high
- Delays from acquiring more information are serious
- More information simply uncovers the truth, it does not actually change the nature of truth or error

Maximizing on evidentiary standards is appropriate when:

- The consequences of failure are high
- The value of the truth is low
- Delays from acquiring more information are benign
- Acquiring more information increases the value of or decreases the harm

While there has been some implicit respect for this approach in drug regulation – for example the “accelerated approval” regulations lower the evidentiary standard for “breakthrough” drugs it is almost the direct opposite to the current way that diagnostic tests that go through FDA are regulated. In the USA, new, high importance tests, which are not similar to any existing product and which have by definition a high value of a true result have required the most stringent regulatory scrutiny and are delayed the most while high quality studies are run and large amounts of data acquired. Tests of low importance which are most similar to an existing product are treated as low risk and delayed the least.

How did that apparently harmful situation happen? Well the first problem is that the preceding explanation of what maximizes the public good in this situation is not intuitive. What is intuitive [but as you have seen, not necessarily true] is that more regulation leads to more public protection and greater public health. This is compounded by the second problem: that our regulatory authorities do not receive the support they deserve to do this difficult job. They have to operate and survive in a harshly critical and blame-oriented environment, imposed on them by society and politics – and BP’s oil-spill and the financial meltdown didn’t help. The “more regulation is good” strategy is therefore a reasonable response to avoid blame and criticism; if an unimportant test fails nobody cares much. If an important test fails then there will be congressional hearings and the media will be highly critical.

This situation is tolerated by society because the deaths caused by delaying access to important new tests are silent – nobody knows who would have otherwise been tested and saved, and the presumed “good intentions” of the regulator discount this effect even further [even though society is critical of FDA it is generally believed to have good intentions]. In contrast, the harm of a test that doesn't work as well as expected is obvious, it happens to known individuals, and the company marketing the test is obviously responsible. The presumed "bad intentions" [spending less money, making more money] of the test-makers amplifies this perception of harm..

If FDA were to adopt the more permissive Decisionability strategy of satisficing on evidence for important tests, it would mean facing up to the fact that they would probably get blamed more often because lower evidentiary standards go along with tolerating a slightly higher failure rate so that society can receive substantially more health benefits. In such a situation if an important test fails, our culture is not accepting of apparently lame explanations that the benefit of the other successful tests FDA let through more rapidly would have more than made up for the harm from the few tests that didn't work as advertized. Nonetheless, that courageous approach is what is needed to maximize public good. I just don't know how we are going to get there from here.....

Key Learnings from Chapter 4

- You should abandon a decision when the value of success or the harm from failure or indecision is lower than the effort of having to make the decision.
    - This avoids "Decision Debt"
- If your decision has a high value of success and a high harm from failure you should be prepared to spend a lot of time and effort making it if necessary; this is analogous to a high-value stamp on your decision envelope.
- If your decision is extremely urgent then jump straight to a simple heuristic without further ado [chapter 6].
- Your personality and experience can create habits about not deciding (cautious Dick) or always deciding (Decisive Jane). Neither is value added vs. a coin flip [These habits can be overcome with simple methods: see the "safe side heuristic in Chapter 6 or the Decisionability tradeoff method in chapter 7].
- Satisficing is a strategy of settling for something that is "good enough"; you should use it when:
    - Taking more effort than "good enough" methods isn't worth the slight increase in benefits
    - You don't have much time or resources and knowledge are limited
- Maximizing is a strategy seeking and accepting only the best; you should use it when:
    - There is time and resource to evaluate all options
    - When putting in more effort or resources is likely to lead to significantly enhanced benefits
- When delay is destructive or harmful such that the time taken to acquire knowledge is net decision debt, evidence must be satisficed.

Chapter 5

Alternatives and options: what, when and how?

Alternatives – different options for actions

What comes next? You have got to this point because you have found that you cannot make the decision with a rule or principle, you aren't deferring or abandoning it and you've identified a purpose with a "what?" and "why?"and you've chosen a satisficing or maximizing strategy. Now you are ready to seek alternatives for achieving your decision purpose – the different possible different options for action.

When to stop looking for alternatives

At this stage you should think of any alternative options simply as "candidates" for delivering the decision purpose. Like interview candidates, try not to get too attached to any one of them before you have evaluated them properly – the first one might not be the best one. You should start seeking process for alternatives with some sort of a "stopping rule" in your mind. That means you need to define a strategy, rule or idea about when you will stop seeking new alternatives or different variations in the old ones. Your rule should be consistent with your resource limitations and satisficing/maximizing choice. Stop early if you are satisficing, and go right up to your resource limits if you are maximizing. Many of the simple heuristics discussed in the next chapter come with their own stopping rules, so if you use them you do not need to make up your own rule. In general, those methods are of intermediate performance; this means that they are fine for satisficing approaches or for maximizing that is significantly bounded by resource, time or knowledge limitations. If you are intending to maximize and use a method that doesn't have a rule, you will need to make one. This may be to continue seeking alternatives until you have reached the boundary of knowledge or it may be to keep seeking them until you have reached the limit of the amount of time or number of people that are available. Remember not to get into decision debt; habitual maximizers especially love seeking the best even if the effort exceeds the value of the decision. If you aren't in a hurry, are maximizing, and your stopping rule is lenient then it is a good idea to think, muse and discuss with friends, family, advisors or stakeholders for days or more on what possible alternatives there might be.

I will illustrate this with a brief example of the effect of time on identifying alternatives – and the diminishing returns. Here I considered a common decision purpose of a very simple type to illustrate the effect of "thinking time" in a condensed fashion.

The example is that I am driving around in Boston and have become lost; I need to decide what the best way is for getting back on my way in order to complete my journey in good time? In the absence of a stopping rule I timed myself and my ability to come up with alternatives:

30 seconds thinking:

- Stop and ask a passer-by for directions
- Stop at a gas station and buy a map
- Keep going without stopping and hope to find a signpost
- 5 minutes thinking:
- Stop at a store and buy a GPS
- Follow the sun and drive in a particular direction until I hit a major road
- Retrace the route back to the last place where I was not lost

1 day thinking:

- Phone home and ask a family member to do a Google Maps search for me on a named street
- Look at the maps on my Blackberry [why didn't I think of that earlier?]
- Ask a policeman

Although I still came up with a couple of good options after a day – which would be far too long to help that particular situation – there are a number of alternatives identified within the first 30 seconds that are "good enough" for this low value low harm situation. However, if I had had the time and the situation was not time-sensitive, the alternatives that I came up after a day's thinking should be included in the evaluation. Note that many of the alternative options are specific actions, but they can also be processes "keep going without stopping" is a process and there are many occasions where processes will be viable options for action. I will return to this example when discussing how to identify the features that differentiate between alternatives.

What is on an alternatives list?

Here is a list of the 5 different potential end-results of a search for alternatives with examples of each:

1. One fixed alternative vs. no action
   - My unborn baby has a fatal congenital malformation: abortion vs. no abortion?

2. One variable alternative with a decision threshold: deciding "how much of it?"
   - What level of LDL "bad" cholesterol in your blood should lead to action?
   - How much money should be in the financial bailout package?

3. Several fixed alternatives
   - Brian's "innovation" projects at CR Engineering
   - Treatment options for prostate cancer: radiotherapy vs. surgery vs. chemotherapy vs. hormone therapy

4. Many fixed alternatives
   - People available for marriage
   - Brand and type bread at the supermarket

5. Many variable alternatives
   - Biochemical pathways to be changed and to what extent in order to develop new treatments to cure cancer
   - Different investments and amount of each in a financial portfolio for retirement

Avoiding traps when seeking alternatives

Clearly you must avoid a number of traps in order to get a good end result. The first trap is failing to involve the right people. According to a recent McKinsey survey, good decision outcomes occur when "the right skills and experience are included in decision making, decisions are based on transparent criteria and a robust fact base, and ensuring that the person who will be responsible for implementing a decision is involved in making that decision. Even though such surveys based on post-hoc narratives are despised by Taleb in "The Black Swan" I am not quite as skeptical as he, because some systematic and data-driven research of decisions by academics like Paul Nutt ["Why Decisions Fail"] does show that a failure to involve relevant stakeholders when discussing alternatives, or even earlier when discussing the purpose of the decision is a key risk for decision failure. If they haven't been involved already, now is the time to consider broader participation in your process to improve the acceptance of the decision, even if you don't think you need them to generate ideas. The lesser error is to over-involve stakeholders rather than to under-involve them.

The second potential trap you need to avoid at this point is failing to identify important opportunities that actually exist because you don't have the expertise or knowhow to know that they exist. In the first example in the list above there appears to be only one option vs. nothing – to abort or not to abort an unborn baby with a fatal congenital abnormality. If the person responsible for the decision has a non-compensatory principle against abortion under any circumstances, there may seem to be only one option – the do nothing option. However, because the harm of the wrong decision is very high and therefore a maximizing strategy would be appropriate, this decision would support considerable effort – including perhaps getting input from a lot of experts. The experts might come up with new options, for example perhaps the abnormality could be corrected *by in-utero* surgery or surgery immediately after the birth, or perhaps the abnormality isn't always fatal. So experts are needed to identify unknown options even when there seems to be only one, and should be brought in for high value high harm decisions even if it costs money, time and effort.

The third potential trap here is if you accidentally over-simplify the alternatives. In the prostate cancer example there appear to be only 4 treatment options – surgery, radiotherapy, chemotherapy and hormonal therapy. However, that is an oversimplification, because one, two, three or perhaps all 4 can be used in combination or sequentially, which means there are more than 64 therapy combinations, and within each one are different approaches, doses of drugs, choice of drugs so the actual number is probably several hundred. This is another high-value high-harm situation where incremental benefits are probably meaningful and it supports a highly resourced maximizing strategy. If you have ever been in the situation of seeking the best cancer treatment, it certainly creates a strong desire for "unbounded maximizing" for cancer treatments and it is frustrating and frightening to run up against the boundary of knowledge – because science can't discriminate between the 64 different combinations in this case. Unfortunately, this is true for most diseases: the almost inevitable limitations on knowledge prevent meaningful discrimination between all of the options. So although I complained that 4 individual options for prostate cancer was too few, and unrepresentative of the key combination approaches, I am now complaining that 64 is too many. So I am suggesting that they be simplified because of the knowledge limitations of the current state of the art, but to the key combination options not just single treatments. In this case the experts would probably help identify ~6 key options for which we could create meaningful descriptions of benefit and harm, but some would be single therapies and some would be combinations.

I've identified what the available alternatives are, what next?

If you are satisficing in a low to moderate value and low to moderate harm situation then that's it. You can move to choose the most appropriate heuristic in the next chapter. Even the heuristics which benefit from knowledge of the features of your alternatives [features being the good or bad characteristics or effects of each alternative] do not require you to list or rate them in advance.

However, if you are maximizing in any situation, or if you are satisficing in a moderate to high value or harm decision then you will need to take pen to paper and create some kind of table which associates each alternative with its features. There are a couple of different ways of doing this which will be described in turn.

Creating a table of alternatives vs. desired features.

In the process of defining your decision purpose you already created lists of the current state and the desired future state. This will enable you to list the key features of each of your alternatives so you can compare them. A sample table is shown on the next page for a downsizing of a house decision. Note that at this stage you are merely describing the information not rating it.

Desired features	House #1	House #2	House #3
Price less than $300k	$250k	$240k	$300k
Easy work commute	10 minutes	30 minutes	15 minutes
At least 3 bedrooms	4	3	5
On school bus route	Yes	No	Yes
In a safe area	Yes	No	Yes

It is not a terribly efficient process because all alternatives have to be described against all features even if there are some that don't discriminate between any of the alternatives. Also, as you do this, keep an open mind and add features that might not have been in your previous description of the desired future state: the very process of looking at the alternatives generates new ideas about what features might be important to you and which discriminate between options. These features may well have been missed when you imagined your desired future state earlier; there's nothing like looking at practical alternatives to generate new ideas. For example in actually looking at the three houses above you might have realized that one of the neighborhood schools is rather better than the others but you didn't actually put that in the desired future state the first place because you assumed they were all similar.

As a final reminder, and I promise not to say this again, I still don't recommend that you call these features "objectives", because it creates the expectation that a "good" decision will fulfill all of them. In practice this is usually impossible because of uncertainty and random variation, so having that expectation leads to guilt and regret. Stick to the "desired features" nomenclature, and think of them as attributes of value, but only one thing is certain: you aren't going to get all of them all of the time.

The alternatives vs. consequences chart

There is an inherent problem with merely listing how the alternatives fare against your “desired future state”, as this misses out an important issue: some of the alternatives may be associated with harmful and unintended consequences as well as the desirable and intended ones. If you don’t have any of these, then stick to the table above, but if you do then you need to create an “alternatives vs. consequences” chart, which simply includes unintended and undesirable effects in the same chart as before. For example, perhaps one of the alternative houses above is next to the landfill, or perhaps a neighbor is a registered sex offender – neither of which would have been included as a desired feature. Now the chart [below] has been modified to include the bad things which were discovered when looking at the alternatives:

Consequence	**House #1**	**House #2**	**House #3**
Price less than $300k	$250k	$240k	$300k
Easy work Commute	10 minutes	30 minutes	15 minutes
At least 3 bedrooms	4	3	5
On school bus route	Yes	No	Yes
In a safe area	Yes	No	Yes
Next to landfill	No	No	Yes
Neighbor is a registered sex offender	No	Yes	No

The differentiating features strategy.

Instead of listing all the features, an economical approach where you are not maximizing is to list only those features which differentiate between your alternatives. If I go back to the simple example of being lost in Boston from earlier in the chapter, I might have defined my desired future state as getting back on track within a certain time, but that fails to discriminate well between the options. If you ask me why I don't stop and ask for directions it comes down to the following issues: embarrassment, shyness, reluctance to admitting being wrong, cost/time, and the fact that what I do might not work [probability of success]. Clearly those are not objectives of a decision but they are key features that differentiate between alternatives. These are shown in the table:

Alternative	Admit Error?	Overcome Shyness?	Time and cost	Probability of success
Stop and ask a passer-by	Yes	Yes	5 min; free	Medium
Get a map at a gas station	Yes	Yes	10 min; $5	High
Keep going	No	No	Time??? $free	Low
Stop and buy a GPS	No	No	15 min; $200	Very high
Retrace the route back	No	No	10 min; $free	Medium
Phone home search	To family	No	5 minutes $free	High
Blackberry maps	No	No	5 min; $free	Medium

Identifying the differentiating features can be time consuming and difficult – it sometimes involves analyzing the origin of a vague emotional feeling about one of the alternatives and asking why is it there? However, if you are good at self-analysis and identifying hidden reasons then this will be your method of choice. It can also include the unintended consequences that weren't readily apparent in the "alternatives against objectives" strategy.

Using T.H.E. Decisionability triangle

If you are maximizing, and therefore want to ensure that you have done a holistic assessment of the features, then it is a good idea to recall the Decisionability triangle and to ask whether there are any features in the alternatives in technical, human and economic categories which weren't immediately obvious. For example, the previous table on house choices mostly focuses on technical issues such as number of bedrooms and proximity to the landfill, it includes one economic issue in the price, and one human issue – proximity to a sex offender. When forced to identify things in the relevant categories more issues might surface – such as dislike of the appearance of house #2 as a human issue. In practice I have found that people usually focus on one of these three domains, with a bit of lip service to one of the others, while forgetting completely about the third.

How this information is used in the choice of methods

Assuming now that you have identified a reasonable set of alternative choices for your decision, it is worth a quick review of the decision purpose to check that you don't want to modify it now that you have looked at alternatives and features and are ready to select the decision making method. The methods are described in detail in the following chapters but here are some basic recommendations:

- If you are under extreme time pressure and there is no time to get more knowledge – use the "safe side" heuristic
- If the decision is of modest value and harm and you can rank or approximate the value of the features of each alternative:
    - "Take the best" heuristic
    - "Even Swaps" method
- If you are maximizing in a high value high harm situation and some of the features aren't 100% probable
    - Decisionability tradeoff method
- If you are maximizing for a high value/harm decision in a low trust environment
    - Multi-criteria decision analysis

Why "risk tolerance" is missing.

Books on decision making processes usually require you to assess your risk tolerance, or to score a decision on a "risk tolerance" rating. I am not asking you to do this because you have already thought about the harm of decision failure and the value of success and these factors have figured in defining the resources and strategy so far.

Key learnings from chapter 5:

- Select the key alternatives – different options that deliver some or all of your desired future state.
- Involve key stakeholders in the decision, or key people whose acceptance will be needed.
- The differences between alternatives should be identified by:
    - Alternatives vs. features charts
    - Alternatives vs. consequences charts
    - A differentiating features approach

Part 2

Choosing and using the right methods

Introduction to part 2

In part one you created the decision envelope, wrote the characteristics of the sender and the recipient and destination of the decision. You also ensured that the stamp, the motive force for the decision was sufficient to support the anticipated size and weight of the contents and you applied a "satisficing" or "maximizing" sticker to the outside of the envelope.

Now you are ready to put something inside the decision envelope: the assessment of the alternatives using the chosen method and most importantly, the results.

In this part, I will describe recommended methods that are part of the Decisionability system; the key is that they are methods that can be used every day without computer models or experts.

Chapter 6

Instincts and simple methods

Instincts, intuition and "gut feeling"

There really is useful information buried in your subconscious brains that you can't access other than through emotion or feelings. The information may be as simple as recognition, but usually comes in the form that there is something bad or something good associated with a decision, an alternative or an action, but you don't know what it is. Occasionally the information emerges as a specific idea – a new action, a previously unknown alternative or action that you didn't know your unconscious mind was working on. Sometimes the information is simply that you made a decision but don't know how you did it.

Jonah Lehrer in "How We Decide" proposes that the unconscious brain be left to solve complex problems in its own way. I disagree. We've all had revelations in the shower but there is no statistical evidence that this actually works reliably, in fact it is a surprise when it does happen. Maybe your intuition is better than mine but I'd rather rely on something I can analyze. The mental short-cuts – heuristics – that I describe later in the chapter certainly do work, but I am asking you to bring them out of the unconscious, and to replace habitual use with a slightly more disciplined choice. Even though there are many situations where heuristics work well, this only happens when the heuristic matches the environment where it is used – this is called “ecological rationality.” If left to the unconscious brain the question of environment matching to the method isn’t considered. Another problem with purely unconscious methods is that that there’s misinformation stored in the brain along with the real information and misunderstanding stored along with correct logic: the gut reacts to spicy food as well as real risk. Well known biases of the subconscious brain include an over-aversion to loss vs. gain, a tendency to over-value “status quo” and a dread of serious consequences causing overestimation of their likelihood.

Because you don’t do statistical tests on them we can’t know how good or bad the performance of our gut is when compared with random chance – you will often be right just by chance but you almost never assign chance as the cause of being right in your mind. This means that you and I are likely to consistently over-estimate our abilities – the “95% of us are above average” fallacy. Humans also have a well known tendency to create narratives assigning fact and logic where there is none – “the narrative fallacy” as excoriated by Nassim Taleb in “The Black Swan”.

I am not recommending that you dismiss nonspecific feelings entirely, rather that you take the time to interrogate bad or good feelings of unknown origin. They can be treated like a crying baby: follow a sequential list of possible wants. Is the baby crying because she is hungry, needs a diaper change, is too hot/cold or needs a cuddle? Try creating a mental checklist of possible causes of the feeling, and presenting each one to the unconscious mind – the culprit sometimes can be identified. Time also helps a feeling to become associated with its conscious definition. However, reliance on feelings and emotion entirely to make important decisions isn’t appropriate unless perhaps the benefit of the decision is also entirely feelings and emotion – such as falling in love for example.

How heuristics fit into your Decisionability

The purpose of my naming and describing heuristics is to bring the selection of them from your unconscious to your conscious thought so you can optimize their use. This requires a common language and understanding of what they are and what they do.

When you use heuristics to enhance your Decisionability you need to be able choose consciously which heuristic you intend to apply, ensuring that your intended use matches the environment where it works best, and that its performance is good enough for your decision. You also need to have the discipline to avoid using a favorite or habitual heuristic where the match is poor or its performance is not good enough. The extension of mental heuristics onto paper that I will explain later in this chapter will enable you to broaden their utility and application beyond the small number of pieces of information that your brain can handle [with no intended insult to your brain, that's just a known problem]. Finally I want you to know when to avoid heuristics altogether, when to "let go" of instinct and use something more sophisticated.

While there are probably hundreds of variations on heuristics I have chosen only a few for this chapter: the ones I recommend have either been tested in research [mostly by Gerd Gigerenzer at Max Planck and the ABC Research Group] or have strong mathematical logic behind them. So that you get the picture of what a heuristic is, I am going to show a couple of background examples before moving on to the ones that you will find yourself using every day in decision making.

Women and Children First

HMS Birkenhead sank off the coast of South Africa on 26th February 1852. The ship was carrying 480 British troops and about 26 women and children. When the ship foundered, the captain shouted "every man for himself", but the soldiers' leader, Lieutenant-Colonel Alexander Seton intervened and told them to 'stand fast!' The soldiers and sailors complied and allowed the women and children to make use of the few lifeboats. About 400 of the 600 soldiers and sailors on board were drowned or eaten by sharks, but all the women and children survived. The "women and children first" ethos was later called the 'Birkenhead Drill' and was celebrated in verse by Rudyard Kipling in the poem "Soldier an' Sailor Too":

To take your chance in the thick of a rush, with firing all about,
Is nothing so bad when you've cover to 'and, an' leave an' likin' to shout;
But to stand an' be still to the Birken'ead drill is a damn tough bullet to chew,
An' they done it, the Jollies - 'Er Majesty's Jollies - soldier an' sailor too!
Their work was done when it 'adn't begun; they was younger nor me an' you;
Their choice it was plain between drownin' in 'eaps an' bein' mopped by the screw,
So they stood an' was still to the Birken'ead drill, soldier an' sailor too!

When the Titanic sank, women with children had a 70% better chance of survival than men, and as recently as January 15th 2009, when a US Airways jet with 115 people on board crash-landed onto the Hudson River, women and children on board were the first to emerge - thanks to the survival of the "Birken'ead drill" to this day.

This is a decision short-cut that plausibly has a hidden and potentially complex statistical benefit that isn't necessarily obvious, but which works under specific circumstances. Instead of using it, Lieutenant-Colonel Seton could instead have performed a cost-risk-benefit analysis. Perhaps children are highly valuable to society because they have the most life-years ahead of them. Perhaps women are more valuable than men because their future reproductive potential is more capacity-limiting to a growing population than a man's. Perhaps women's clothes in those days were obstructive so they were most at risk whereas the men were likely to be stronger swimmers so the risk to them was lower. However, had the Lieutenant-Colonel taken the time and effort to do this assessment, everyone would have perished or followed the captain's advice of "every man for himself". Although this is the first clearly-documented use of this heuristic, it is possible that evolutionary pressures had already created the brain's hard-wiring to be more receptive to this command that then became codified as the ultimate expression of "gentlemanly behavior" in England such that Englishmen were more likely to perish on the Titanic than other nationalities. If my theorizing about preservation of reproductive potential and life-years is correct, evolutionary pressure would be high to genetically program a bias towards such behavior that competes with self-preservation heuristics.

When looks are everything

Remember Don from chapter 2 - the 28 year old hoping that a new car would get him a girlfriend? Don was shy and claimed that he didn't get many opportunities to meet people. Nonetheless I managed to persuade him not only to keep his Ford Focus but also to try a different approach to his loneliness and lack of sex problem: speed dating. Speed dating involves groups of men and women racing through a series of "mini-dates" each lasting about five minutes. Participants can then invite whoever takes their fancy to get in touch with them again. He didn't even have to pay an entry fee – a researcher: Dr Alison Lenton was based near his home in Edinburgh and was carrying out a research study. She had it all organized, all he had to do was sign up and attend. At the first session, Don was in a small group – there were 7 women to meet for 5 minutes each. His first meeting was awful, he thought the first young woman was gorgeous, but he was nervous and she seemed disinterested in him, answering his pre-prepared questions with "yes" "no" or "maybe" and 5 minutes seemed like hours. To cut a long story short, there was a woman called Naomi that he liked who wasn't the best looking but she was lively and they talked about things that neither of them had thought out beforehand, and the 5 minutes seemed like 30 seconds. Needless to say Don didn't invite the first girl for a date, but did go out with Naomi a few times, after this session. In fact he wasn't going to attend the second session because they were going steady, but then she dumped him because she thought his Ford Focus was too boring to be seen in [oops!].

The second speed-dating session was a lot bigger than the first – now there were 16 different women to meet. Don wasn't so nervous this time, but he found it hard to keep track of all the different women he had met, and what characteristics he liked. He invited three of the best looking women to future dates but they didn't invite him, so he went home without a date, vowing to get some new car brochures.

While Don is fictitious, the research project was real. What Dr Lenton did was to study 118 speed dating sessions with groups of between seven and 36 people. For apes and birds, the chances of a non-contender being chosen as a mate increases as groups get larger, and she wanted to determine whether this was true in humans. In fact she found the opposite: as the size of the group of humans grew, a small number of the most attractive individuals received all the offers. Some candidates ended up with few invitations or none at all. Dr Lenton believes that in smaller groups, people can trade off different qualities in prospective mates – physical attractiveness for intelligence, for example. When they are in large groups and overwhelmed by the complexity of making tradeoffs, humans searching for a partner seem to attempt to use a single characteristic – attractiveness. As a result, no amount of clever chat-up lines can make up for a lack of looks.

Once again this is a heuristic: limiting the search and using a single important reason for choice [attractiveness] in the face of time pressure and overwhelming numbers of other factors – and in this case it didn't work very well!

What heuristics do we know are useful for every-day decisions?

I like to think of Gerd Gigerenzer of the Max Planck Institute the uncrowned "King" of heuristics. He, along with the "ABC Research group" studied the actual utility of a number of "fast and frugal" heuristics. Usually heuristics had been judged against the "gold standard" statistical test called multiple linear regression. The "gold standard" is indeed sophisticated: complex computer programs that include equations and statistical distributions that describe how each factor influencing a decision is expected to behave. In the past, heuristics had always appeared inferior to multiple linear regression, but Gigerenzer identified a key problem with that conclusion: there was no external "truth standard". So if the "gold standard" wasn't really gold, if the multiple linear regression models weren't 100% perfect then if a heuristic gave a different answer it was possible that sometimes the heuristic was performing better. Different does not necessarily equal worse. So a novel aspect of the research was that both heuristics and multiple linear regression models were compared against a known "truth standard", when a real outcome was known. Gigerenzer also found that heuristics had previously been tested only in fixed experimental situations where searching for information wasn't necessary; once again this had tilted the scales against heuristics because one of their key advantages is that they can handle information choice problems, such as when choice is overwhelming or not much of it is available.

I am now singling out 3 specific heuristics that you will find incredibly useful when used in situations which match their strengths. As you gain Decisionability you will correctly select the appropriate one and use it with discipline. They are:

- The recognition heuristic
- The "safe side" heuristic
- The minimalist, "take the last" and "take the best heuristics [note these are grouped because they are different flavors of the same strategy].

I have also included in this chapter 2 other simple methods that are paper and pencil extensions of heuristics:

- Even swaps [the extension of Franklin's rule]
- Dawes' rule

"The devil you know is better than the devil you don't know": the recognition heuristic.

Frank has never been to Tokyo before, but on his way to his first meal with his Japanese hosts, he appreciates the efficiency of the transport, he is dazzled by the visual assault of the super-color advertising displays making the evening streets flashier than stroboscopic sunlight through trees, and he feels welcomed by the smiles and politeness of everyone he has met on his first day here. Now he is sitting in an expensive Japanese restaurant, surrounded by his Japanese colleagues who have already ordered, and the smiling waiter is hovering, waiting for Frank's choice. Even though they have given him a menu with English translations, Frank is lost. He is quite a conservative eater – meatloaf is his favorite – but he doesn't know what to choose. His hosts explained earnestly what some of the dishes were, but they seemed to be strange objects that once lived at the bottom of a pond or they are made of uncooked fish. Even though he has never tasted either, he does recognize the names of two dishes: Stone Fish which he has a bad feeling about [actually it contains a neurotoxin that can be harmful if the fish isn't properly prepared] and Teriyaki Chicken, which he has heard of but doesn't know if it is good. With relief, he chooses the chicken.

The human mind has a huge capacity to store simple recognition information – people are able to recall whether they have encountered something before with surprising accuracy. In the 1970s psychologists such as Standing and Shepard showed that when thousands [even 10,000] pictures were shown to people, 48 hours later they could correctly discriminate between pictures they had or had not seen before, with remarkable accuracy between about 80 and 90% even if the pictures weren't particularly striking. Humans are also pre-programmed genetically with some recognition of characteristics – the layout of the human face, and the taste and smell of rotten food for example.

In short, the recognition heuristic is simply determining whether an object/issue is known and ascribing greater value to known objects than unknown – at its simplest there need be no further knowledge than recognition, although recognition associated with "good" and recognition associated with "bad" or "good" is not far behind in terms of simplicity. So far, this is not surprising. What is surprising that this, the simplest of all decision-making strategies can work amazingly well in some situations. Gigerenzer showed that simple name-recognition of stocks in the stock market could sometimes lead to surprisingly good returns. The problem is that the performance of this heuristic varies; if you are completely ignorant, or if you are an expert then you cannot use it because you recognize none of the stocks or all of them. What also appears to happen is that the heuristic delivers a performance that is better than ignorance or chance, but not as good as that of an expert; in the stock market performance experiment, experts in the US stock market did beat the recognition heuristic used by a panel of lay-people when choosing US stocks. However, when US experts were asked to choose non-US international stocks, where they were knowledgeable but not expert, the recognition heuristic used by lay-people beat easily beat the experts. This is an example of the "less is more" result that Schwarz explains in "The Paradox of Choice". If you know you are partially ignorant, then be satisfied that you can beat chance but not the experts and don't bother trying to maximize to reach the best possible decision, when you don't have the knowledge or expertise. If you know you are relatively knowledgeable, don't try and use simple recognition to make a decision related to your own domain because you know too much. If you are an expert, don't get carried away and think your expertise will generalize to other areas related to but slightly outside your field. The recognition heuristic can also be thought of as a prelude to some other heuristics – for example if you recognize a number of things but have to choose just one, the recognition heuristic eliminates the unrecognized ones first, and then other heuristics can narrow the choice further.

Use the recognition heuristic when:

- You are partially ignorant
- There isn't time to do something more sophisticated or if the decision isn't worth the effort

Don't use the recognition heuristic when:

- You are very knowledgeable or completely ignorant
- Somebody might be trying to trick you

<u>*The "safe side" heuristic*</u>

Fear and caution ruled on the Hill, "Constituents vent fury at House members jittery about losing their jobs. Even supporters of the rescue package are tepid"

Los Angeles Times, September 30th 2008. By Doyle McManus

President Bush lobbied. Treasury Secretary Henry M. Paulson pleaded. Vice President Dick Cheney worked on conservative Republicans; House Speaker Nancy Pelosi coaxed liberal Democrats. Barack Obama lobbied gently. John McCain worked the phones and boasted about how effective he was.

But all that leadership failed to command much loyalty in either party Monday. When the financial rescue plan came to a vote, two-thirds of the House's Republicans and two-fifths of its Democrats ignored their leaders' pleas and voted no.

The surprise defeat of the Bush administration's financial rescue plan was a product of the waning influence of a lame-duck president and the nervousness of members of Congress, whose institution is even less popular and who faced a flood of angry messages from constituents. McCain and Obama are more popular, but neither candidate embraced the bailout measure enthusiastically before the vote.

Their cautiousness, combined with the unpopularity of other senior political leaders, left rank-and-file members of Congress free to draw their own conclusions about how to react to public skepticism of the bailout, coming only five weeks before Election Day.

"We're all worried about losing our jobs," Rep. Paul D. Ryan (R-Wis.), who voted in favor of the plan, said in a speech in the House. "Most of us say, 'I want this thing to pass but I want you to vote for it, not me.' "

This proposal is stunning and unprecedented in its scope and lack of detail," Dodd said. "It would allow the [Treasury] secretary to intervene in the economy by purchasing at least $700 billion of toxic assets. ... It would do nothing to help even a single family save a home."

Republican conservatives protested that the bailout is little more than an expensive giveaway to big corporations, as well as an irresponsible government intrusion into the private sector.

"This massive bailout is not the solution. It is financial socialism, and it is un-American," Sen. Jim Bunning, R-Ky., said at a Senate Banking Committee hearing at which members of both parties spent five hours grilling top administration officials.

Following the above article in the LA Times, the markets reacted predictably and fell worldwide by hundreds of points at the news. As we now know, the package was passed in the end, and even that wasn't sufficient, requiring further bailout packages later.

You have to have some sympathy with the critics – the actual uses of the money weren't clearly specified, it seemed like "throwing money at the problem" because that's exactly what it was. But what do you do if you don't have the time or knowledge to discriminate between any of the alternatives, and you can't use the recognition heuristic because you recognize all of them or none of them? In some situations you can simply use what you know already about the harm of decision failure to narrow down your alternatives or to choose approximately what to do. As a heuristic, it really only works on a simple A vs. B decision – for a more sophisticated tradeoff approach in complex decisions where you do have some knowledge about the alternatives, see chapter 7.

Here's how it works in the financial bailout example, and it requires asking two questions about decision failure. Many decisions can fail in two directions: you did something that was wrong vs. you failed to do something that was right. You did too much vs. you did too little. You thought something was true when it was false vs. you thought something was false when it was true. Statisticians - with their vivid imaginations held forcefully in check - call these "type 1" and "type 2" errors. What you need to do is to ask about the two types of failure, in this example:

Which is the worst error?

- Financial stimulus package is too big
- Financial stimulus package is too small

This requires imagining the consequences of each type of error. I'm going to guess that if representatives and senators were asked individually [in-private, off the record], even if they disagreed about the amount of the package, they would agree that "too small" a package that leads to a financial meltdown, massive job-losses and bank failures would be worse than "too big" a package that costs the taxpayer more money than necessary and increases government debt. The safe-side heuristic simply biases choices towards options that are associated with the error that is less harmful, in the absence of any estimates of probability. Trying to get a "just right" stimulus package would be attempting to choose the center of the statistical distribution of errors which would have an equal possibility of each type of error. "Being on the safe side" therefore involves biasing the choice towards the least bad error – in this case over-generosity by choosing a "surprisingly big" stimulus package, not even attempting to get the "just right" package.

A simple algebraic supplement to this heuristic/instinct that we've used routinely is to compare the harm of the errors, in this case:

- How bad would it be if the financial stimulus package was too small?
- How bad would it be if the financial stimulus package was too big?

Let's say that the "too small" error is about 10x as bad as the "too big" package. Knowing that one kind of error is 10x as bad can further shape the decision. The least cost to society would be reached if the likelihood of the less harmful error is greater than that of the most harmful error by the ratio of their seriousness. In this case that would be balanced if the "too big" error was ten times as likely as the "too small" error. So legislators, rather than listening to their constituents and trying to get a package that has equal numbers of contributors to re-election campaigns complaining in each direction, or equal likelihood of failing in each way, they should have been trying to get 10x as many complaints about the package being too big vs. too small. Of course they wouldn't have been re-elected but that's another story. So although this method doesn't tell you the exact size of the correct package, it does say that in the absence of good knowledge about the correct answer, to be on the safe side it should be too big 10x as often as too small. This is discussed in more detail around setting decision thresholds in chapter 8. A note of warning – if there is considerable emotion or vivid imagery associated with one of the failures and an abstract or simple economic failure on the other, then our ability to properly evaluate which failure is worst is compromised and this method should not be used [but unfortunately it often is].

A more human example of this tradeoff between seriousness and probability is demonstrated by research into whether men perceive women to be interested in them or vice-versa. Generally in surveys of people who knew each other it was found that individual men overestimated the real interest that a woman had in them, while individual women underestimated the real interest that the man had. The proffered explanation for this is that the probabilities x seriousness of each type of error balance one another out.

For the man, the errors and their consequences are:

1. Failing to recognize that a woman is really interested in him
   - Missing an opportunity to have sex and reproduce genetically
2. Imagining that a woman is interested in him when he is not
   - Getting rebuffed by the woman

For the man, the seriousness of missing an opportunity to have sex and reproduce genetically is far more serious than of getting rebuffed; this is therefore balanced by increasing the probability of the lesser error in order to decrease the probability of the greater error – so the male overestimates the degree of interest of the female in him.

For the woman the errors and their consequences are:

1. Imagining that the man is more interested in her than he actually is
   - Having sex and getting pregnant by a man on a one-night stand
   - Being left as a single parent to raise the offspring alone
2. Failing to recognize that the man is interested when he really is
   - Failing to take advantage of the potential for a long term relationship and raising offspring together

For the woman it is argued that – at least when evolutionary pressures were developing the instinct even if not today – the seriousness of raising the child alone after a one night stand was greater than the other error, of failing to take advantage because there are "other fish in the sea". Thus she ensures that the former error is made less probable than the latter by underestimating the interest the male has in her.

In chapter 7 I will explain how to improve on this approach by bringing in estimates of probabilities when you have some information on how often events are likely to occur, and more alternatives than 2 to the same type of thinking.

Examples of situations where the "safe side" heuristic would be applicable:

You just got off a plane and picked up your car, and are about to drive home 50 miles but it is snowing. Your gas warning light only just came on so there *should* be enough gas to get you home. You don't really want to face the cold and inconvenience of filling the car with gas as you leave.

- Worst error: Getting stuck in the snow, running out of gas and dying of cold when you forgot to renew your life insurance
- Least error: Filling up with gas in the cold when it wasn't necessary

You are going on a job interview by train to New York; there is a train that arrives in time to get you there 15 minutes before the interview, which would be "perfect" timing, or you can get up an hour earlier and catch the earlier train.

- Worst error: Being late for job interview because the "perfect" train was late
- Least error: Getting up an hour early unnecessarily because the "perfect" train was on time

You are looking after your friend's 4 year old and she is opening a peanut granola bar from your cupboard, you don't know if she has any allergies.

- Worst error: Causing a serious allergy in your friend's 4 year old
- Least error: Denying a 4 year old a granola bar

You are up a ladder and you can't quite reach that floodlight, but maybe if you stand on the top rung and stretch out....

- Worst error: Falling off a ladder and dying or being seriously injured

- Least error: Failing to replace a light bulb that you could have reached

You were sure you had left $10 in your pencil drawer at work and now it isn't there and you think that the person in the next cubicle has taken it.

- Worst error: Accusing an innocent person of theft and ruining your relationship unnecessarily
- Least error: Failing to retrieve $10 and deliver justice

The key problem with this heuristic is that it is inbuilt, probably genetically programmed, and as a result people over-use it, or use it unconsciously so that they do not think to seek better methods. Even when more information is available, perhaps even comprehensive statistics on the likelihood of each type of outcome, the simplicity of hanging on to the heuristic is alluring – and it is perceived as dangerous to relax the approach. Evolution as a process does not anticipate the existence of such improvements as statistics and epidemiology, it is entirely reactive; the relatively recent invention in evolutionary terms of sophisticated statistics that improve substantially upon our key risk-management heuristic causes an internal conflict. This problem is compounded if there is dread of one kind of outcome and not the other, even if they aren't very different in their harm. A good example of this is the fear of autism with the Measles, Mumps and Rubella vaccine, which I will explain in more detail.

The measles, mumps, and rubella (MMR) vaccine is a combination vaccine that was approved by the FDA in 1971 to protect children against measles, mumps, and rubella. These diseases are serious and can be potentially deadly. Each year in the United States, nearly 10 million doses of the vaccine are distributed.

The Center for Disease Control (CDC) continues to recommend two doses of MMR vaccine for all children: dose 1 at ages 12-15 months and dose 2 at ages 4-6 years. The recommendation from the CDC is clear: *"people who decide not to vaccinate their children because of religious or personal beliefs put their children and others at risk for getting these diseases"*.

Because signs of autism may appear around the same time children receive the MMR vaccine, some parents worry that the vaccine causes autism. For example – entering "MMR vaccine and autism" on "Google" delivers a list of over 100,000 "hits". Because of these concerns, many parents decided to be "on the safe side" and did not have their children vaccinated. Their perceptions are likely to be the following:

- Worst error: being personally responsible for causing autism in my child through giving them a vaccination
- Least error: failing to vaccinate my child so they get measles

The results of this perception are clear: "There is an unprecedented increase in measles cases in England and Wales" says Mary Ramsay from the Health Protection Agency. The number of cases of measles in just one month [November 2008] was the same as seen in the whole year a decade earlier. Complications of measles include pneumonia, encephalitis [inflammation of the brain] and a fatality rate of about 3 per thousand in developed countries.

Perhaps it was reasonable to use the safe-side heuristic when these concerns first emerged. At that time there was no definitive proof that autism and vaccination were not linked, few studies had been done and therefore the probability of each of the types of decision failure was unknown. However, now that knowledge has moved on, it is currently wrong – and dangerous – to continue to ignore the statistics and depend on the safe-side heuristic when many carefully performed scientific studies have found no link between MMR vaccine and autism. In this case, the parents' dread of being personally responsible for causing autism in their child outweighs their perceptions of harm from their child "randomly" acquiring measles, and the reduced trust in the medical establishment reinforces this behavior. In summary, the warning signs for mis-applying the "safe side" heuristic in this situation are: good statistical knowledge exists but is not being used, people dread one of the consequences but not the other, and there is lack of trust in the recommendations of the establishment. In this particular case there is also the possibility of the "selfish" effect: the perfect vaccination strategy for me is if everyone else in the population is vaccinated; I can't possibly get sick as the disease won't exist and I don't have any of the risks of vaccination either.

There are a number of past and current applications of the "safe side" heuristic that meet some of the same danger signals including silicone breast implants, nuclear power and genetically modified foods in Europe. One paradox is that initially when a new risk is identified by a hypothesis-generating statistical analysis or through public fears, there is inevitably insufficient scientific research to show a risk is a low probability event or simply isn't present: it is much harder to show the absence of a risk than to raise a red flag that one might be present. The "safe side" heuristic justifiably operates to treat risks as if they were true because failing to act on a real risk is perceived by modern society as a worse error than falsely acting on a risk that isn't real – the "precautionary principle" has become a part of European law after all. If the action is taken driven by this heuristic, for example to ban a substance, then the scientific evidence of its safety or otherwise will likely never be acquired because it is banned. There are three upsides to that approach: firstly it manages public fears and is therefore politically popular, secondly it eliminates the harm of the risk if it is real and thirdly if there is a decision error it will never be discovered because the science will never be done. The downsides are that the benefits of the substance are denied to society, the costs of replacing it are borne by the consumer and these may be unnecessary because the perception of risk may be false. The bottom line is that the safe-side heuristic is important but has a transient application; as data and statistics become available for a decision it should be replaced but that this will feel uncomfortable to many.

Use the "safe side" heuristic when:

- You are satisficing in a low value low harm situation OR you are maximizing in a high value high harm situation but there is too little time to acquire more knowledge about the probability of different types of error, or where these estimates would be mired in complexity
- When there are 2 types of decision failure and their seriousness is substantially different
- When you don't know the probabilities of one kind of failure over the other

Don't use the "safe side" heuristic when:

- You could get information to estimate probabilities of each type of error
- When you have time, knowledge and resources to evaluate the alternatives properly
- When there is substantial emotion [good or bad] and a vivid outcome with one type of decision failure and a more abstract or boring outcome on the other

Stop at the first feature that is better: the minimalist heuristic

Tina is a college student and she has just spilled her cup of coffee on the keyboard of her laptop computer. The burning smell and blank screen are enough; even though she isn't an expert she can tell that needs to buy a new one. This is urgent as she can't bear to be away from Facebook for even a day. She usually asks her older sister Gina [her parents liked rhyming names] for advice because she is really into computers, but unfortunately, she is climbing a mountain in South Africa and won't be online again until next week, and Tina can't wait that long to change her Facebook status or to look at what parties her friends have been going to. A simple phone-call to her loving parents where she carefully stressed the importance of having a computer for her college work secured her a $750 transfer into her bank account. She knows her constraints – the maximum price and that it must connect wirelessly to the internet. She also knows her freedom – to choose any brand in her price range but she has already unconsciously used the recognition heuristic to narrow her choice down to 3 brands that she recognizes – HP, Compaq and Dell. They all seem to have slightly different features for the price – the features that she recognizes are: hard disk space, integral Wi-Fi card, battery life, screen size and "RAM" memory. There are other features that she doesn't recognize such as clock-speed, and processor type but she eliminates these, again using the recognition heuristic. She is standing in Wal-Mart but isn't enjoying staring at the computers; while she has heard of these features, she doesn't really know how they will affect performance for the tasks she wants to do, and she doesn't want to ask the sales-guy as she thinks he will just try to sell her something more expensive or get her 'phone number. So she decides to go through the features she recognizes one by one and stop when one computer seems better. She doesn't know which feature is most important to start with, so she picks randomly. The first thing she looks at is hard-disk space – and all 3 brands have the same 120 GB drive, so she moves on. The next thing she looks at is the memory; here 2 of the brands have 2 Gb but there is a special offer on the HP that day with 4Gb at no extra charge. Her search is over; she buys the HP without looking at any of the other features. It is also available in pink, her favorite color!

This is an example of the use of what Gigerenzer calls "the minimalist heuristic". The strategy is – after applying the recognition heuristic if you can – to pick features that might discriminate between your choices in any order. The only requirement is that the features themselves are known to be linked to some kind of benefit or harm, but you don't need to know how much – just the direction, whether they are good or bad. Then choose the features one by one, in any order you like. If the first one does not discriminate between your choices then continue to the next one, and so on. The stopping rule is that the search is over at the first feature that discriminates in favor of one of your alternatives. This is the most "frugal" heuristic after recognition – it enables the search to be stopped as soon as one alternative "wins" and doesn't require any experience or knowledge as to which factor is the most relevant.

If you have made the same decision before, a variant of this approach is to start with the feature that you found discriminated last time. In the situation above, if Tina needed to buy another laptop next week because the one she just bought was stolen, she would start with the comparison of memory rather than hard disk size because that was the factor that stopped her search before. This is a bit more frugal, because on average the search will stop a bit earlier. Gigerenzer calls this approach the "take the last" heuristic.

On the face of it, these strategies seems ridiculous – aren't you supposed to look at all the differences between things and compare them all? Isn't Tina throwing away useful information by not even looking at what processors the computers had? Shouldn't she feel ashamed or guilty that she didn't make the best use of her parents' money?

Well, firstly the "frugality" can be an advantage, particularly under extreme time pressure – if you were asking yourself "which is the nearest emergency exit?" in that downed plane on the Hudson River, then if there were two exits the same distance away you might rapidly select the next comparison "are there obviously more people who are in front of me at one exit vs. the other?" – and then act immediately. That would take a lot less time than identifying and evaluating all the factors that might impede your exit before acting. Secondly, the performance of this heuristic can be better than you think if the features aren't independent. For example, a computer that is made with more memory is also likely to have a better processor and more hard disk space – or at least no worse than the competition. Choosing the factor you think of first isn't really throwing away information if all the features are correlated. Thirdly, trying to evaluate all the information can be confusing, and even linear statistical models can start to go wrong. In practice, Gigerenzer found that where there wasn't much information available, these simple heuristics performed as well as the complex multiple linear regression models. When there was more information to build a good model, the regression models were better but not by a huge amount – 72% correct vs. 66% correct in one test gives you a rough idea, with the "take the last" slightly better than “mimimalist”. One obvious effect of using the minimalist heuristic is that the order in which the features are seen affects the results, and the order is dependent on the environment. Because there is no conscious effort to rank order the features by importance, their visibility tends to affect whether they are included in the decision. High visibility features that are seen first will be used to discriminate more often – a feature well known by advertisers and supermarkets who manipulate the environment, and this is likely to degrade the performance of this heuristic when compared with the academic test settings.

Use the minimalist heuristic when:

- You are under extreme time pressure in a high harm high value situation, or when satisficing in a low value low harm decision
- You know whether the features are good or bad
- Some of the features are likely to be related to each other
- The number of alternatives is manageable [e.g. 2 to 50]

Don’t use the minimalist heuristic when:

- You are maximizing and have access to resources and knowledge
- Somebody might be manipulating the environment to get you to see particular features first

The "Take the best" – heuristic

Tina's older sister Gina gets home from her climbing trip in South Africa, and she proudly shows her the new computer that she bought all on her own. She is hoping that Gina won't tell her to return it and get a different one. Gina doesn't care what brand it is, she is focused on performance, and she manages to conceal her disgust at the pink color and examines the features that it has. Her experience and knowledge of Tina's computing needs tells her that the most likely cause of dissatisfaction with a computer would be, in rank order of importance:

1. Not having a spill-resistant keyboard
2. Not having a built-in high-speed Wi-Fi card for her to connect to the internet without using an easily-damaged add-on card
3. Not having enough memory to handle all the simultaneously open windows that Tina habitually has
4. Not having enough hard disk space to store all her photos and videos
5. Not having enough battery life for her to use it in the classroom away from a power outlet
6. Not having enough processing power

Gina does a better job of looking for alternatives than Tina and isn't so brand-conscious, so she identifies 6 alternatives in the price range – as opposed to Tina's 3. Note that Gina didn't use the recognition heuristic because she was an expert – she recognized all of the brands so it was of no use. She starts at the top of the list and compares the first feature of importance with other computers in her price range – none of them have a spill resistant keyboard so her computer is no worse than the others. Her computer has a built-in card but one of the 6 does not and is eliminated. Moving to the third feature, of the remaining 5 alternatives, only one has the same memory and the remaining 4 are eliminated. Examining disk space, Tina's computer has 20Gb more than the one remaining alternative. Gina therefore stops at that point, ignoring items 5 and 6 and smiles at Tina – "good job Sis", keep this one, but I'll order you a spill-resistant "skin" to go over your keyboard!

This is an example of what Gigerenzer calls the "Take the Best" heuristic. It is a bit different from the minimalist heuristic – which used the features in random order – or the "take the last" heuristic which used the one that was successful last time first. Here the features are ranked in order of importance based on experience, in particular their individual ability to predict success or failure in a situation and environment like the one being faced – "ecological rationality". The method also assumes there is knowledge of the direction of a "good" effect and a "bad" effect [e.g. more memory is good, more cost is bad].

The rank order could alternatively be based on statistics – for example in this case Tina could have used it without Gina if only she had seen a magazine survey that correlated which features in a computer most often caused dissatisfaction for consumers like her. Otherwise the heuristic is the same as for the minimalist approach – the search continues through the features in rank order until one alternative is superior and stops at that point without the need to consider the remaining features. The features can be compared in either a "satisficing" mode, where they are made into a binary or dichotomized "good" or "bad" or "better" or "worse" outcome, or in a "maximizing" strategy, a minimally important difference can be defined in advance - for example, perhaps a difference of 1Gb in hard disk space isn't defined as a meaningful difference but 20Gb is.

Once again this would appear to be a suboptimal process – leaving out features at the bottom of the list no matter how good or bad they are is another example of a "non-compensatory" strategy like the rules we discussed earlier. However, once again this heuristic can perform surprisingly well: in fact Gigerenzer's stunning result was that it outperformed multiple linear regression models by a few percent when both were used in a dichotomized fashion and applied to new data such as predicting high-school dropout rates [accuracy of 60% vs. 54% for linear regression] or professors' salaries, despite being economical with data and fast to apply. He and colleagues could not believe how good the result was, so they thought that perhaps regression models would improve when they used continuous data rather than dichotomized data. They were right, regression improved its performance but so did the heuristic, in those situations they were equal in performance!

There are a number of possible reasons that the "take the best" heuristic equaled or bettered the "gold standard" of multiple linear regression. Firstly, even the best statistical models based on the past don't predict the future as comprehensively as they explained the "training" datasets they were developed from. This is inevitable, because of natural variation in the data from the past to the future. Secondly, the less important features that are included in the statistical model but left out of the heuristic are often adding more noise than signal, and the statistical model learns the noise – this effect is called "over-fitting. Thirdly, linear statistical models based on normal distributions of the data may not represent reality – as Taleb points out in "The Black Swan", linear statistical models often don't perform well in real-life applications, indeed he calls the bell curve that they depend on "that great intellectual fraud". So the key reason that the heuristic generalizes so well is because it makes very few assumptions about the statistical distribution of the inputs. Unlike the minimalist heuristic, it is also relatively resistant to the order that features are seen or their visibility to the eye because knowledge or experience is used to rank the order of the features, not simply the order they appear. In theory, when information is very abundant, the "take the best" heuristic would not be as good as some other methods which actually use all the information, such as Dawes' rule, but for many decisions there is a restriction on the availability of information which plays to this heuristic's strength. There are quite strict limitations of the mental version of this heuristic – how many features and how many alternatives can we hold in our heads? The answer is thought to be about 7 pieces of information which is only 3-4 features for 2 alternatives! This can be overcome by using a pencil and paper to create a ranked list rather than attempting to hold all the information in your head.

Use the "take the best" heuristic when:

- Information is only moderately abundant
- You are satisficing in a high resource situation or you are maximizing in a knowledge-limited situation
- You can rank the most important features of your alternatives
- Highly ranked features are "non compensatory" - MUCH more important than low ranked features
- When some of the features are correlated

Don't use the "take the best" heuristic when:

- You are maximizing and have lots of knowledge
- The features are completely independent
- Different features are of equal importance

Franklin's Rule – on the way to "even swaps"

In 1772 Benjamin Franklin outlined what he called "moral or prudential algebra", a process for making a decision based on listing pros and cons of a particular option. In a letter to his friend, Joseph Priestly he described how, over several days deliberations he would write down pros and cons of a particular decision option. He doesn't explain about how it might apply to multiple options so I'll assume that it is for a simple A vs. B decision with only two alternatives. Having written the pros and cons, he proceeded to give each a mental weight or currency [without actually writing it down], and when he found a "pro" that was the same weight as a "con", he would cross them both off. Alternatively he might combine two less important issues from one side as equivalent in "moral algebra" to one more important issue from the other side – in which case all 3 would be crossed off. The end result is at least one remaining pro or con on one side or the other, which drives the decision. Note that the nature of the actual remaining issue isn't important, indeed it should not be regarded as any more or less important than any other issue; it remains on the page as a piece of currency that isn't balanced by something from the other side.

This method is mainly included for historical interest, but you can use it if you have a simply structured decision with two alternatives, and you are satisficing for a low to moderate value and low harm decision. It assumes that your subjective weighting is reasonable and rational, and that you can therefore estimate the currency value of each pro or con. If some of the pros or cons are uncertain – in other words if they aren't 100% likely to happen, then the inaccuracies of this estimation process will increase as you try to judge the seriousness and the likelihood of each pro or con and compare that with the seriousness and likelihood of any other. That is beyond my mental arithmetic and it's not much more complex to assign numbers as shown in the next chapter in Decisionability tradeoffs, so I don't recommend attempting it where there is uncertainty.

Even Swaps

Even swaps is an extension of Franklin's rule with a bit of actual algebra but it is simple enough to use a calculator or write on the back of your decision envelope. It extends the rule to more complex decisions with multiple alternatives. The table below was used in chapter 3 features of 3 different alternative houses:

Desired features	House #1	House #2	House #3
Price less than $300k	$250k	$240k	$300k
Rank	2	1	3
Easy commute	10 minutes	30 minutes	15 minutes
Rank	1	3	2
At least 3 bedrooms	4	3	5
Rank	2	3	1
On school bus route	Yes	No	Yes
Rank	1=	3	1=
In a safe area	Yes	No	Yes
Rank	1=	3	1=

I've added to the table a simple ranking system that shows how each feature was ranked in the alternatives, with 1 the highest and 3 the lowest.

House number 2 is outranked by house #1 on all features except price. It is also outranked by house # 3 on all features except price. Given that all the houses were within the "good enough" price range, the decision can be simplified immediately by eliminating house #2, as it is said to be "dominated" by the other two alternatives – it is ranked behind them on every feature.

Now the comparison is between house #1 and house #2. The last 2 features – school bus route and safe area - were equivalent for both the houses so can be crossed-off as equal as in Franklin's rule. The 5 minutes difference in commute time can also be dismissed as too small to be meaningful. The revised table below shows what's left:

Desired features	**House #1**	**House #3**
Price less than $300k	$250k	$300k
Rank	2	3
At least 3 bedrooms	4	5
Rank	2	1

In order to make a swap, either price has to be traded for a bedroom, or bedroom for price – it doesn't matter which. If the family really only needs 3 bedrooms, and the 4th one is already spare, a 5th bedroom might only be worth $20k to them. So making that swap in the table we can add an imaginary bedroom to house #1 and eliminate that differentiating feature from the table, as long as we add $20k to the price of house #1 for the imaginary bedroom we "bought". We are left with a price of $270k for house #1 and a price of $300k for house #2, so house #1 wins. As with Franklin's rule, the last remaining decisive feature it is not necessarily the most important because the prior trades may have eliminated many more important features. They haven't ceased to be important, but they have ceased to contribute to the balance in the decision process. It is also important to look at the incremental change – adding a 5th bedroom to a 4th is a less valuable increment than adding a 3rd to a 2nd.

As with Franklin's rule, this process is too simple to deal with uncertainty. Also it depends on the veracity of the "swap" process, but it is a simple method of narrowing down the numbers of alternatives and the numbers of desired features.

Use the "even swaps method" when:

- You are satisficing in a low to moderate value and low to moderate harm situation
- The number of alternatives is small [e.g. 2 to 20]
- Some of the assumptions for alternatives such as the "take the best" heuristic are not met e.g. the features are truly independent or are of similar importance to each other

Don't use the "even swaps method" when:

- You are maximizing in a moderate to high value or moderate to high value situation and have access to resources and knowledge
- It is not 100% likely that the features, advantages or disadvantages will occur

"Weight and Rate" Decision Matrices

This is one of the commonest methods of decision-making so you may have experienced it before. However I do not recommend it as I view it as inferior to all the other methods in this chapter. I am including it simply because of its common usage.

It starts by making a matrix table of the alternatives you are considering and the features that are important – much as was done for the even swaps method. You score each alternative on how well it addresses each feature, with a perfect score for that feature being at the top of the scale and absence of that feature with a zero. Common scales would be a 10 point scale with value from 0-10 or a 100 point scale. Large scales would be used where there are subtle but meaningful differences between alternatives that would be missed by a smaller scale when scored on that feature.

However, this method recognizes that some of your alternatives' features are more important than others, so you give each feature a relative weight. You give the most important features high weights and the least important low weights using a 0-10 scale where a weight of 10 is the most important. In practice you create weights by identifying the most important feature first and ascribing it a full scale score – for example 10 on a 0-10 scale. Then you weight every other feature in relation to the first, with an effort to keep the scoring linear, so that your weighting of 5 really is half as important as you rating of 10, and a weighting of 2.5 really is a quarter as important.

Finally you just multiply the two numbers together - the score multiplied by the weight for that feature, so each feature for each alternative gets a weight-adjusted score. Then you just add up the total scores from all the features for each alternative. The alternative with the greatest total of weighted scores is the best.

Unfortunately the method depends on some quite fundamental statistical assumptions which are almost never met! Hence my reluctance to recommend it. The first assumption is linearity; for any given input score your weighting factor is assumed to act in the same manner over its entire range. A one point increment at one end of one of the scale on one feature is supposed to equal to a one point increment at the other end of the other feature discounted by the constant weighting. The key problem with this approach is that the relative importance between different features varies in real life, they aren't two nice straight lines. For example, take the number of bedrooms in the house that you just looked at in the even swaps method. You might give that a fairly high importance rating in your fictitious family, but is it linear? – No, absolutely not! A one bedroom house would have no utility to your fictional family, a two bedroom house very little utility, a three bedroom house would have a lot of utility, and a 4 bedroom house only a bit more than 3, and a 5 bedroom house no more than 4. So what kind of weighting would you give to the number of bedrooms when its importance in relation to other factors in the decision varies nonlinearly? Many of the factors that you commonly come across have such a non-linear utility scale. This is not such a problem in even swaps because you are scoring the utility without making any linearity assumption.

Dawes' Rule

One way around the "weight and rate" problem of incorrect weighting from non-linearity is to avoid the weighting completely, and just add up the number of positive or negative features for each alternative – this is called "Dawes Rule". Each feature is either present or absent, or above a threshold or below a threshold. For "good" features if they are present or above the threshold a score of +1 is ascribed. For "bad" features if they are present or above the threshold a score of -1 is ascribed. A "not present" gets zero. The total score for each alternative is simply added up. I think of Dawes' rule as an extension of the minimalist heuristic without the stopping rule; the requirements are the same – simply knowing what the alternatives are and how they compare between alternatives. Presumably the minimalist heuristic has to stop looking for alternatives early because of the brain's limited capacity, whereas Dawes' rule doesn't have that limitation because it uses pencil and paper.

Use "Dawes' Rule" when:

- You are maximizing and knowledge is abundant but there is time or resource pressure
- You are not choosing the "take the best" heuristic because the features are not very different in importance to one another, or you don't know if they are different
- The importance of a feature may be nonlinear along its range

Don't use "Dawes Rule" when:

- There is significant uncertainty about one or more benefits or risks
- One or more features are "non compensatory" – then use the "take the best" heuristic

Ecological Rationality – Recap

Although each method has a checklist of how it best fits a given environment I thought it best to reinforce the key differences here.

Gigerenzer's "take the best" heuristic assumes that the best feature is worth more than all the rest put together, that the second best is worth more than all the remaining ones, and so on down the ranked list of features until a choice is made, but the method does not require you to actually say what the differences in importance [weights] are. As mentioned before, this characteristic is described as "non compensatory" because benefits of features that are ranked lower cannot compensate for a deficiency in a feature ranked higher.

The "weight and rate" decision matrix approach assumes that you can subjectively weight each feature based on what you know and requires you to do so, and is "compensatory" – any combination of beneficial features can be used to overcome any combination of non-beneficial features. Although it is compensatory, if one or more features are more important than all the others they can be ascribed a very high weight in the process, so could produce a similar result to a non-compensatory process.

"Dawes Rule" assumes that the weights are all the same, or that the error in ascribing weights exceeds the benefit in doing so, and just adds up the number of pros and cons it is entirely compensatory. Because the weights are the same and all the features are included, not having any one "good" feature can be overcome by having any other "good" features or the absence of a "bad" feature.

The "Take the Best" approach is the method of choice when there is sufficient knowledge of the features to give them a clear rank order of importance. It beats "Weight and Rate" in situations where there is insufficient knowledge about the constancy of the ratio of importance between features. It also beats "Weight and Rate" even if you do know the importance ratio when time or resources are scarce because it is quicker and requires less knowledge.

Dawes' Rule is the method of choice when the features seem to have similar importance to one another, or where the importance is unknown or cannot be agreed upon. It also applies where the importance is known but there is insufficient knowledge to use "weight and rate" because the ratio of importance between features is not known to be linear across the whole scale. By avoiding weighting Dawes' Rule avoids the errors in weighting but it also loses the benefits of weighting when some features really are more important – hence our choice of "Take the Best" when the features are clearly weighted differently. It is also fairly simple to use and can cope with large numbers of features; in knowledge-abundant situations it performed well when tested by Gigerenzer, in knowledge poor situations it was beaten by "take the best".

The decision matrix "weight and rate" is rarely the method of choice. When the differences in importance between the features are significant but not large enough to be viewed as non-compensatory, and where knowledge is abundant so many features can be taken into account it can be used, but it requires sufficient knowledge that the ratio of importance between features is constant; under those circumstances it approximates to multiple linear regression statistics. In actuality the knowledge about constancy of ratios of importance is very difficult to imagine or test without doing complex statistics. And if there are many features, the over-fitting errors of multiple linear regression also apply to this method – some features just contribute noise. So I almost never use this method but use Dawes' Rule where features are compensatory and "Take the Best" where features are non-compensatory or at least very different in their importance.

The BIG limitation here is that for all of these methods we've imagined that uncertainty doesn't exist or can't be predicted adequately. We've assumed that that the pros and cons or the intended benefits and undesirable features are all certainties – i.e. that they will occur 100% of the time. If there is modest uncertainty but you are satisficing in a low or moderate importance decision, then you can ignore it. But if there is uncertainty about whether you will get some or all of the benefits or risks and you have a high importance decision that you are satisficing or a moderate to high importance decision that you are maximizing then you can't use these any of these methods and will need to proceed to the next chapter.

Decision tree for highest performing methods showing choices between "Dawes Rule" "Take the Best" and "Weight and Rate" depending on the environment.

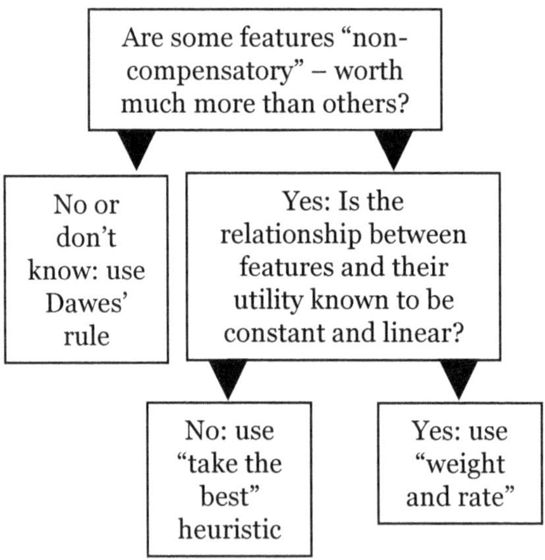

Key learnings from chapter 6:

- Simple heuristics can work surprisingly well but only if you match them to the right environment.
- When knowledge is low and time pressure high, simple recognition, "minimalist" and "be on the safe side" heuristics work well, but should be abandoned when knowledge increases.
- When knowledge is higher but the decision is of low to modest harm and value:
  - Even Swaps and Dawes rule are good methods if features are compensatory [similar in value]
  - "Take the Best" heuristic is the method of choice when features are non-compensatory [some much more important than others]
  - "Weight and Rate" is the method of choice only on the rare occasion when there is sufficient knowledge to determine that the relative importance of each feature is constant across the scale used for rating features.
- These methods do not account for uncertainty about achieving the outcomes or consequences of the decision – see next chapter.

Chapter 7

Damned if you do, damned if you don't: decisions and tradeoffs in the face of uncertainty

When is the Decisionability tradeoff method useful and why?

The methods described in the preceding chapter make the assumption that everything is certain. That's OK if everything is actually certain. It is even OK when things are uncertain but you can live with imprecision because you are working in a low value situation, or where resources are not available to do better.

The decisionability tradeoff method is designed to help you handle differences in likelihood when thinking about the risks or benefits of different alternatives – in other words when there is a less than 100% probability of achieving good or of causing harm from a given alternative.

Thankfully you don't need to know statistics in order to use this method and it can lead directly to the process of identifying the specific actions that are most efficient when resolving risks – this is useful in running an efficient business, and often at home too. It does require moderately more time and effort than the "even swaps" method, but can be done on a calculator, with a pencil and paper or ideally an Excel spreadsheet.

Because this method takes a bit more effort, I am assuming that you are in one of the following situations:

- You are facing a high harm high value situation but the knowledge, time or resourcing aren't available to build a custom statistical model.
- You are maximizing but the decision isn't a high harm high value situation so extra resources aren't warranted to build a statistical model
- This is a high value/harm situation but it is a personal or life decision [i.e. not a business decision] so the idea of building a statistical model is ludicrous

The concept of "harm" and tradability of probability and seriousness

In chapter 3 I mentioned briefly that I use probability and seriousness as important components that drive the concept of "harm". I didn't make up this concept but it has provenance in many areas such as accidental release of radiation from nuclear power plants, occupational health and environmental protection.

The idea of the tradability of seriousness and harm got a boost from a public enquiry into the building of "Sizewell B" a proposed new nuclear power-plant in the UK in 1972. At the public enquiry, the industry and its opponents presented highly complex data tables and statistics to support their opposing positions, causing the judge to famously declare "go away and come back with something that a reasonable person can understand".

What the industry came back with were graphs that used probability multiplied by seriousness to create a boundary for allowable events. Events with low seriousness that happen frequently such as kicking over a bucket of mildly radioactive water can be viewed as equivalent to extremely rare events with a much higher seriousness such as a reactor shut-down. These events could be compared with other known events such as chemical factory accidents or even car accidents. I call this concept the "harm" - the probability of something bad happening multiplied by its seriousness.

The concept of "harm":

- Harm = probability of an adverse event [risk] x seriousness of the event if it occurs [hazard]

Another point that arose from the nuclear reactor inquiry – and radiation exposure regulation still uses it today – is that you can accept a satisficing approach even in a "high value high harm" situation. As long as your harm is below some predefined level you are "safe enough" and do not have to spend any money, time or resources in getting it lower or in increasing the precision of your estimate.

Overall the principle is to use harm as analogous to debt, it takes away value from the outcome of your decision. Harm can be due to "collateral damage" of the decision or can simply be that the hoped-for value of the decision is not completely met. Your approach here should be to:

1. Characterize the harm for each alternative for a decision
2. Use the harm as a discount to that alternative's value
3. Use the discounted [residual] value of each alternative to decide between them.

Only the perfect alternative which delivers the entire benefit with no possible negative consequences would have no harm. Any choice which has costs, consequences or which fails to deliver all of the benefits has harm from each of those issues.

Example, obtaining good vision: glasses vs. contacts vs. laser surgery.

My first example is a situation where the benefit of each alternative is the same but the risks and costs are different: the choice between glasses, contact lenses and laser-surgery. The purpose of the decision is: "to choose the most cost and risk effective method or procedure in order to obtain good vision". I start by defining the current state: that I don't have good vision unaided today. The key feature of my desired future state, good vision, is the same from each alternative: glasses, contact lenses or laser surgery. My next step is to acquire information on all the possible harm that might be associated with each alternative – and harm is defined very broadly including: failing to deliver on the benefits, the appearance of a new type risk, or a cost of the procedure. As usual I am using the holistic "T.H.E. Decisionability triangle" assessment approach to the alternatives that I introduced in chapter 5. In this case I am maximizing because I think my Decisionability "window" shows an upwardly sloping line - that extra effort will lead to a significantly better decision. I am fortunate that there is a large amount of factual information on the likelihood of such issues published on the internet for each alternative, so I am not limited by knowledge or data. My task is also made easier because the only person I need to accept the information is me, so I don't need to form a committee for the purpose of promoting acceptance of the decision, or to provide input on the subjective issues but I would certainly get input from my wife as a sanity check. Because the intended benefit is the same for each alternative, I can start simply by comparing the negative consequences for each of my options. The table below shows these from my personal perspective.

Negative consequence	**Do Nothing [keep wearing glasses]**	**Corrective Laser Surgery**	**Contact lenses**
Technical	I have limited peripheral vision and internal reflections from glasses that are annoying when I play tennis	The procedure might not work well, I might still need glasses all the time	I might not tolerate contact lenses, switch back to glasses
	My nose gets sore from the nose rest	I might still need reading glasses	I might still need reading glasses
		I might have glare in my night vision so I have difficulty in driving at night	I might still need to wear glasses ~30% of the time
		I might have permanent dry eye needing eye drops	I might get an infection leading to permanently damaged vision such that I can't drive a car
		The procedure might cause permanently damaged vision such that I can't drive a car	
Human	I look less attractive with glasses on	I am afraid of the Lasik procedure	I don't like the idea of putting something in my eye
	I keep losing my glasses and I waste time looking for them		Time and Inconvenience of putting in and taking out lenses, getting supplies
Economic	\$300 per year over 10 years = \$3000	\$3500 cost of procedure	\$400 per year over 10 years + extra checkups = \$5000

The next step is to examine how probable and how serious each negative consequence actually is. Let's do each one in turn, starting with the seriousness.

Rating the seriousness of different types of failure

What you need to do is to create a seriousness rating scale that is transparent, that makes an effort to be linear, where zero really is zero, not just the lowest score, and which creates a currency which you can used all consequences of different types. This isn't as hard as it sounds. For decisions about finance or pricing, a dollar value can be used. For decisions that are primarily about the way that humans think, feel or act, you can use a "quality of life" [QOL] scale, where you rate the approximate impact of the issue on your quality of life. For adverse effects in this example, a 100% impact on the quality of life means that this issue if it occurred would be actual death, or a life so miserable it is equivalent to death. For business projects that do not involve human life the same concept can be used – the virtual "life" of the project which is very analogous to the human QOL – what percentage of project value is lost from a risk, delay or increased cost. For projects that are principally about economics, then actual currency- willingness to pay or actual costs - can be used. I am going to take you through the 6 simple steps in this example.

Step 1: Create an upper-end anchor point with the one of the worst consequences.

In this case, I chose permanently damaged vision as my worst case scenario for an unintended consequence of any of my choices [in this case from laser surgery]. I scored it like this: I think that being totally blind in both eyes would probably be a loss of 50% of my quality of life [my accidental death and dismemberment life insurance policy rates it as such too], so I am going to rate damaged vision such that I can't drive a car as a loss of 25% of my quality of life, about half as bad as being totally blind.

Step 2: Create a lower end anchor point with the most trivial consequence

Now looking at the other extreme I see a difficulty – how do I rate a "continuously sore nose", which is the least bad consequence in my choices [in this case from glasses rubbing the bridge of my nose] compared to the upper end which was so serious? Well, let's start by giving the sore nose a trial score of 1%, the lowest single digit score. However, to check the linearity of my trial score I would ask whether 25 continuously sore noses [with a score of 25%] is the same as one damaged vision [with a score of 25%]. That doesn't seem enough of a difference to me so I settle on 100 continuously sore noses as equal to 1 damaged vision. I could equally have gone for 1000 but when the seriousness scores are that small it isn't worth worrying too much as they won't contribute significantly towards the total. That means a sore nose has an effect of ¼ of a percent on quality of life, as that is 1/100th of 25, and 25% was the score I gave to damaged vision.

Step 3: Create another anchor point somewhere in between.

Now I have got 2 anchor points on our scale for this issue. I am now going to make another one somewhere in the middle. I am choosing to rate "night vision glare" at 5% - I'd be saying that 5 night vision glares was worth one daytime damaged vision, or

20 sore noses. Obviously no single person could have 5 glares but it is still a health economic comparison that I can evaluate subjectively.

Step 4: Rate the seriousness of all the other negative consequences in relation to the anchor points.

Now you work down your list of all possible negative consequences and put them on the scale in relation to your anchor points. A point you should remember is that this is individualized – I rated the distortion and peripheral vision issues from glasses quite high because I play tennis, an airplane pilot friend of mine cares less about that but he would have rated the night vision glare far more highly than I because he would have to give up flying. Another slight peculiarity is that the fear of the laser procedure occurs only once, and does not come back once the procedure is over. The day before the procedure, the fear might cause me such misery and incapacitation that my quality of life [QOL] might be impacted by 80% if I was frozen with fear that day, but that is only one day in the 10 year assessment. So it figures as pretty close to zero when amortized. While it doesn't figure in the cost because of this, it could be regarded as a non-compensatory decision "gate" and not included in the overall calculation: simply that if I can't overcome my fear then this choice isn't available to me.

Regarding the economic costs, these are not in QOL points and I must convert them from dollars into a QOL percentage. For those, I used my accidental death and dismemberment insurance policy as a guide. As I am well insured my insurance payout for complete blindness [a 50% loss of QOL] would be $1M. I therefore estimated that to me, the permanent damage of 25% would therefore be "worth" $500,000 and a 1% change would be worth $20k. The economic costs are pro-rated into % change using that formula. For projects in corporations, the "common currency" desired may actually be $, so the conversion could equally well be performed in the opposite direction – QOL points into dollars - so that all the ratings were in dollars.

An Aside: why pick a perfect result and rate the seriousness of not getting it?

This is a bit of a trick. The alternative to picking a good result [such as "good vision"] is to pick a mediocre result and score outcomes that are better and worse than the reference level and add up the positives and negative harm scores like credits and debits. The problem with that is that humans don't rate benefits and risks in the same way – we tend to be more "loss averse" than "benefit seeking". This means that for any given degree of harm, most people would seek about twice the benefit to offset it – perhaps this is an extension of our natural "safe side" heuristic. Thus, if you try to rate the seriousness of benefits or improvements and deterioration or harm for the same issue you will run into the directional difference between subjective scoring of harm and benefits. Because of this, my recommendation is to define a near perfect outcome and rate all the possible factors that would cause the outcome to be less than perfect, because then all the scoring is in the same direction. The perfectly viable alternative is to define the worst possible case outcome and score all the factors that might improve that case as benefits but it just doesn't seem as much fun to do that, and if most of your scores are closer to perfection than disaster your estimation errors will be less because you are operating over a shorter scale difference.

Step 5: Assign probabilities to each of the negative consequences

For the glasses alternative, the probabilities are easy, because all of the negative consequences are certain – i.e. 100%. For the other alternatives there are published data on their likelihood – for the sake of simplicity here I have not attempted a literature review on the actual incidences, but have merely used plausible figures [for example a 1 in one thousand chance of damaged vision].

In practice, if there are no published figures for likelihood then you should find an expert, but it has been shown that – whether expert or novice – human likelihood estimates are more accurate when asked as a natural frequency instead of a probability. For example, one might describe a probability as a 9 out of 10 frequency, or a 1 in 10, or a 1 in 1000 rather than a 90%, 10% or 0.1% probability. The neutral way of asking this question that Gigerenzer recommends in "Calculated Risks" is in the format below:

"If you were to consider 100 projects exactly like this, how many of them do you think would have this scenario come to pass" or "If you were to take 100 people having this procedure, how many of them do you think would have the issue?". If the issue is rarer than 1 in 100 you will have to increase the number of people in your question to more than 100, such as "If we were to take 1000…". Even when you ask yourself or others the question in this neutral way you still have to convert it to the percentage fraction to use in the calculation.

Step 6: Multiply the seriousness by the probability to get a harm rating.

When you multiply the seriousness by the probability fraction you discount it to something less than 100%. You can actually view this in 2 ways, as **a probability** that has been adjusted by seriousness, or as **a seriousness** that has been adjusted by probability. For now we are using the latter, but the former has some other uses which we will return to later in this chapter.

I created a chart for the "good vision" example on the next page. I started with the Quality of Life scores from the earlier steps, and multiplied each by the probability as a fraction. To get the total harm for each of the three options I just added up the harm scores for each option. This simple addition works when you are treating these numbers like a seriousness score that has been adjusted by probability, or when the numbers are small as above. If the percentage numbers are large [more than 20% harm total or when you need a quantitative calculation, they probably stop being simply additive – the next examples use a different approach where they are treated like probabilities and are not simply added, but hold that thought for now.

It is clear from the totals that for me, glasses are the worst option; switching to either contact lenses or laser surgery would deliver a 5% improvement in my quality of life [QOL] – the difference in harm between glasses at 7.79% harm and either of the other two options at around 2.5%. While contact lenses looks like the best option, it is only one quarter of a percentage of QOL better than laser surgery and that difference isn't really meaningful, and may not even be a true difference as my errors in estimating scores are undoubtedly larger than that.

Here is how the alternatives look:

Glasses	**QOL %**	**Probability %**	**Harm %**
Poor peripheral vision	2.5	100	2.5
Sore nose	0.25	100	0.25
Look less attractive	5.0	100	5.0
Cost of glasses	0.04	100	0.04
TOTAL			**7.79**

Laser surgery	**QOL %**	**Probability %**	**Harm %**
Still need glasses	7.83	10	0.8
Reading glasses	2.0	50	1.0
Night vision glare	5	5	0.25
Permanent damage	25	0.1	0.025
Permanent dry eye	0.25	20	0.05
Fear of procedure	0	100	0
Cost of procedure	0.5	100	0.05
TOTAL			**2.63**

Contact lenses	**QOL %**	**Probability %**	**Harm %**
Still need glasses	7.83	10	0.8
Reading glasses	2.0	50	1.0
Permanent damage	25	0.1	0.025
Fear of lenses	0.1	100	0.1
Time, inconvenience	0.25	100	0.25
Cost of lenses	0.06	100	0.06
TOTAL			**2.38**

If in doubt about whether a difference is real, try changing one or two options within a range that you still consider to be plausible and within "natural variation" and if the scores can be reversed they are indistinguishable. If this happens – as for contacts and laser-surgery in the current example – I could pick either one randomly and not worry about having missed the better opportunity; the decision method would be telling me that there is no harm in picking between the two best options with a roll of the dice. However in this case that isn't necessary as the alternatives can be performed sequentially – I can pick contact lenses first because the costs of contact lenses are not all upfront like those for laser surgery – my contact lens costs are spread out over years. If I start with them and find that the negative consequences for contacts are higher than I expected I can then switch to laser surgery for little penalty of having tried contacts first. Switching does not mean I made a mistake, because many of the adverse consequences are uncertain and I can't know in advance whether they will affect me personally, even if the likelihood figures from a population view were accurate. There is actually a whole mathematical approach to switching called "real options" that is beyond the scope of this book, but suffice to say if switching is any more complex than the case above you will probably need expert help.

Situations where you need to establish the weight of evidence.

The previous example calculated a "burden of harm" for each option and simply added it up. That approach treats the harm number as a seriousness score discounted by probability. It is well suited to evaluating "how bad would it be?" and providing a relative [not absolute] harm score. But if you want to ask a different question: "how likely is it", or if it is important to have an absolute score that is truthful, then the simple addition of harm doesn't work well. In that case, the score is best treated like a probability discounted by seriousness, rather than a seriousness score discounted by probability. That might seem like nonsense now, but I hope to shed some light on what the difference is and why it is important in the following examples.

To show how this works I am going to use an example of evaluating the "weight of evidence" for something. This is useful if you are trying to decide whether to believe something that you are being told, for which there are a number of conflicting pieces of evidence, some of which you aren't certain about. This may be a scientific hypothesis, a course of action in business or even a verdict in court.

In this approach, thankfully for simplicity's sake, most of the method is exactly the same as before. I am still intending to rate each option for seriousness and probability, and use the same probability x seriousness to get a harm number for each. At that point it gets a little different: instead of simply adding up the total of discounted harm, I am going to treat the harm number as a probability that has been discounted by the seriousness. That's the opposite of my prior example with improving vision where I treated the number as a seriousness that was discounted by probability and simply added up the total. In that example we wanted a seriousness output.

Use the harm number as a "total burden" and simply add up the sub-components if:

- You are simply comparing relative harm of one alternative to another, you don't need an absolute value
- The total harm is modest
- There are 5 or fewer causes of harm
- You are seeking the relative assessment of a "seriousness of something"

Use the harm number as an adjusted probability and make a sequential calculation if:

- You do want an absolute number for the harm
- The total harm is high
- There are more than 5 causes of harm
- You are seeking a relative or absolute "probability of something" assessment

In this example, I want a probability that something is true or not; instead of adding up the seriousnesses to get a "burden of adverse effects" as I did before, the new approach allows us to treat the numbers as sequential risks and to do a deterministic calculation for an overall probability of failure. That sounds complicated but it isn't really, I will take you through the steps one at a time. The choice between these approaches depends on what type of answer would be most useful to you, although if the harm numbers are big I think the second approach is more accurate – either way it is still simple enough to be done on a pocket-calculator.

Example: establishing guilt or innocence

On October 4th 1995 I was sitting in the cafeteria of the Smithsonian Air and Space museum in Washington DC when suddenly a loud cheer and the sound of many people screaming ecstatically erupted from the kitchen, followed by much excited talking from the staff. The people eating in the cafeteria sat for a moment in shocked silence before murmuring in low voices: the OJ Simpson "not guilty" verdict had been announced. Clearly the amateur juries around the country had already reached their verdicts based on their own cultural and ethnic perspectives – which were interestingly reflected in the reactions of the staff vs. clientele in the cafeteria.

Let's imagine that I am a part of that historic jury, and I am going to use the Decisionability tradeoff method to calculate a probability of guilt or innocence. Initially, I'll take each of the pieces of evidence in turn and use the method to score the harm each piece of evidence in the same way as for the glasses vs. contact lenses vs. Laser surgery example. As with that example I'll establish the seriousness of the evidence if it was true and then assign a probability that it is true, and then simply multiply to get our harm number. However, after getting the harm number in this case I am going to treat it like a probability (adjusted by seriousness). I can't simply add up probabilities to get a total but I will show the simple calculation needed to get an overall absolute estimate of the probability of guilt or innocence.

There were seven key issues used in evidence:

1. OJ Simpson's history of violence towards Nicole
2. Hair present at the scene
3. Blood present at the scene
4. Cuts on Simpson's hand
5. A glove at the murder scene and another at Simpson's house
6. Shoe prints at the scene
7. Simpson's "slow motion" flight in his Ford Bronco.

I will go through each of these in turn using the Decisionability tradeoff method.

1. OJ Simpson's history of violence towards Nicole

a. Seriousness if true – i.e. if OJ really was violent how seriously does it affect the murder case

Even though about half the people who are murdered by their spouses have suffered previous violence at their hands, this is a red-herring in terms of demonstrating guilt – it takes guilt as a presumption and asks the question backwards: how many people guilty of murder previously abused their spouse. The real question for a case like this, presuming innocence and asking the question forwards is: how many people who are violent towards their spouses do **not** murder them? Given that about 2 million people per year assault their spouses but only a few thousand are murdered and many of them aren't spouses, only about one in a thousand people who assault their spouse also murder them. The seriousness in terms of establishing guilt is therefore only 1/1000 or 0.001. That's too small to register on my scale so I have counted it as zero.

b. Probability of history of violence being true

A history of violence was known to be true and admitted by the defense, so the probability of it is 100%

c. Harm in murder case deduced from this issue

Seriousness if true = 0%
Probability of truth = 100%
Probability x Seriousness = 0%

2. Hairs of a similar type to Simpsons were found on a cap and on Ron Goldman's shirt.

a. Seriousness if true

The seriousness of the presence of Simpson's hair at the crime scene in establishing guilt is quite low because the detectives used a blanket from Ms Simpson's home to cover the body, and it could have had Simpson's hairs on it by contamination. Let's say it is only 5% seriousness.

b. Probability of being true

Given that the hair type fits 10% of the population, the probability of the hair truly being Simpson's could only be estimated if we knew the local population of people with this hair type who could possibly have reached the scene of the crime as alternatives to Simpson himself. That's likely to number in the hundreds of thousands, so the chance could be said to be one in several hundred thousand. However, because of the contamination issue it was quite likely to be his hair, say 20%.

c. Harm score

Seriousness if true = 5%
Probability of truth = 20%
Probability x Seriousness = 1%

3. **Blood evidence: blood of the same blood type [0.5% of population] dropped at crime scene, blood at crime scene contained Simpson's genetic markers, blood in Simpson's home and driveway, blood on socks in OJ's home.**

a. Seriousness if true

Ordinarily the seriousness of truly finding the victims' blood at Simpson's home and Simpson's blood at the crime scene would amount to very strong evidence of guilt – close to 100%. However, the defense scored well here – they were able to cast doubt on the way the blood was handled and to raise the possibility that a racist detective had planted blood. The sock bloodstain wasn't what would be expected if the socks had been worn. Let's say they reduced the seriousness to 50% - by establishing that it was equally likely that the blood was planted vs. came from Simpson at the scene.

b. Probability of truth

The probability of it truly being Simpson's blood with early DNA testing was high. Maybe not as high as today's tests, but let's say 90%

c. Harm score
Seriousness if true = 50%
Probability of truth = 90%
Probability x seriousness = 45%

4. Simpson had fresh cuts on his hands the day after the murder.

a. Seriousness if true
The seriousness is low – Simpson claimed the original wound wasn't enough to drip the amount of blood found, and that he had reinjured it on a glass before being interviewed by police. The mere presence of a cut on the hand does not establish guilt. We'll score that at 5% seriousness.

b. Probability of truth
The probability of Simpson having a cut on his hand was 100%

c. Harm score
Seriousness if true = 5%
Probability of truth = 100%
Probability x seriousness = 5%

5. A left glove was found at the murder scene and the right one at Simpson's house. Nicole had bought a pair in 1990 and Simpson was known to have worn gloves of this type.

a. Seriousness if true
The seriousness of the presence of a glove truly owned by Simpson would have placed him at the murder scene, an important but not definitive indication of guilt – say 50%.

b. Probability of truth

Although Simpson was known to have had gloves of this unusual type, and one was found at his house and the other at the scene the probability of the glove truly being owned by Simpson was cast in doubt by the defense who claimed it could have been planted by a racist cop and by the glove not fitting Simpson's hand in the courtroom... "If the glove don't fit you must acquit". The probability of this being truly Simpson's glove is therefore discounted to 50%

c. Harm score

Seriousness if true = 50%
Probability of truth = 50%
Probability x Seriousness = 25%

6. Shoe prints of the right size for Simpson were found at the murder scene.

a. Seriousness if true

The seriousness of truly finding Simpson's shoe prints at the crime scene would have been high, establishing his presence [unless he was being framed] although not proving that he committed the crime. It would be similar to the glove evidence - 50%

b. Probability of truth

However, the probability of the shoe prints truly being Simpson's is not high. This would have been higher if the shoe had been found and been shown to be Simpson's, but in the absence of that we only know it was the right size and a relevant brand. The number of shoes of that size and brand sold to people with access to the Goldman home is not known, but is likely to be a few. If 5 people with access had shoes like that and we knew Simpson owned a pair the probability of them being his would be 1 in 5. However, he did not admit to owning a pair so let's discount that to 1 in 10 or 10%

c. Harm score
Seriousness if true = 50%
Probability of truth = 10%
Probability x Seriousness = 5%

7. Simpson's flight in Ford Bronco

a. Seriousness if true
This question needs to be addressed in the same way as for the violence question: instead of saying how many murderers would run away from Police [which presumes guilt], we'd need to know how many high-profile people who didn't murder their ex-wives but who felt under suspicion by police in a similar situation would choose to run. We don't know that but it is not going to be zero. Unless only guilty people run and only innocent people don't, Simpson's flight doesn't demonstrate anything concrete about actual guilt other than a weird state of mind and fear of suspicion that might have occurred whether he had been the murderer or merely the ex-husband of somebody murdered. The seriousness of this is not calculable but is close to zero.

b. Probability of truth
The probability of the truth of Simpson running was 100%

c. Harm score
Seriousness if true = 0%
Probability of truth = 100%
Probability x Seriousness = 0%

Using the harm scores to estimate guilt

I can use these figures to calculate an overall probability of guilt in this case, or technical, human and economic success in more general cases. I am now treating the probability x seriousness as a probability that has been adjusted by seriousness, so I don't just add up the risks - if there were 3 different risks of 50% each that would add up to more than 100% [statisticians reading this, please don't laugh, for mere mortals this isn't intuitive].

Instead, I treat the "virtual life" of a project, or OJ Simpson's innocence like a probability of survival calculation. For example if you have 3 risks of 50% each, there is a 50% chance of surviving the first one, which leaves a survival fraction of 50% of your "virtual life". If you have a half a life left and then apply the second risk of 50% only to your remaining half of a life, then that will give you half of a half - 50% of 50% - which brings your remaining "virtual life" down to 25%. Then when the third risk factor of 50% is applied only to your remaining 25%, then half of 25% leaves 12.5%. So your probability of surviving all three risks of 50% each is 12.5%. Even if the three risks were very different from each other, the order you apply them in the calculation doesn't matter, the final percentage works out to be the same. Clearly if you just subtracted 50% three times you would be left with -50% of a life which isn't possible.

Now I can do the calculation of OJ Simpson's guilt; this is explained in simple terms in the table below starting with the presumption of innocence at a 100% life-equivalent score that will be discounted by guilt.

Issue	**"Harm" - probability adjusted by seriousness**	**Remaining Innocence "Survival" fraction**
History of violence	0%	**100%**
Hair at scene	5%	**95%**
Blood at scene and home	45%	45% of 95% is 44% guilt; innocence fraction is 95% less 44% guilt = **51%**
Cuts on skin	5%	5% of 51% is 2.5%; innocence fraction is 51% less 2.5% = **48.5%**
Glove at scene and home	25%	25% of 48.5% is 13%; innocence fraction is 48.5% less 13% = **35.5%**
Shoe prints	5%	5% of 35.5% is ~2%; innocence fraction is 35.5% less 2% = **33.5%**
REMAINING INNOCENCE		**33.5%**

So this method suggests that given the doubts raised by the defense, the probability of innocence was ~33% and the probability of guilt was therefore 100% minus the innocence factor of 33% which leaves a guilt or ~66%. Now obviously these are my subjective scores based on summaries of the evidence, but they suggest how somebody like me (I happen to be Caucasian) in a jury seeing the same evidence pattern could have rated the person's likelihood of guilt systematically without being over-influenced by emotional issues or racial stereotypes.

The numbers do not appear to me to be sufficient to meet the "beyond all reasonable doubt" criterion for a criminal trial, but would be sufficient to meet the lower burden of proof in a civil trial – as proved to be the case. It also suggests that the common arguments made in the media that the jury was protesting against a history of white oppression of African Americans is doing them a disservice – their verdict was reasonable based on the evidence in the case, although admittedly that was significantly and cleverly devalued by the defense attorneys' theatrics, allegations and actual evidence of racially-based police tampering with the evidence. However, the impact of human emotion on the perception of guilt or innocence was substantial – I will take a bet that not many people at the time would have agreed with my number, the US population was probably bimodal with many people believing he was guilty with 99% surety and many believing he was innocent with 99% surety. A systematic and methodical calculation like the one above can therefore reduce some of the adverse emotional impact on rational decision making.

Applying the same process where the value of each option is different

It is not much more complex to apply the same process where value and risk are different – in the first two cases I simply fixed the value. In the good vision example, all 3 options had the same intended outcome of good vision, and the value was therefore the same across all options. In the guilt or innocence example the initial value was simply 100% innocence.

Now I am going to vary the value of each alternative as well as the risk. However, I am going to start with a small cheat to make it simple. Here's how it goes: in my glasses vs. contacts vs. laser surgery perhaps that visual acuity with laser surgery was slightly better than the others, I could still have used the exact same method as before by defining the outcome as "perfect vision" and by treating slightly less than perfect vision as a new kind of harm associated with the two methods that can't deliver it. This broadens the application of the simple method to any decision where a perfect outcome can be defined and is the same across all the alternatives. As I mentioned before, creating a perfect outcome and discounting it by harm is a useful trick to avoid human shortcomings in comparing benefit and harm on a level playing field. This is illustrated more fully in the next example.

Choosing the right job

My friend Samantha called me because she had to make a decision about a new job urgently. The company she works for currently has had a substantial fall in income, and they had informed her a few months ago that she'd better start looking for a job or she'd be laid off. Given that she is skilled, intelligent, hardworking and likeable, she had quickly obtained 3 offers for 3 different jobs, a quite remarkable feat in the current environment – but now she was having trouble choosing between them. She didn't pre-specify objectives for her choices, but having visited and interviewed at several companies she now has a good idea of what features are important to her and her family. The following table of alternatives vs. consequences shows the details. Each company [Co #1, Co #2 and Co #3] has slightly different advantages and disadvantages, and Samantha has identified the key differentiating features:

	Town Geography	Job Environment	Husband employment	Job Security	Relocation Package
Co. #1	Seattle – Sam and her husband like it and lived and worked there before [Rank 1]	Great team, nice company culture and position relevant to skills [Rank 1]	Good – he has worked in the area before and there are many opportunities [Rank 1]	Risk of takeover which might cause layoffs [Rank 3]	Best, [Rank 1]
Co. #2	1000 Oaks CA – cost of living is higher, few attractions [Rank 3]	Good position and relevant to skills and interests [Rank 2]	Not much [Rank 3]	Company has few projects. Laying off people [Rank 2]	OK [Rank 2=]
Co. # 3	Boston – not bad but not as nice as Seattle [Rank 2]	OK position but not in Research, [Rank 3]	In between [Rank 2]	Big but not immune to layoffs [Rank 1]	OK [Rank 2=]

They are all quite straightforward except for the fact that company 1, the likely favorite based on looking at the ranks, is currently the subject of a hostile takeover bid. This is not certain to go through and the effects of it if it does so are also uncertain. If Samantha ignored that uncertainty, rank ordered the importance of the features, and used the "take the best" heuristic, company 1 would win 4/5 times depending on her order of importance of the features - every time unless she placed job security as the most important factor in her choice. If she decided that the features were too similar in importance, to use the "take the best" then she could apply Dawes' Rule (which weights all the same, simply counting all the features for each alternative) would also put company 1 top every time as it has more top ranked features than any other choice.

However, given that moving her family and choosing her working environment is a high value high harm decision, and that putting more effort into the decision is likely to lead to a significantly better outcome [the imagined Decisionability window shows a steeply increasing value with modestly more effort] Sam's correct decision strategy is to maximize. She has a lot of knowledge about the choices, some time to evaluate the choices and to consult with friends and experts and she can incorporate all the information she has and make a more sophisticated choice with a lower probability of failure. She could use the "even swaps" method described in chapter 4 to trade some of the benefits of company 1 in exchange for job security and then eliminate that factor. For example if the extra benefits of the town environment from company 1 vs. company 2 or 3 are equivalent in value to the difference in job security then that swap can be made and job security eliminated from the factors, along with the town environment factor which then becomes equivalent. Company 1 would still win on the remaining factors.

There is a bit of a difficulty in using "even swaps" here because of the uncertainty of the effects of the hostile takeover. The takeover might have no effect [hurray], she might have to move again to the HQ of the company taking over [OK], or she might lose her new job completely [boo]. So even though the even swaps method includes a subjective job security factor, it doesn't actually quantify the effects of those different possibilities and she might not be capturing their effect.

To estimate the effect of uncertainty with more precision I am going to use the Decisionability tradeoff method. This is a case where each alternative has a different value – even if the salaries are the same, the quality of life features aren't. I will start the process by defining the attributes of a perfect job that would have 100% value:

- In Seattle
- Employment opportunities for Jane's husband
- Great team environment and position in development
- Great relocation package
- Good job security

I will take any deficiencies on these factors as discounts to the value of each alternative – so each alternative will have a value that is less than the starting point of 100% perfect score. I will use a Quality of Life [QOL] scale as explained earlier, to estimate these deficiencies' effects on Samantha's family and score each deficiency in terms of seriousness and probability. Because I want an absolute estimate I will be treating the harm scores as probabilities as for OJ's guilt or innocence. I will start by creating a table of "harm" to the perfect outcome:

	Town, Geography	Job Environment	Husband employment	Job Security	Relocation Package
Co. #1	No harm, perfect score	No harm, perfect score	No harm, perfect score	Seriousness: 30% Probability: 50%	No harm, perfect score
Co. #2	Seriousness: 30% Probability 100%	Seriousness 10% Probability: 100%	Seriousness: 30% Probability 100%	Seriousness 10% Probability 100%	Seriousness: 5% Probability 100%
Co. #3	Seriousness: 15% Probability 100%	Seriousness 20%, Probability 100%	Seriousness: 15% Probability 100%	Seriousness 0%	Seriousness 5% Probability 100%

Using the deterministic "survival" calculation method used in the guilt vs. innocence issue outlined earlier, here are the scores:

- Company 1 gets a perfect score except for the job security discount of 50% of 30% =15% harm = an overall **85%** score [100% less the 15% harm].
- Company 2 gets **47.5%** [100% less sequential harm scores of 30%, 10%, 30%, 10% and 5% from the preceding table]
- Company 3 gets **55%**. [100% less sequential harm scores of 15% 20% 15% and 5%]

However the job security discount can be looked at in another way – if I really am maximizing and trying to do the best with the information I have, instead of a separate harm factor for job security, it would be more precise to regard it a potential or uncertain loss in the other factors. To evaluate the effect in that way, let's evaluate what would happen under the hostile takeover scenario. There are three possibilities:

<u>First Scenario for Company 1</u>

Well first of all, nothing might happen, Company 1 might be left alone – let's say there is a 30% chance of that happening. In that scenario, company 1 gets a perfect score across the board as we've taken off the job security issue as a separate issue.

<u>Second Scenario for Company 1</u>

The second scenario is that the takeover goes through and the new parent company requires Samantha to move with her family to Chicago to the new parent company HQ. They don't rate the town as highly as Seattle but they do have family there so rate it as only 10% worse. She estimates the probability of this as 40%. The job environment would be slightly less amenable but still as good as for company 2 and the employment for her husband similar to company 3.

<u>Third Scenario for Company 1</u>

The third scenario is that the takeover goes through but the new parent company lays Samantha off, so she might be in Seattle without a job, although with 4 months' severance. The seriousness of that would be 80% on her job environment - she didn't rate it as 100% because she has already demonstrated her marketability to get a job in a few months and Seattle has many opportunities. The probability of this actually happening is only 30% though. Sam's husband's employment and the town itself would be unaffected. The relocation package would be unaffected by any of the 3 takeover scenarios so that is also left out of this assessment. The new harm score for company 1 will include all the components of harm applied sequentially from each of the three scenarios: follow the numbered steps below.

Scenario 1, job unaffected by takeover or takeover doesn't go through (30% probability):

1. 30% probability, no seriousness, value remains at **100%**

Scenario 2, takeover goes through, job moves to Chicago (40% probability):

2. Town, environment – 40% probability @ 10% seriousness = 4% harm
    - Starting job value fraction = 100%
    - Remaining job value fraction = 100%-4%=96%
3. Job environment – 40% probability @ 10% seriousness = 4% harm
    - Starting job value fraction = 96% [from 1 above]
    - Remaining value = 96% less 4% of 96% = 92%

4. Employment for husband – 40% probability @ 15% seriousness = 6% harm
   - Starting job value fraction = 92% [from above]
   - Remaining job value fraction = 92% less 6% of 92% = 92%-5%=**87%**

Scenario 3, takeover goes through, Samantha is laid off (30% probability):

5. Job environment – 80% harm @ 30% probability = 24%
   - Starting job value fraction = 87% [from 4 above]
   - Remaining value = 87% less 24% of 87% = 87%-22%=**65%**

Doing the sequential deterministic calculation for these probabilities in the 5 numbered steps above I get an overall score for company 1 of 65%. This could be done in any order such as putting scenario 3 first, the final percentage ends up the same. That 65% score is notably more conservative than the other approaches but is still substantially more than the other companies' scores and is the most reflective of the true situation. Samantha can therefore be confident that this is still the best option – but Sam can manage her own expectations using the 65% score. Her option of choosing company 1 is on average going to deliver her only 65% of a perfect outcome, but it is better than the other alternatives.

This means that Samantha shouldn't feel guilt or self-blame if one of the less than desirable scenarios comes to pass because she included them in her calculation – and she should expect an average 35% deficiency in the outcome of her decision.

This point is where my assertion of “painless” decision making comes from: when expectations are realistic and the most appropriate method has been used then self-blame [if and when one of the less desirable outcomes comes to pass] is reduced, if not quite painless.

This realistic expectation also enables something else: planning for failure. Now that Samantha realizes she is likely to get only 65% of her perfect outcome, she can start working right away to mitigate the risks of her new job being eliminated by cultivating new potential job contacts in Seattle as “insurance” right from the beginning of her new position! [See next chapter]

The same approach would be applicable in different situations - instead of a hostile takeover, perhaps she has only a verbal job offer from company 1 but has written offers from the other 2 companies – she could create scenarios for what would happen if she waited for an offer – one scenario is that it arrives, another scenario is that it doesn’t but one of the other offers she rejected is still available and the third is that she’s unemployed. The calculations would be the same as those we’ve just shown.

In the above example, I used the Decisionability tradeoff method for companies with different value by creating an idealized perfect score across all alternatives. However, sometimes the alternatives are completely independent and cannot be adequately described by a single ideal outcome – if the outcomes are different for each alternative. That only requires a slight tweak in the method and is explained next.

Deciding between alternatives with different risks AND different values

To show the variation of the method when applied to alternatives of differing value and different outcomes I am going to return to Brian's innovation program at CR Engineering. Remember that his task was to discriminate between a number of research projects to spend a $500k annual budget. Rather than going through the whole portfolio, I will take a single project and evaluate it – Brian's committee would have to repeat this for each alternative.

The proposed project description for just one of Brian's investment alternatives is shown next, and is loosely based on a real example.

Project title: Create a low-cost intelligent packaging system for drugs that captures the time and date that the tablet was taken, with information that patients can see and which can be transmitted to the physician from the pharmacy.

Background: most people on long-term medications aren't very good at taking their tablets. This varies with the type of disorder, but it is common to find that half the people are regularly missing doses of medication. When they go to the doctor, this information is invisible to the physician – who may decide to increase the dose of drug because it doesn't seem to be working as well as expected, so that on days when the person does take the tablet the dosage is too high and they get side effects, but this compensates for the day they miss. From the payor's perspective, the most expensive drug is the one that isn't taken – with no health benefits.

Proposal: create an electronic blister-pack that drug companies would license to package their drugs inside. The package would collect the time and date that the blister was broken, and via a simple RFID chip would transmit this data to the pharmacy by holding the old package over a reader at the pharmacy at the time when the new prescription was collected – and this information could be emailed to the physician. A small LCD screen on the pack would tell the patient when they last took their tablet and would flash or beep when the next one was due. The packaging cost would depend on volume but to be viable must be plausibly reducible to less than $5 per one-month package.

Estimating value of the project

If you have a project that is at a very early phase in its life and/or very innovative it may not be possible to predict actual value to you or your company. In that case you can still do the risk estimation I just did for glasses, OJ's innocence and Samantha's job by just assuming that the value is the same across all such projects and give it "100%" before discounts.

For many business programs and plans, a "net present value" will have already been calculated, and if this meets reasonable standards then it can be used for each project or alternative to be compared, and the harm calculated as I have shown above, and used as a discount as per the guilt/innocence example but starting with the actual value not a simple 100%.

If neither of these is true, and you don't or won't have the resources to get a financial expert to calculate, you will have to start by making some simple calculation of value for your business project or life decision.

For the packaging project at CR Engineering on the previous page, the team estimates that they would be able to license the technology to a large manufacturer for $10M in 3 years time, and that the development costs to the point of licensing it would be $1.5M. Their feasibility project costs $100k.

The calculation of value isn't as simple as taking the $10M and subtracting off costs. Firstly, $10M in 5 years isn't as good as $10M today – accountants apply an annual discount rate to it. This is akin to the interest that you would have earned had you taken the $10M today and invested it wisely and the effect of inflation on the money. To make it easy I usually use a rate of 10% per year and take that off each year into the future; this approximates to the "cost of capital" – but not the risks, which we are calculating separately.

So with this example, the value 3 years ahead is $10M and taking off 10% each year, $10M in 3 years is worth $9M in 2 years, $8.1M in 1 year and $7.3M today. If the other competing projects subtract taxes then that should be done, but for simple approximations between projects that can be regarded as a constant. The remaining $7.3M is the value if successful, and that needs to be discounted by the probability of failure – which is where the Decisionability tradeoff calculation comes in: in the same way that "guilt" discounted innocence, the probability of failure can be used to discount the value.

When I asked the proposing team to determine the project harm, using T.H.E. Decisionability triangle they came up with the following assessments:

Technical

- CR Engineering might not be able to create the product within the performance specifications: seriousness – 100%, probability 10% [harm = 10%]

Human

- Patients might not want the packaging, or could find it annoying to be reminded: seriousness = 50% probability = 30% [harm = 15%]
- Patient privacy advocates might declare this to be an invasion of civil liberties and lobby against it; seriousness 50% probability 10% [harm = 5%]

Economic

- Payors might not be willing to pay for better packaging; seriousness – 100%, probability 10% [harm = 10%]
- Competitors are working on the same project and might get there first; seriousness – 50% loss in market share, probability 50% [harm = 25%]
- Physicians or pharmacists might want to be paid to convey and receive the information but nobody is willing to pay them; seriousness 80%, probability 20% [harm = 16%]

Starting with a probability of success of 100% and multiplying those harm figures in the same sequential way as for guilt, we get a final figure of **51%** for the probability of success.

Recall above that the value of the project discounted to today was $7.3M, I discount that again for the probability of failure – I get to keep only the 51% success which leaves a final number of 51% of 7.3M which is **$3.7M**.

I haven't taken off any of the project costs yet – I'll say that I'll spend these whether it is successful or not, and I spend them at today's dollars, so I'll take off the $1.5M that the team estimates as development costs and I am left with a final residual value of this project of $2.2M. Although this is an approximation, it is good enough!

The sequence of discounts is shown below:

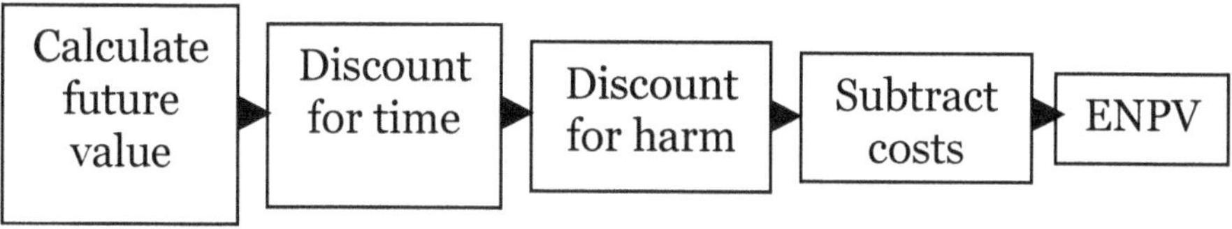

The "ENPV" is the expected net present value. In my experience the commonest way of including risk in this calculation without using the Decisionability harm calculation is to ask the team the probability of success is. They usually say "80%", whatever the reality, so this is a much more precise way of including real risks in such a calculation.

Assuming that Brian at CR Engineering can persuade the teams proposing each new project to use this approach, the committee can compare the project I just assessed to the rest of its project portfolio that might look something like the one in the table on the next page – simplified to compare only 3 projects:

	Intelligent packaging project [$M]	**Project 2**	**Project 3**
Future value	10	50	20
Today's value	7.3	35	18
Risk discounted value	3.4	3.5	9
Cost subtracted value	2.2	-1.5	6

The intelligent packaging product is as I described above. Project 2 is a high value but high risk [90%] and high cost project that ends up with a negative value, and Project 3 is a high value modest risk high cost project. On the face of it, project 3 has the highest residual value, our intelligent packaging project comes in second, and Project 2 should not be performed because it has negative value.

Those conclusions are correct if I can't change the risk assessments, or if they would be very costly to change. However, if there was something inexpensive that could be done to Project 2 that might resolve a large component of its risk, it could transform the value of that Project. Intuitively humans do try to identify alternatives with mitigated risks, but this can often be suboptimal because there are just too many factors to keep in our heads; not only are we trying to identify alternatives but we are trying to spot differences between them, look for uncertainties and mitigate the risks. We just can't do it all: it doesn't take many alternatives or issues to overwhelm our mental abilities.

In chapter 8 I will advance the intelligent packaging project through a risk mitigation process that shows how much of its risk can be changed through a small pilot project. When you are maximizing and knowledge is abundant you should take that approach - so that when you actually compare your alternatives, it is a risk-mitigated comparison; this is akin to taking out insurance for your decision envelope!

Risk Tolerance and Portfolio Risk Balance

If you are selecting just one alternative then the economist would pick the project with the best residual value after the preceding process. However, if there are two or more alternatives which have similar residual values but quite different risks, then you will need to examine which one best suits the risk tolerance of the environment you are in; for example a high value high risk project might have the same residual value as a low value low risk project. If you can do only one then you need to examine the following issues:

- What are the consequences of failure of a high risk project in your environment?
- What are the consequences of only modest success of a low risk project in your environment?
- What is the cost per success of projects like the ones you are considering? Does your company have that much money?

The answers to these can be paradoxical; for example in drug development success of a modest return project is not necessarily viewed as a good thing because modest projects don't pay the R&D bills even if they are successful.

The cost per success is an interesting sorter – in the table above for the 3 projects at CR Engineering, Brian's project cost $1.2M and had a success rate of ~1 in 2 [we calculated its harm at

~50%], so the average cost per success the company would incur if it chose all projects like that is $2.4M per project. This is because it would have to pay the costs of two projects on average to get one to succeed. The second listed project in the table had costs of ~$5M and odds of success of only 1 in 10. That means the cost of one success when pursuing projects like that is $50M. The third and apparently best project has a cost of $3M but will succeed only half the time, just like Brian's project but the cost per success is $6M – a lot higher than Brian's project. Even though the third project had the highest discounted value, if CR engineering doesn't have a budget of $6M to spend over the next couple of years, then it should not choose projects like #3. It might "get lucky" on the first project for only $3M but it should know that on average is most likely to spend the money for no result. So if the company is cash rich, choosing project 3 is good, whereas if it is cash poor it should do Brian's project.

If you or your company is choosing a select number of opportunities from a large group you don't have to choose a single representative risk that best fits your environment you have a portfolio of risk and return to play with. In that case you might deliberately choose to include high risk high return projects as well as low risk low return projects – as is commonly done for stocks and bonds. Given that you have used the above process, you know 4 things about each opportunity:

- The value undiscounted for harm/risk
- The value discounted for harm/risk
- The amount of harm/risk
- The cost per success

There are three possible combinations of value and harm: high value low harm, low value low harm and low value high harm –

and a balanced portfolio will have representatives of each. The cost per success becomes relevant if the budget is small in relation to the costs.

Are these numbers right? How have they been validated?

The commonest question that people give me when they see these numbers when I have used this method: "how do we know they are right?" The answer is that actually we know that they are wrong, but nonetheless they are useful. They are inevitably wrong because they are probability-adjusted. In real life most of the issues that we include in our "harm" list will either happen or they won't – a binary outcome, whereas our estimate that is "something in-between" is practically impossible. Nonetheless, when averaged over a number of decisions, the numbers are mathematically correct as long as the inputs we gave are correct and our assumptions are met. The second answer is that I've done a number of these evaluations in the pharmaceutical industry and they do create numbers that are similar to historical averages for the industry, that are much more realistic [i.e. lower] than the usual guesses from teams. The third answer is that it doesn't matter if they are somewhat wrong, as long as they are better than the best available alternative assessment method or they are the best you can do with your knowledge and resourcing constraints. Given that guessing or using generic historical averages that can't be customized to an individual project is the usual alternative, this is an easy to beat!

When people don't have these calculations they usually just guess. As a result, overestimating the probability of success is almost ubiquitous. I consulted for one organization where each R&D team was "required by finance" to create probability of technical success scores for each drug project. That statement was the first warning sign – teams should be estimating and managing their own probability of success because they want to know, not because "finance says so". The second warning sign was that the teams were told their estimates had to be between 90 to 100% or the project couldn't go ahead. With industry averages in their specialty at 10% to 20% success those numbers were clearly ridiculous. Indeed, everyone knew it was a game they were all playing – but they had to keep playing because if any one of them alone had entered more realistic numbers based on industry averages their project would have been penalized. The result was that all their projects had probabilities of success between 90 and 98%. Interestingly they welcomed the Decisionability process because their expertise was put to work in making good evaluations of how the projects might be harmed and everyone was doing the same thing at the same time. It was also obvious who was accountable for what numbers so individuals felt responsible. Needless to say, the new survival estimates ranged from 6% to 40%!

Interestingly, this approach is somewhat resistant to corporate game-playing. You know exactly who made what estimates of risk, so accountability for the numbers is transparent. So if people try to play games by covering up risks initially to get their project funded, but their project fails later for an obvious risk, you know whose head is on the block.

Communicating harm with pictures and charts

You may have loved the preceding simple calculations, probabilities and percentages – or you may have hated them. If the latter, then you will find it very helpful to display these harm values as pictures and charts because the results aren't necessarily intuitive – for example, most people would be most worried about damaged vision from laser surgery, but I calculated that the harm from that issue is actually almost the lowest negative effect, and the right kind of "harm" chart will illustrate not only what the harm is but also why it is high or low. In contrast to a "preference" method, this approach can enable a new understanding and can actually change the perception of what people should be concerned about. Communicating the risks and issues is as important as calculating them.

The chart below is the simplest view of harm. There are 4 quadrants of harm and you can simply list issues for your alternatives separately under each heading.

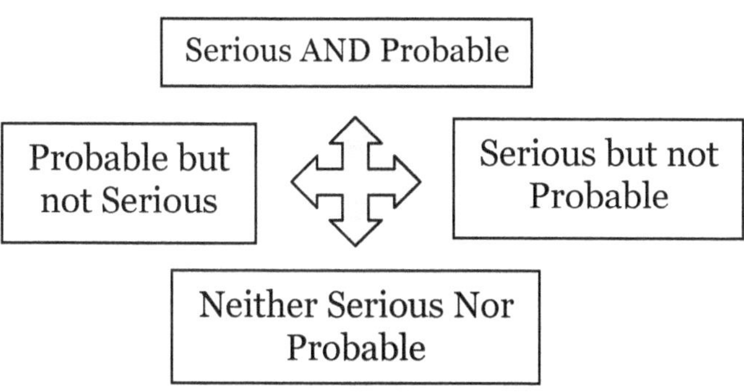

The second type of display, a little less simple is to create a bar chart. The trivial causes of harm (neither serious nor probable)

can be eliminated because they aren't worth the effort of discussing and the chart used to show the upper three quadrants. I like to show the left side bars for probable but not serious, the right side for serious but not probable and the center for serious and probable so the overall effect is the Decisionability "harm mountain" with a "summit" [high seriousness high probability], a "north face" [high seriousness but rare] and a "south face" [probable but low risk].

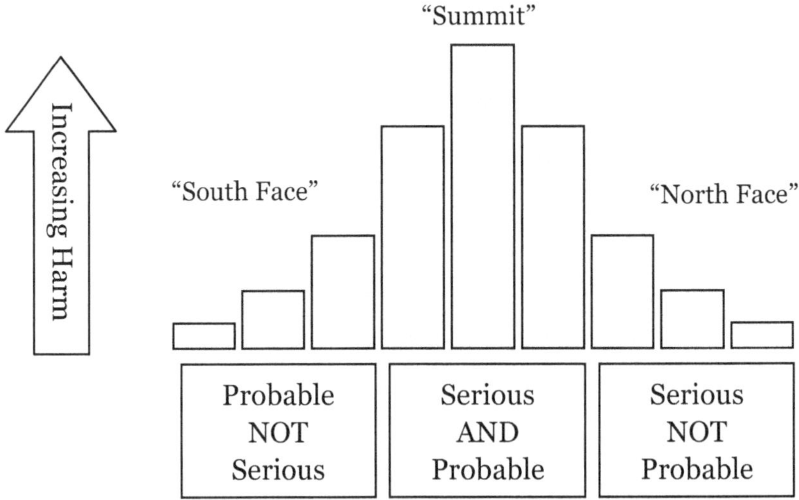

The Decisionability "Harm Mountain"

This type of chart is very useful for communicating the magnitude of the harm to a project or a person as well as the drivers for that harm – seriousness vs. likelihood. Given that the typical human tendency is to subjectively over-amplify the likelihood of serious but rare events, this display is a necessary counterbalance. In the laser surgery example we would all rate "permanent vision damage" as the thing to worry about if we could not see a chart, so it can change perceptions. The other nice thing about a chart like this is that you can add a bar in the chart as a reference or comparison for something else in a better-understood context – for example "fatal car accidents" is a serious but not probable bar that could be added to a drug side effect chart that would enable people to compare the likelihood of dying from a drug to that of being killed in a car.

I've assumed above in both case studies that you can represent each negative consequence by a single number for seriousness and a single number for probability. This is often the case but I'll briefly consider how to do a harm profile. This is necessary if your community doesn't agree on a single harm score, or if the issue itself has a range of real severities and probabilities.

If the decision-making community doesn't agree on the probability, or doesn't agree on the seriousness, but there is an overall consensus on the amount of harm, then this is not a problem. For example, if two people score the same issue at 25% seriousness sand 50% probability and 50% seriousness and 25% probability they are probably just looking at the same thing slightly differently, but their harm number [of 12.5%] is the same. You can simply use the 12.5% as a fair representation of harm and each will be satisfied. You don't quite know whether to put it on the left or the right of the chart, but the height is the most important feature.

However, if the community disagrees, you have 2 options: firstly you can average the scores and pretend that the variability from disagreement doesn't exist. Secondly you can show the distribution of the scores and include ranges in your overall assessments – the graph could have error bars on the columns for example. The former is acceptable when you are satisficing and the disagreements are not from key stakeholders. It is also acceptable when the answer isn't going to make much difference to the decision, perhaps when alternatives to the one being scored are much better or much worse so precision isn't needed as it doesn't change the decision. However, if you are maximizing and there is a close competition between your alternatives but you find a harmful issue for one of them that really is variable, then a harm-profile can be created. Instead of attempting to use one number to capture the harm for the entire issue, the breadth of the effect can be divided and probabilities assigned to each subdivision. I already did this in the example above for Samantha's job, where one alternative – Company 1 – really did have 3 different outcomes of different seriousness, it wasn't just that there was a simple disagreement over the same issue. Our process split the variation into scenarios, assigned a probability for each one coming to pass, scored each one and then amalgamated the score.

If you are maximizing and you need to create communication materials to show the participants what they produced or convince the recipients about the alternatives, you can create fully quantitative harm displays, but that is beyond the scope of this book.

Key learnings from chapter 7:

- Probability x Seriousness = harm.
- If you trade probability for seriousness or vice-versa you are in good company; this is commonly used in environmental protection and the nuclear industry.
- Start by defining a near-perfect outcome or value of the decision.
- Seek to identify harmful consequences of each alternative using T.H.E. Decisionability triangle.
- Rate the seriousness of failure from each consequence an absolute "quality of life" or "project life" scale using anchor points to improve linearity.
- Rate the probability of each consequence.
- Calculate the harm of each consequence by multiplying probability and seriousness.
- Use the harm as a discount to the value of each alternative.
- If there aren't many consequences and a relative comparison is all you need then just add the harm for each alternative.
- If there are lots of consequences and you want an absolute calculation of value discounted by harm then treat the harm as a probability and do a sequential "survival" calculation.
- The Decisionability "harm mountain" plot has a summit where issues are probable and serious, a "south face" where issues are common but not serious, and a "north face" where issues are serious but not common.

Chapter 8

When to mitigate your risks and when to trust to luck

Decision insurance – why and when?

Do you ever get to the counter at the post office and get asked "do you want to insure this package?" I almost never do, but if there is something very valuable in the envelope I do. I might also do it if I can't predict the environment that my envelope might be traveling in – or when I do know that the environment will be hostile.

Now that you have created, addressed and stamped your decision envelope, and put inside it a decision outcome and its supporting information, your job may not be done. If you are satisficing for a low or modest value or harm decision then the simple answer yes, the job is done and you should execute the decision using that choice.

When you are maximizing for a high value high harm decision you should find out if you can mitigate your risks. This is particularly useful if some of your benefits or negative consequences are uncertain. You might have given them an average score in the tradeoff method in the last chapter, but what if you can improve those scores by taking some simple actions?

The ideal time to do this is before finalizing the winning alternative because one or more of its close rivals could potentially win if its risks could be simply and cheaply mitigated. It is also good practice even if you have already picked the winner, because you may be able to improve its benefits and reduce its risks with some simple actions.

Identifying the risks

The simplest case is where you have already identified the risks because you've used the Decisionability tradeoff method in Chapter 7. If you used even swaps or another method to choose your winning alternatives then you will need to go through the risk identification procedure described in the last chapter by seeking the issues [across all three domains of the Decisionability triangle] for each alternative that would cause a less than perfect outcome of your decision. The end product is the same as the input for the Decisionability tradeoff method: a list of risks and each is scored for seriousness and likelihood to get a harm score, which is the probability x seriousness.

Creating ideas to change the risks you have

When you have this list of factors that might harm your decision, start by eliminating all the rare and trivial risks as not worth worrying about. For the remaining issues, consider using your group of stakeholders to be creative and to generate ideas about how they could be changed. For issues that are harmful because they are both likely and serious, you can attack these by changing either the likelihood or the seriousness or both. For issues that are harmful because they are highly likely but only moderately serious, try to identify ways that they could be made less likely. For issues that are harmful because they are very serious but only moderately likely, then you will seek ways to make the issues less harmful if they occur.

Picking a simple example, remember Samantha's new job choices in chapter 7? The key issue was that company 1 that was offering her favorite job choice was the possible subject of a hostile takeover bid, so that Samantha might be laid off from her new job within months of starting. The other risks had only caused only slight discount to the theoretically perfect outcome, but there was 24% harm from this specific issue. This issue is dominated by the seriousness [80%] so that's where Samatha looks first – what can she do that would mitigate the seriousness if this scenario came to pass and she was laid off? Here are her ideas for things that she could do now that would be beneficial in reducing the seriousness of the consequence of being laid off:

- Get an academic appointment at the University so she is already known by them if she is laid off – there might be job opportunities there
- Do some scientific presentations at forums where local companies are in attendance so that she gets some local contacts who might be hiring
- Live in a modestly priced house –at least initially- so that her husband's income would be enough to support them both

Samantha thinks that these actions would reduce the seriousness from 80% to 60%. She can't change the likelihood of the hostile takeover itself, but perhaps she could change the likelihood of being laid off if it went through:

- Cultivate contacts in other departments that might survive the takeover so they might move her internally

- Talk to her boss about other opportunities within the company that might survive the takeover
- Talk to her contacts within the parent company responsible for the hostile takeover and see if they would take her on.

She's not convinced that these actions would really change the likelihood though, and although she intends to do them, she leaves it at its original 30%. The original harm of this issue was 24% and with a few simple actions Samantha has reduced it to 18% [30% of 60%]. This doesn't change her ranking but it could have - we didn't show whether the other alternatives could be improved in the same way. If you are maximizing and you have the time and knowledge to risk-mitigate each of your chosen options and re-compare them before making your final decision, it is worth doing.

Now I'll take a more complex example where there are some costs involved in changing the risks, and costs involved in resolving uncertainty. In contrast to Samantha's actions which were all simple and of no cost other than a small amount of time, these actions might or might not be worth the cost – our job is to estimate the value and cost of acquiring knowledge about risk and of reducing risk, and see if the cost is greater than the value. If the value of reducing the risk is greater than the cost of doing it then the risk should be mitigated. If the cost of reducing the risk is greater than the value then the risk should be left alone, trusting to luck.

Mitigate risks when:

- The value liberated by risk reduction is greater than the cost and effort of mitigation

Tolerate risks and "trust to luck" when:

- The effort or cost of risk reduction is greater than the value liberated by doing it

Monetizing risk reduction

The most straightforward way of seeing if a risk reduction is worth the effort is to create a common currency for the cost and the benefit of doing so. Recall the intelligent packaging project at CR Engineering, which had a value in today's dollars of $7.3M, which was discounted to $3.7M because of the 49% harm I calculated. From those numbers I know that my score of 49% harm is responsible for a discount that amounts to a $3.7M value reduction when compared with a perfect outcome. Doing some simple math, I could equally say that if I could achieve a 1% reduction in harm it would liberate 1% of $3.7M in value, which is $37,000.

I can now make the risk mitigation argument like this: as long as I spend less than $37,000 to get a 1% harm reduction I am in profit. Allowing for a safety margin for the approximations and errors in our approach, I can use that kind of calculation to compare the cost-effectiveness of different ideas for risk mitigation. This is a nice balance to the natural temptation to put the most effort into changing the biggest risks. The problem with that is: what if the biggest risks are insensitive to change? In that case you might be better off leaving the big risk alone but tackling some of the more modest risks that you could change without much cost or effort.

The most efficient place for your effort and resources is where you can liberate the most value by changing the greatest amount of risk for the least effort or cost.

Nonetheless, if you are the decision-maker but you have no control or influence over what happens after the decision is made then it is not worth going through a mitigation exercise, simply choose the alternative with the highest residual value after it has been discounted for time and risk, and the costs subtracted. This situation sometimes happens with investors, who put in money but have no control over the organization afterwards. However, if you have more influence than a "fund and run" investor, you can mitigate those risks.

Estimating the change in harm resulting from the proposed mitigation action.

Imagine that CR Engineering team has been asked to design a harm mitigation proposal for their intelligent packaging. The key technical risk they identified was that the product might not meet specifications at the desired cost. They rated this issue as 100% seriousness and 10% probability.

Their first proposal is therefore to spend $100k on piloting a prototype in order to address this risk. After they finish their pilot study the seriousness of failing to meet specifications won't change [it is still 100%] but the probability will either be 2% or

80%. Why that number? If the engineering approach really is successful they think their pilot study will correctly show this almost all of the time. That almost eliminates the possibility of technical failure later, reducing their estimate of likelihood to 2%.

The results of the pilot study aren't quite life or death to the project however. If the pilot study shows that the technology doesn't work the team thinks that most of the time that will be impossible to overcome [i.e. death to the project], but 20% of the time they might be able to fix the problem later on; so instead of saying a negative pilot study signals a 100% probability of failure they tone it down to 80%. So the harm estimate after the completion of their pilot study either increases by 70% [from the current 10% to the future 80%] if the pilot doesn't meet specifications or decreases by 8% [from the current 10% to the future 2%] if it does.

"Good harm" and "bad harm" – the value of knowledge

Now the team has an uncomfortable dilemma. Some team members say that the pilot study is bad for their project because there is greater scope for increasing the harm than decreasing it: averaging +70% and -8% gives them an average **increase** in harm for this approach of +31%.

Unfortunately this is kind of thinking is often followed – I have often heard the mantra: "don't hurt the project". However, the team is NOT really creating new harm when the number is increased because they are simply uncovering the truth. If the engineering approach doesn't actually work, the company needs to know that early, before spending a great deal of money. If the team doesn't discover it now then they will discover it later when a lot more investment will go down the plughole. In other words it is "good harm".

"Good harm" and "bad harm"

- "Bad harm" is created when an action or an omission leads to a new and harmful unintended consequence
- "Good harm" is created when an action leads to the exposure of a harmful truth

So how can I convince the team that this kind of action should be taken? The first step is a philosophical one - acceptance of the principle that uncovering unpleasant truths is an important organizational principle. The second step is to calculate what this effect is. In the current example I can address this for my actions in uncovering the truth – "good harm" - by ignoring the directional change in harm in the value calculation, accepting that this kind of knowledge is incredibly valuable as whichever direction it is in, it will help us manage the project. Note that after the truth is known, and if harm from an unpleasant truth really is uncovered, it really does harm the project and needs to be included in any subsequent risk and value calculation; it is only before exposing such a risk when planning which action to take that it is counted as a benefit of that action.

In contrast, if you take an action that increases the harm due to incompetence or negligence, you cannot ignore the direction of change. If you create this "bad harm" then you do have to take the direction of change as increasing the total harm.

Assuming that the CR Engineering team thinks that the pilot study will either reduce the existing harm if the engineering approach works or will create “good harm” if it doesn’t, they can proceed to calculating the results of their experiment. If they don’t know what the chance of success vs. failure is, they can start with guessing that it might be equally likely to fail as to succeed. In that case, the average change in harm after their experiment would be the average of the two numerical changes – ignoring the direction of the change – which is 70%+8% divided by 2 = 39% beneficial change in harm. In contrast, as mentioned above if we had taken the “all harm is bad” approach then the experiment would have increased the harm by 31% [average of -8% and +70%] and the natural [but incorrect] conclusion would be that it should not be done.

If the team does have reasonable estimates of likelihood of success and failure based on something other than wishful thinking and faith, perhaps their statistical track record, then they can use them in the calculation. For example if they have succeeded in overcoming engineering problems 90% of the time in the past, their estimate would be that this technology has a likelihood of success of 90% and will fail 10% of the time. If they ran 10 projects 9 of them would have a -8% change in existing harm and only one of them a +70% creation of good harm. The average is [[9x8%] + [1x70%]]/10, which is 14.2% beneficial change in harm.

Interestingly, this shows that the more successful they are likely to be, the less valuable the pilot study is – the change in harm has gone down from 31% to only 14% when the probability of success has changed from 50% to 90%. This makes complete sense – in the ultimate case if they are completely sure of success [0% failure] the pilot study becomes useless – they might as well do the whole development program with the final technology from the beginning without wasting time and effort on a pilot study. In contrast, this type of approach shows that when the risk of failure is high, a pilot study becomes more and more valuable – and you don't need to create a computer model to do this for every new project.

Choosing the most cost-effective actions within a single alternative or project.

You can repeat this process for different risks for different decision alternatives, or for different ideas to address the same risk within a single alternative. If you just want to choose the actions within the same alternative that are most cost effective in terms of their ability to reduce harm or to create "good harm" then you don't need to do anything other than repeat the above process for each possible action and rank them from best to worst in terms of change in harm per unit cost of the action. Then you can simply choose the actions that are at the top of the list respecting any constraints as to sequential order and create the project strategy.

Selecting the best actions within one project or alternative:

- Within a project the most cost effective actions are the ones with the greatest effect on reducing existing harm or increasing "good harm", for the least cost.

Monetizing risks to choose actions across alternatives, and to ensure that actions are worth more than they cost.

Things get more complicated when you are comparing different actions across different projects. In fact for results like the one above where the result is asymmetric [a -8% or a +70% change in harm] if you are maximizing and have the resources you'd need to create a statistical model – and that is beyond the scope of this book.

There are some situations where you can do without the complexity of a model, either because the situation is simple or because it is more complex but you can accept an approximation because your resources don't allow you to create a model.

Taking the simplest case in the intelligent packaging example, recall that the pilot study cost $100k and is able to change the harm by 39% when failure and success are equally likely. Using those two numbers we can calculate the value of a 1% change in harm using that approach as $100k/39 = $2500. In the case where success is much more likely, and the harm was only 14.2% the value of a 1% change in harm is $100k/14.2 = $7000. If you don't know or can't calculate the value of your project then this is all the calculation needed – you simply select the actions with the greatest harm reduction per unit cost and do them, and don't do the ones which have a negative value.

Monetizing reductions in "bad harm"

When you do know the value of the project then harm can be monetized. In this example, we estimated initially that a 1% reduction in harm had a value of $37,000 by looking at how much the net present value was discounted by the harm and simply dividing the loss in value by the % harm. In situations where there is no "good harm" creation then you can simply do this for all opportunities to mitigate harm and compare the cost of the harm reduction with its value. You can do it both within and across projects. You will need to calculate the amount of harm reduction by substituting the new harm % – post mitigation – for the old number in the deterministic calculation and re-doing the whole harm calculation. For example, in a project that had 3 harmful issues each worth 20%, the total harm would be calculated as follows:

First issue – 100% less 20% gives a residual "project life" of 80%
Second issue – The remaining 80% life is discounted by proportionate 20% which is 80%-16%=64%
Third issue – The remaining 64% life is discounted by proportionate 20% which is 64%-12.8%=51.2%

The project life has been discounted to 51.2% of its original, which gives the harm as 48.8% as this is 100% minus the surviving fraction of 51.2%

Now let's say that you have mitigated one of these issues from 20% to 10%. Repeating the same calculation with 20%, 20% and 10% [in any order] gives a new number for the surviving fraction of 57.6 and a total harm of 100-57.6= 42.4%. In other words, mitigating one of the issues by 10% reduced the overall harm by 6.4% - not the same as simply subtracting 10% off the total unless you only had one risk. If the value of a 1% change in harm is $37,000 then this change would "liberate" $236,000 worth of value - $37,000 multiplied by 6.4.

If you have mitigated all 3 risks, then you will need to decide whether you are going to value them one at a time, as if you can afford to do only one of the proposed mitigation actions. Perhaps you can do any 2, or all 3 of them. The overall calculation is the same for each situation – and must be re-done for each - but if you are doing 2 or 3 risks together, you will need to apportion the value increase to each risk. For example if you mitigated of 2 risks, one with a 5% harm reduction and one with a 10% harm reduction and you calculated your total value liberation as $300,000 for mitigation with both approaches then this would be apportioned $100,000 for the 5% mitigation and $200,000 for the 10% mitigation.

A word of caution – while this approach is good discipline, don't treat the estimates as exactly equivalent to real money. It is good for comparing alternatives, and a rough idea of value, but it contains too many assumptions to be regarded like cash, rather it is a marker of monetary value. For that reason, I suggest leaving a safety margin of at least twofold between the value and the cost, so actions that cost half as much as the value they purport to liberate start to arouse suspicion.

Monetizing increases in "good harm"

For projects where you do create good harm by uncovering an unpleasant truth that changes the percentage substantially you have 2 options. Firstly, you can ignore the good harm part and just estimate the value for true harm reduction. In the example the harm reduction from a successful pilot study was 8% for a price of $100.000 which is $12,000 per percent harm reduction. I showed that 1% reduction is worth $37,000 so it looks like good value – liberating 8 x $37,000 which is $296,000 for a cost of $100,000.

However, I don't like ignoring the creation of "good harm" because it is the type of action that might not happen if it wasn't valued – it's called living in denial! The problem is that you don't know the value of "good harm" because if it is large you terminate the project and that particular project becomes valueless. However, you do actually create real value by terminating projects with "good harm". All the futile expenses and resources that would have been consumed by that project are saved. You are also freed up to move on to new value creating projects more quickly, so including an approximation for good harm value is desirable. I can make a simple estimate of this if just pretend that the value of the good harm is similar to the bad harm reduction. In my example I'd say that a 1% increase in good harm was worth $37,000, just like a 1% reduction in bad harm. By doing this I am saying that if I reveal the truth that happens to be harmful, then this creates value that is similar to what I would have obtained from reducing the existing harm by the same percentage. Of course I don't know what the real value of that is without a model, but this approximation is surely better than not including it at all.

Whether you choose to pretend that creation of "good harm" doesn't exist or whether you include it as approximately the same value as reducing "bad harm" depends on your environment. If you need to create incentives that will enable people to be motivated to be curious about revealing unpleasant truths [such as the pharmaceutical industry] then you will need to include creation of good harm in your risk measurement and tracking.

Unfortunately this is not very common: business owners classically have numerous metrics for costs, business performance and numbers of projects that all incentivize teams to keep projects alive and not to be terribly curious about risks. If the processes are well known and risks are rare, then perhaps measuring "good harm" creation is not necessary.

Redefining "the right thing" to do when making decisions that involve risk

To recap the overall approach to risk mitigation: identify value, discount it by harm, and to seek cost and effect of mitigation actions. This is quite simple but it is not often practiced. Actually I'm being kind – I've NEVER seen it practiced without help, but perhaps there are some industries that we haven't worked in where it is the norm. Quite often an organization or a person seeks to maximize one element of value, cost or risk and pays lip-service to the others. Organizations or people that focus on managing risk may pay too much for trying to reduce risks that are not sensitive to change – that's the argument used by the Bush administration for not signing-up to the Kyoto accord on climate change. A focus on value may lead to exposure to risk because the company is reluctant to detect and expose risks that actually exist, lest they be viewed as destroying value. That's the accusation that was laid at Merck's door by tort attorneys over the withdrawal of Vioxx, a pain drug that was associated with increased risk of heart attack. A focus on cost leads to cheap programs that are not liberating the full value or exposing all the risks, which is a criticism sometimes leveled at the biotech industry. It is only by including all three elements in the process that these factors can be balanced, and my assertion is that even if this involves some approximations, it is better to do it imperfectly than not to do it at all.

Cost-risk-benefit management

- The "right thing" is to liberate the most value through resolving the greatest amount of risk at the least cost
    - Identify the value
    - Discount it by harm
    - Identify risk mitigation actions and their effect on harm
    - Create "good harm" by revealing unpleasant truths
    - Reduce "bad harm" by reducing seriousness or probability of driving issues
    - Execute the actions with the greatest effect on value and risk per unit cost

Making risk-risk tradeoffs that aren't monetized; example - mitigate your personal health risks for cardiovascular disease

If you live in or near Massachusetts, Framingham does not seem such an extraordinary place. However, if you are a health-care professional the name does have a special significance, being associated with a dramatic improvement in the understanding of cardiovascular disease [CVD].

In 1948, one of the most important epidemiologic studies into cardiovascular disease was started: the Framingham Heart Study. The National Heart Institute (now known as the National Heart, Lung, and Blood Institute or NHLBI) commenced a long-term study of the residents that has now covered 2 generations, has expanded the collaboration with Boston University and is starting the third generation of studies. At the time, little was known about the general causes of heart disease and stroke, but the death rates for CVD had been increasing steadily since the beginning of the century and had become an American epidemic.

One of the major research achievements was to use the epidemiologic data to create a scale that predicts 10-year cardiovascular risks – of heart attacks, angina, stroke and peripheral vascular disease – from common demographic information and simple diagnostic tests such as blood pressure and cholesterol. You can look up the scale on www.framinghamheartstudy.org if you want to predict your own risk of getting cardiovascular disease in the next 10 years.

Let's say I am a typical middle-aged American and here are my results:

Factor	**Result**	**Framingham Points**
Age	50	8
HDL ["good" cholesterol]	40	1
Tot Cholesterol ["bad" cholesterol]	210	2
SBP [Systolic blood pressure]	140	2
TOTAL		**13**

If I am a male non smoker, and I am not diabetic, my Framingham score of 13 points – according to the website – predicts my 10 year risk of significant cardiovascular disease or stroke to be 15.6%. Of course without knowing my genetic and environmental factors this score is not individualized but it is a reasonable guide. And it's a scary number – 16 people out of a hundred like me, or about one in 6.

So I have a talk with my physician about reducing my risk factors and I hear about the following ways of mitigating my risks:

1. Take a generic statin to lower my cholesterol by ~30-40%
2. Take a patent protected statin to lower my cholesterol by 40-60%
3. Initiate a diet and exercise program to lower my blood pressure and increase my good cholesterol
4. Take blood pressure medication to lower my blood pressure

None of these sounds terribly attractive – I don't like the idea of taking drugs and diet and exercise seem equally unappealing. However, my doctor explains that if I did these things, the Framingham equation predicts that I could halve my risk of CVD from nearly 16% to 8% or maybe even better if I respond well. Before agreeing to anything, I go home to think about the impact of these things on my life, using a risk mitigation process.

There are a series of reasons that drive me to maximize: decisions about my cardiovascular health have a high value of success and high harm of failure. Through my imagined "Decisionability window" on the relation between effort and decision performance I see that increased effort in making this decision could lead to a much better decision. There is a lot of knowledge available and I don't need to be expert to get it. Finally, the Framingham equation shows that for me, results in all of the diagnostic tests show increased risk, improving any or all of them will affect my risk.

However, I am just not sure that I can do all of those things at once. In fact, I know that I just cannot face doing all of them; but I might do some of them. Each of the alternatives changes the value and each has a different cost on my life, so I decide to go through them individually, as shown below.

The first option, of taking a generic statin reduces my cholesterol by 30% or more and buys me 2 points on the Framingham score. I see from the table on the internet that this translates into a reduction in the probability of a serious cardiovascular event from 15.6% to 11.2% - or 4.4% probability, or to put it another way, in 100 people like me about 16 would get CVD within 10 years but this would be reduced to about 11 if they reduced their cholesterol with a generic statin.

Having scored the benefit, the next step is to score the cost to me – the impact of having to take this drug every day for the rest of my life. The drug is generic so doesn't cost me anything on my current medical plan, but there are side effects and emotional costs to include. Research on the internet shows me, that aside from some muscle fatigue and occasional liver monitoring requirements, these drugs are pretty safe. I therefore try to assign it a quality of life [QOL] score: how much of my entire benefit of being alive is lost through taking a tablet with this safety profile? Perhaps 1%, the apparent minimum would be appropriate? Is that true for me – initially perhaps it doesn't feel like enough? But then I think how few minutes a day would I actually suffer when taking this tablet even though I don't like the idea of it? I decide to allocate it a cost of one percent. This option therefore gives me the value of a 4.4% reduction in risk for the cost of 1% of my quality of life.

The second option, of a statin that is still patent protected and therefore more expensive than the first, is of no more benefit than the generic as far as the Framingham equation is concerned. Does my doctor think I get any more benefit from another 15% to 20% reduction in cholesterol that isn't shown by the Framingham equation? The answer is "perhaps", but my physician can't answer this question exactly. However, my prescription plan still covers this drug 100%, and the risk of muscle side effects and liver side effects are probably a bit lower. I therefore give it the same benefit of a 4.4% reduction in risk [with the possibility of more but I can't score that precisely] but do lower the quality of life cost to 0.5% of my quality of life because of the reduced side effects. If I were paying for it myself, there would be added costs, but given that I am maximizing and there is no financial cost to me because of my health insurance plan, this is invisible.

Option 3, diet and exercise would potentially give me 2 to 3 points on the Framingham score, which moves me somewhere between a 4.4% reduction and 7.2% reduction in cardiovascular risk, an average of about 6%. However, I have tried both of these options unsuccessfully before, so I discount the value by 50% for the probability of failing to adhere to the regimen – my benefit is therefore 3% risk reduction when discounted for failure. I have also found that the diet and exercise negatively impact my quality of life; I love food and feel miserable when dieting, so I score the cost of this option as 10% of my quality of life. I therefore get a 3% risk reduction for a 10% cost to my quality of life.

Option 4, to take a blood pressure medication is another option that scores me 2 points on my Framingham score, lowering my risk by 4.4%. The tablets' side effects are a little more than for statins so I score the cost as 1.5% of your quality of life.
Looking at the scores, I have created a rank-ordered list from best to worst:

Rank:

1. Option 2: taking a patent-protected statin: 4.4% risk reduction for 0.5% cost to QOL
2. Option 1: taking a generic statin: 4.4% risk reduction for 1% cost to QOL
3. Option 4: taking a blood pressure medication: 4.4% risk reduction for 1.5% cost to QOL
4. Option 3: diet and exercise: 3% risk reduction for 10% cost to QOL

If I pick the highest statin option [option 2, patent protected statin] and the highest blood pressure option [option 4] then I get the biggest benefit for least cost. Both of these give me a much greater benefit for less cost than the diet and exercise option, so I choose to continue to be a couch potato and not select option 4. I don't know exactly what the risk reduction will be for me personally, but in a population of people like me it would approximately halve my risk – a reduction of 8% – at a cost of only 2% of my quality of life. If I added diet and exercise the cost would be 6 fold greater on my quality of life than my selected options but the benefit would only be another 3% in absolute terms, about a third in relative terms, so I don't think is worth it.

I also don't know exactly whether I would convert a 1% reduction in my quality of life into a 1% reduction in risk, but I don't have to worry about precision here because the numbers for cost [2%] and benefit [8%] are quite far apart. I might have to pay more attention to the conversion of QOL to risk perhaps if diet and exercise was the only option available to me because there the QOL reduction of 10% is numerically greater than the risk reduction of 3%. But thanks to those big bad pharmaceutical companies, some of the most cost-effective medical treatments ever devised have been invented for cholesterol lowering and blood pressure treatment so I don't have to.

I therefore tell my physician that I will take a patent protected statin and will treat my blood pressure but I can't honestly commit to diet and exercise as I don't believe it is cost effective for me and I don't think it would be likely to succeed. The doctor says my choice is fine, he wouldn't have believed the diet and exercise kick for me anyway – but unless I watch my weight, at least don't gain any more, I might get diabetes which is another 3 points back on the score, undoing all my good work with taking the tablets! So I decide to be a bit more careful with food, but not to make myself miserable by dieting aggressively.

In other words I just made health choices that are similar to those of millions of Americans like me – and the method has enabled me to explain those choices in simple terms of risk-risk tradeoff calculations. Perhaps more importantly I personalized the scoring so that people different to me don't necessarily need to do what is average, but for them what would make the most sense.

How to manage risks when probability is low and unknown: "Black and Gray Swans"

Much of Nassim Taleb's book "The Black Swan" is about failures of prediction. There are many causes of such failures including:

- You may assume a probability distribution and linearity that isn't true
- You may be guessing but pretending you are predicting
- There is more random noise than you think

- You make excuses when you fail, and create narratives about how you were almost right

Taleb tells us that where you anticipate that such situations you should:

"Know how to rank beliefs not according to their plausibility but by the harm they may cause."

Much of this and the preceding chapter has assumed that you can identify bad things that might happen, how likely they are to occur and how much you might be able to change these things. But what happens when this is not true? What happens when you identified all serious risks in the risk identification program that I described above, but some didn't contribute to your score because you have estimated the probability and it is very very low, or because you can't even estimate a probability?

The solution is that you look at those types of risks and if there are any very simple or cheap actions that you could take to mitigate their seriousness then do so. For example, I identified a possibility that a passer-by might be a crazy hatchet murderer in my risk identification for getting directions when I was lost in Boston. This is so rare that it wouldn't score on a harm assessment, but there is nothing to stop me choosing a passer-by that is pushing a baby buggy - at least it excludes hatchet murderers who aren't good at disguises. Alternatively perhaps I just don't open the window all the way and keep the car in gear when talking to them. Even better, get my spouse to talk to them!

The point is that when you identify serious risks that are very unlikely, they score low on harm assessments you can still take simple low-cost actions for some of them.

Looking in more detail at serious risks you can probably safely ignore any action that simply changes the probability of occurrence – paying for prevention when the probability is low or unknown is unlikely to be a cost-effective approach unless you have the resources of a large government. It's not impossible, but Taleb would perhaps argue that there are so many opportunities for risk prevention that when you can't predict the probability it is futile to try unless it is cheap. That leaves only two types of actions: firstly those that enable early detection of a hazard if it occurs, with mitigation of the seriousness by prompt action and secondly actions that reduce the seriousness of the consequence even if you miss early detection. Taleb calls this investing in "preparedness not prediction" Given that early detection methods are often cheaper than mitigating the seriousness, the actions for the former are often more attractive than the latter – for example it is far cheaper to have a hurricane tracking and warning system and a comprehensive evacuation plan for a city than to build levees or sea-defenses that are unbreachable; a colonoscopy is cheaper than treating colon cancer, a smoke detector is cheaper than a fire sprinkler system.

Key learnings from Chapter 8:

- Be creative about identifying ways to mitigate harm for your alternatives, ideally before finalizing your decision but certainly afterwards.
- Monetize the reduction in harm by calculating the % reduction in harm and applying that to reverse some or all of the risk discount to value.
- Choose the harmful issues that are most sensitive to change per unit cost instead of simply choosing the most harmful issues.
- Don't assume that changes in harm from an action are symmetrical: good harm results when a negative truth is uncovered and bad harm results from an unintended consequence of a decision or incompetence.
- Prioritize actions within and across alternatives or projects based on the greatest reduction in harm for the least cost.
- Make risk-risk tradeoffs by scoring the outcomes of health decisions by scoring costs in terms of benefit per unit cost in terms of quality of life.
- When you can't make probability predictions you can still rank risks according to seriousness.

Chapter 9
Decision thresholds

When is an "action threshold" needed?

If something is changing and you need to decide how much it should change before acting then you need to set an "action threshold". This happens when:

- There is an effect that varies in size
- There is an effect that varies in frequency or number of events
- There is an effect that varies in frequency and size
- You wish to define a "normal", "tolerable" or "acceptable" range
- You wish to define an "abnormal", "intolerable" or unacceptable range

Complexities when the effect varies in size

The commonest examples of this type of decision are medical tests such as blood-pressure, cholesterol or any new diagnostic test as well as measurements of pollutants in the environment or food.

Life would be simple if the variable is binary – present in the population where action is needed and absent in the no action population or vice-versa and with no overlap between the two. An example that is quite close to this ideal is the human pregnancy test. It detects human chorionic gonadotrophin [HCG] a hormone that is not normally present at all in a female who is not pregnant because it starts to be produced after a fertilized ovum implants in the uterus and starts to grow a placenta – about 10 days after fertilization. If any HCG is detected, it signals a pregnancy with near certainty. The early tests weren't very sensitive though and they couldn't detect low levels of the hormone that were present very early on, so a negative result wasn't as reliable as a positive result and people had to wait a couple of weeks for hormone levels to increase. As tests have got more sensitive, this issue has diminished. Even with this near perfect test though, we can see that the decision isn't quite binary – if there is a positive result it is a near certain yes, whereas if it is a negative test early on, it isn't equally certain.

This is starting to give us clues about how more complex situations arise. The first type of complexity is that there is some overlap in the middle: you know that a big change means the issue is present, and you also know that no detectable effect or a small change means it is absent or requires no action, but there is a gray area in the middle. If you set the decision threshold to be at the low end of the overlap, you will include some changes that aren't real – the "false positives". If you set the decision threshold to be at the high end of the overlap you will miss some real changes, some of your results will be declared negative but should really be called positive – the "false negatives".

There are two approaches to setting thresholds in a case with overlap between the populations. If your situation is entirely driven by human factors – a key stakeholder has in mind an acceptable number for the false positive rate then setting a threshold to get that rate is what you are stuck with. That is unsatisfactory because you don't know where that number came from but nonetheless it often happens – for example new diagnostic tests are often expected to have a sensitivity of 90% - they detect 90% of the true cases but 10% will be false positives. If you aren't stuck with a formulaic human-based number then follow the list below:

1. Score the seriousness or cost of a false positive result (falsely declaring action when it should be no action)
2. Score the value of a true positive result
3. Score the seriousness or cost of a false negative result (failing to declare action when it should have been declared)
4. Score the value of a true negative result

An action threshold is "good enough" when:

- The number x cost (or seriousness) of false results is less than the number x benefit of true results
- The number x cost of false positive results is similar to or greater than the number x cost of false negative results
- A safety margin between value of truth vs. cost of falsehood must be established if
  - The errors are consequential for individuals
  - One party is imposing the costs of errors on another party rather than themselves
  - There is variability in the measurement

The mathematics of how to achieve all this is out of scope here but it is worth knowing the principles because at least it will convince you that setting a threshold isn't a case of picking a nice round number.

Thresholds for events

The issues for discrete events that vary in number are the same as for issues that vary in size – it is merely the frequency that is varying. Otherwise they have the same problems. Discrete events that vary in frequency include incidences of cancer and road traffic accidents. Simply counting events and determining whether they exceed a threshold is simple but can be problematic where different events have different degrees of seriousness. For example, a decision threshold based on number of discrete events is California's "Three Strikes and You're Out" law – where 3 felonies lead to mandatory life sentences.

The downside of simple event-based thresholds is illustrated by the story of Leandro Andrade: on November 4, 1995, he stole five videotapes from a K-Mart store in Ontario, California. Two weeks later, he stole four videotapes from a different K-Mart store in Montclair, California. His history is rather checkered – he had been in and out of the state and federal prison systems since 1982, including convictions for petty theft, residential burglary, transportation of marijuana, and escape from prison. As a result of these prior convictions, the prosecution charged Andrade with two counts of petty theft with a prior conviction, which under California law can either be a felony or a misdemeanor – the prosecution chose to make it a felony. Under California's three strikes law, any felony can serve as the third "strike" and thereby expose the defendant to a mandatory sentence of 25 years to life in prison. Andrade was sentenced to two consecutive terms of 25 years to life in prison. This seems like a disproportionate response given that 2 of the offenses were for stealing videotapes without violence within 2 weeks, but nonetheless California's right to do this was upheld by the Supreme Court. However I don't think many people would call it a "good decision". The key problem is that a credible seriousness measure isn't included – "felony" – wasn't adequate.

Use simple event or frequency counting thresholds when:

- There is agreement on how many events are and are not tolerable

Avoid event or frequency counting thresholds when:

- There is a significant difference in seriousness between events which are counted as the same

Decision thresholds based on size and frequency

When both the size – or seriousness - and the frequency of an issue vary then the threshold must take into account the harm or benefit based on the product of the seriousness and frequency – the tolerability of risk principle that I mentioned earlier for radiation protection and have used throughout this text whenever I multiply probability and seriousness to get a harm score. In this case all that is required is to define a harm score that is tolerable or not tolerable. A subjective example – unfortunately without quantitation - of such an appropriate threshold is laws for sexual harassment, where a single serious event and pattern of more minor events are viewed as equally harmful and intolerable.

A simple strategy where knowledge is sparse: "go" "no go" and "don't know"

The take home message of the chapter so far is that all this is quite complicated. Nonetheless there is a simple method for setting decision thresholds when knowledge is sparse. It starts with the principle that if you don't know enough to set a single binary threshold then don't! A way around incomplete knowledge is to actually set two thresholds. It is often possible to choose a low level for a variable that is almost certainly safe, acceptable or requiring no action – and a threshold can be defined below which the result requires no action. For the same variable, it is also possible to set a very high level that is almost certainly unsafe, unacceptable or requiring action – that is the second threshold, above which almost certainly does require action. Then there is a "gray" or "don't know" area in the middle, in-between the upper and lower threshold. Results in the gray area get discussed individually by a group of knowledgeable people whereas results outside the two extreme thresholds don't need it. It is far preferable to do this transparently rather than pretending that you do know what a single "go/no-go" threshold should be and putting it in the middle of the "don't know" area.

As more knowledge accumulates over time as to where the threshold should be, then the gray area can diminish in size, ultimately becoming a single threshold, but for some issues perhaps this will never happen.

Setting a threshold based on optimal statistical efficiency

If you have lots of scientific data that links the variable you are looking at with the true outcome that you are trying to predict then you can play around with different decision thresholds – from setting a high threshold that would not detect anything [low sensitivity] but if such a huge change was detected you could be sure it was true [high specificity]. Conversely you could set a low threshold that detects almost everything [high sensitivity] but where many of the results wouldn't be true [low specificity]. When statisticians do this they can create a curve that shows the results called a "Receiver Operating Characteristic" curve or "ROC" curve. There is a place in the middle that is optimally statistically efficient, a threshold that gets the best balance between the tradeoff between sensitivity and specificity.

While the statisticians would routinely choose this route, I think it is rarely the best for managing life decisions. The reason is simple: that the method is only best when a false positive result is equally serious and likely when compared with a false negative result. That situation is not often true. For example, for a test like mammography to screen for breast cancer, the consequence of a false positive result is that the person has to have a biopsy which is inconvenient and uncomfortable and has to live with a couple of weeks of unnecessary fear that they might have cancer when they do not. The consequence of a false negative result, when there is cancer but the test says it is not present is far more serious: the person presents some time later when the disease is more advanced and they have a lesser chance of being cured. These are notably different in seriousness and a statistical efficiency approach would not be optimal – it would be better to equalize the cost [probability x severity] of each type of error by biasing the test in favor of high sensitivity even if that means that there would be less specificity and more false positives.

An example of setting a decision threshold where probability and seriousness vary

Brian's company CR Engineering has successfully completed the pilot study we heard about in the last chapter and is now scaling-up production of its intelligent packaging product. Unfortunately the production process isn't perfect and some packages have an error – some of the blisters containing tablets fail to detect when the package has been opened. The package then reminds the patient to take another tablet when they have already taken one that day. The fix to this error is to increase the sensitivity of the film that covers the blister, but this has an unintended consequence in the opposite direction – some packages state that blisters have been opened when they haven't because just handling the foil can generate a "false positive" signal. These errors are invisible to the patients and doctors who will be using the packaging but they create misinformation.

The company can spend money to reduce the error rate but they have realized that it is unlikely to ever reach zero with the current technology. Brian has been asked to define what decision threshold defines an acceptable error rate. He decides to use the methods in this chapter, and he knows that prescribing physicians are the key stakeholder, so he asks a panel of physicians to evaluate the value of the truth and the harm from each type of error.

The value of the truth – from a fully functional package – is that the patient and the physician have a record of what tablets were taken when, and how good the overall compliance with the treatment was. This will enable optimization of the benefit of the medicine. The physician panel likes this approach but feels that the value will vary depending on the condition, but it will be modest – say an average of a 5% seriousness score. The physicians rated this as the improvement in quality of life from the better treatment effect in the population likely to receive drugs in this type of package.

The harm from failing to detect that the package has been opened and potentially reminding the patient to take a tablet when they have already taken one is viewed by the panel of physicians as substantial – many of the patients will be elderly and won't remember that they already took a tablet that day. Some of the drugs in this package will be powerful and doubling the dose on any given day might cause a toxic reaction. The seriousness of this type of effect should it occur would be a lot greater than the average benefit so the physicians score it 50% - causing a side effect that might require hospitalization, or an issue that is ten times greater than the magnitude of the benefit.

The harm from falsely declaring that the blisters have been opened when they haven't is that the patient doesn't get reminded and the physician is unaware of the fact that they aren't opening their tablets at the right time. Although missing a drug is of significant importance, this isn't as bad as taking a double dose. The physicians rate this as 25% seriousness – five times greater magnitude than the intended benefit.

You can see that one of the 2 errors – failing to detect package opening - is twice as bad as the other, so to comply with our principles it should be made to occur half as often as the other error. The harm is balanced when:

Probability of failing to detect package opening error = 0.5 x probability of false opening error

There is only one type of positive benefit or value in this case and the experts scored it at 5% seriousness. In order to comply with my optimization process I know that the value of the truth must exceed the cost of the errors. So the break-even point when the errors are balanced but exactly oppose and neutralize all the benefits and there is no safety margin would occur in the following state:

The packaging works completely 88% of the time:

- benefit = 88% x 5% = **4.35**%

The false opening error occurs 8.6% of the time:

- harm = 25% x 8.6% = **2.16**%

The failing to detect opening error occurs 4.3% of the time:

- harm = 50% x 4.3% = **2.16**%

In this case the benefit of 4.35% in quality of life is exactly balanced by the two types of harm which cause 2.16% harm each. I am not intending to go through the algebra to support this is but those of you who are mathematically minded can do this on a simple spreadsheet. The end result is that the harm from the failures is equal and opposite to the benefit of successes, and that the percentages where each situation occurs add up to 100%.

I haven't finished yet because this merely creates zero value and zero harm – which would be OK if the product had zero price! Beyond the economic problem, because this situation involves human safety, and a risk being imposed on one person by another, we have to declare a safety margin – how much bigger does the benefit have to be than the risk for this to be acceptable to the patients, prescribers and the regulatory authorities? A good rule of thumb for a product that might be viewed as a "convenience" product would be 100:1 – while there isn't a typical number for medical devices, the Environmental Protection Agency uses similar figures, and Brian's Physician panel agrees. Given the crudity of the assessments, it is also a routine to add an uncertainty factor, so they add another factor of 10, which gives a 1000:1 safety margin. The acceptable error rate for false opening errors would therefore be one thousandth of 8.66% which is 0.09% or about 1 in 1100 packages. The acceptable error rate for failing to detect package opening and giving false reminders would be half that figure because it is twice as serious, or 1 in 2200 packages.

Note that I haven't undertaken a full assessment of the risk here because this chapter is about decision thresholds – but it would be prudent to look at human and economic factors here too – is the reputation of the company at risk if they have even a few failures that result in harm to patients (recent experience with the Toyota recalls would suggest so)? Are their competitors already operating at six-sigma [one in a million] failure rates? In either of those cases the safety margin might be increased.

Anyway, Brian reports back his findings to CR research and the engineers are dismayed as they are currently many times worse than his figures and they don't think they can get near to his numbers. The CEO has been looking for a reason to terminate the project and he eagerly does so; he can tell the board their strategy did not work and focus back on what the company was doing when life was good. Brian loses his bonus for the year "for making the wrong decision in the first place" according to the CEO. Brian feels disillusioned because the pilot study was successful, based on probabilistic estimates of success, and he had no control over the engineering department. He decides to take early retirement.

Key learnings from chapter 9:

- You can set action thresholds for variables, for event frequency or both.
- When knowledge is sparse, you should set 2 thresholds – a low one below which you are certain no action is required, a high one above which you are certain it is required, with a gray area in between which is "don't know."
- If the seriousness of a false positive error is different from a false negative error then don't choose an equal likelihood for each, make the worse type of error less probable.
- Aim to make the probability and value of true positive and true negative decisions greater than the probability and harm of false positive and false negative decisions.
- Create a safety margin to define how much greater the value of truth should be than the harm of failure.

Chapter 10

Capturing human preferences: when to use experts wielding sophisticated methods.

Although the scope of this book ends when the method isn't doable on a pocket calculator or a simple Excel spreadsheet, there are some more complex methods that are accessible through online vendors or software products and I'd like to point you in the right direction for situations when the methods you've so far mastered aren't adequate. The methods you've learned about so far are not appropriate when the following criteria are true:

- You are maximizing in a moderate to high value and high harm decision and have the resources, time and access to knowledge to do something more sophisticated
- Features or issues are difficult to quantify so human judgments must be made
- Experts or trusted individuals can be identified and are willing to participate
- The simple quality of life or seriousness assessments in the Decisionability tradeoff process or "even swaps" aren't likely to be precise enough to deliver your maximization
- There are too many dimensions or layers to a decision for the simple processes to work well
- Trust is low or there is a blame culture

One approach to the perception of limitations of the preceding methods is a method named "BOGGSAT" In the words of John Saunders, Information Resources Management College:

"BOGGSAT is an abbreviation for Bunch of Guys and Gals Sitting Around Talking. This is often how major decisions are made. A group vested with a decision, for example selecting a vendor or establishing a security policy, convenes in a conference room. They proceed to spend hours throwing around the pros and cons of one approach versus another, rehashing old points, rarely recording the discussion or process (what process!) and surfacing old feuds. The group also typically suffers from domination by one or two outspoken (yet often also poorly uneducated in the topic) members. Somehow miraculously, 5 minutes before the conclusion of the scheduled meeting an unholy "consensus" is formed. It is unlikely that many in the meeting could tell you how they got there – they just did. And it is also unlikely that they could provide you with more than one or two sketchy reasons on why they made the decision!"

This clearly isn't an adequate improvement on the prior methods you've read about.

Building a statistical model

If there is a lot of actual technical data around then it is very tempting if you have access to statistical resources to simply have the statisticians make the decision for you, using multiple linear regression or analysis of variance. This only works if the decision you need to make is solely based on the technical data – think back to T.H.E Decisionability triangle – are you sure that no human issues are relevant to the decision? If the statistics is going to be an analysis of technical data then are you sure no economics comes into play? If the model is of the economics then are you sure that no technical issues should be included?

Even if you can overcome these shortcomings, then such models can fail because they assume a normal distribution of the data which might not be true [read "The Black Swan" if you want to be scared about statistical assumptions].

Use a statistical model when:

- You have the resources create a model
- There is a lot of statistical data that can be analyzed
- Human factors aren't important
- You can be sure that the assumptions of the model are met by the data you have

Don't create a statistical when:

- Any one or more of the above criteria is not met

If the reason you weren't sure about a statistical model was that it couldn't include the human issues, two human methods that have decent provenance as solutions: Multicriteria Decision Analysis [MCDA] and War-Games or "Business Design Simulation".

Multicriteria Decision Analysis [MCDA] – what is it, how does it work?

MCDA was invented partly as a response to the dysfunction of committees and partly as a response to the human limitations when faced with complexities. The human tendency to reduce the number of choices and leave out information is often quoted by decision theorists as a motivator for using this approach, but as you've seen that is an oversimplification: heuristic-based choice reduction can be efficient and effective and should not be simplistically mocked. Nonetheless, I've accepted that the limits of the methods in this book can be reached and are sometimes found to be inadequate so I will look in a bit more detail at what MCDA is and does.

The commonest type of MCDA is the Analytic Hierarchic Matrix, developed by Thomas Saaty in the 1980's; its key innovation was to create a common metric for people to compare very different issues by means of a series of pair wise preference ratings. These issues to be compared can be entirely qualitative, semi-quantitative or quantitative – but the usual emphasis is on qualitative and semi-quantitative inputs. As its name suggests, the first part of the process after convening a suitably qualified group of individuals to give their opinions is to build a hierarchy. At the top of the hierarchy is the intended objective of the decision – you could substitute the purpose statements that were discussed in chapter 3. In a complex hierarchy there might be a series of purposes but let's stick to a simple one here as the intent of this discussion is to direct you to the right approach rather than to enable you to do it yourself. The next layer of the hierarchy is what we've called "differentiating features" or just "features" – these are called the criteria. Below that are the sub-criteria – features can often be split into different elements below them. Finally the alternatives are mapped to all the criteria and sub criteria. A hierarchy for Samantha's job, the example used in the preceding chapter is shown on the next page.

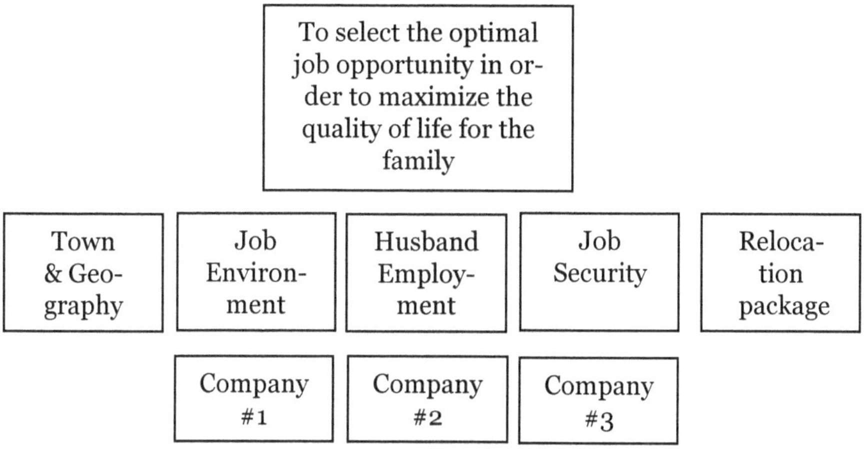

To select the optimal job opportunity in order to maximize the quality of life for the family

Town & Geography | Job Environment | Husband Employment | Job Security | Relocation package

Company #1 | Company #2 | Company #3

3-Layer Analytic Hierarchy for Samantha's Job

The next step of the process is to look at the criteria [I called them features] in the second layer of the hierarchy such as town/geography, job environment etc and to give each of them a "priority" which relates to their importance – but all the priorities need to add up to a total of 1. The clever part about the process is the way such priorities are established through a series of comparisons. For example each of the 5 criteria in our hierarchy would start with a default priority of 0.2 because 5 x 0.2 is 1. But then the software that is used to manage the process requires the participants to make a series of paired comparisons. The first might be: is town/geography more or less important than job environment? The group responds using a scale, traditionally a 1-9 point scale with 1 meaning equal importance, through to 9 being extremely important difference in favor of the first element. This is repeated for each criterion in turn, and internal logic and consistency checks are made so that participants get a warning if they've made some illogical preferences such as: a is better than b, b is better than c, c is better than a.

The software then generates an adjusted weight for each criterion – with the total adding up to 1.

In many hierarchies, sub-criteria can be generated – for example job environment might have sub criteria of company culture, relevance of Jane's skills and job title. The paired comparisons would be done as before for each of these and priorities established for them – but they would add up only to the weight of the "parent" which in this case would be the priority of job environment as a whole. For example, if the priority of job environment remained at 0.2, the sub criteria might have priorities of 0.1, 0.05 and 0.05 respectively – the exact values determined by the preference scoring and the software.

The final piece of the puzzle is to evaluate each of the alternatives, in our hierarchy the third layer down: companies 1, 2, and 3 against the criteria and sub criteria. Once again the preference scoring method is used for each alternative against each criterion. The software then calculates a final score for each alternative.

There are a number of strengths of this method. The use of paired comparisons with consistency checks represents a substantial advance when trying to create a scale – consider how much more sophisticated and precise it is than simply asking people to estimate a quality of life score as I did in a number of examples earlier. It and its variations have a well-established provenance for decisions in many different areas from environmental protection to nanotechnology safety and from government to large corporations. It provides a great framework for a group discussion – and the discussion itself is one of the key benefits of the technique as the participants all feel that they contributed to the scores. While it has its critics, if an organization performs this type of analysis with well-accepted experts from relevant stakeholder groups, it would be difficult for others to criticize. It is therefore useful when there is low trust or where there is a risk of blame if the decision doesn't work out as expected.

However there are some limitations: probability and seriousness are not split into different components, the experts just score them together; this will mean that human traits and biases such as the safe-side heuristic will operate invisibly on the scores. They will truly represent current preferences of the stakeholders; the process will not change their position away from human traits as is possible with probability x seriousness methods and some of the graphical displays. Remember how surprised we were that the harm from damaged vision from Laser surgery was so small because the probability discounted the seriousness? Our preference scores within Multicriteria Decision Analysis would not have delivered such unexpected results.

Another limitation is that the default position is that the analysis is compensatory – deficiencies in one element can be compensated for by gains in others; for many environments this will be just fine, but for some it won't be as good as a non-compensatory method, although the experts have ways of handling this issue. Some concerns among experts exist about accommodating new information, particularly if it changes the existing ranking of information but this appears to be a minor blemish rather than a flaw.

Another issue is that the method also just selects the most preferred opportunity, it doesn't produce an estimate of risk of failure – remember how useful Samantha found her 65% estimate of achieving a perfect job outcome? Well she won't get that from this method and it won't deliver cost-effectiveness estimates or risk mitigation valuations either. Finally, some have criticized AHP as flawed because if a number of "indifferent criteria" for which all alternatives perform equally are included or excluded it changes the priorities and it shouldn't logically do so. Nevertheless, it does have a distinct and powerful contribution to make in the decision-making landscape – the sophistication of different variants has not even been touched in this simple overview. Software is also widely available from online vendors, along with training and education products. If the advantages are necessary and important for your situation and the limitations aren't important then it is an excellent process.

Use multi-criteria decision analysis when:

- You have the resources to call an expert or to obtain training and software
- You are maximizing in a moderate to high value/harm situation
- You need to be seen by others to use a defensible process with real provenance involving inputs from experts - a low trust, high blame environment
- Your most important input is human preferences, especially if regarded as the "truth standard"– either there is little quantitative data or you aren't trying to change preferences

Don't use multi-criteria decision analysis when:

- You are satisficing in high value/harm or are maximizing in low to moderate value/harm
- You want quantitative estimates of cost effectiveness
- Your most important input is quantitative data
- You want to change preferences by revealing something unexpected

Wargames or "Business Design Simulations" – what, when and how?

The term "war-game" in this context means a realistic simulation of a business issue that is either real and ongoing or which is theoretical but might happen. As an illustrative example, I helped to create and run a wargame at Pfizer in 2007 with the assistance of the Institute of Alternative Futures, Washington DC. Pfizer was seeking to understand what its strategy in diagnostics should be; as a pharmaceutical company it could see that in the future, as personalized medicine becomes more widely accepted, it would need access to diagnostic tests to identify the best patients to receive drugs targeted at specific sub-populations. As Pfizer does not own a diagnostics company – unlike some of its competitors – it was seeking the best options for access to this capability. The questions to be addressed were:

- Could Pfizer's needs for diagnostic tests be taken care of by a series of strategic alliances with diagnostics companies?
- Could Pfizer and diagnostics companies reach "win-win" agreements for such alliances?
- What were the different flavors of acceptable deals?
- Would the deals be viewed as acceptable by an internal management committee?
- Would external circumstances affect the relationships between Pfizer and the diagnostics companies?
- What if the USA moved to a single-payer healthcare system?
- What if Pfizer bought a diagnostics company of its own?
- What if an existing diagnostic test had a major and public failure?

- What do other stakeholders think about the deals and alliances?
    - Regulatory authorities, pharmacists, physicians, payors

As you can see, the issues are complicated and quite human-oriented. If we had tried to create a multi-criteria decision analysis it would have been difficult to get experts to agree on a consensus opinion owing to their differing values. We therefore created a 2-day simulation where 6 real diagnostics companies were invited to participate and negotiate simulated deals with "Pfizer deal teams". We also invited a panel of other stakeholders such as pharmacists, physicians, retired regulators and payors to get their observations and to give inputs. Finally we created a virtual management committee that would look at the proposals and give its approval or rejection.

In order to get the negotiations started we had to create a simulated portfolio of diagnostics products that Pfizer wanted, so that the diagnostics companies could say what components they could provide. This required us to survey the real drug teams to find out what they actually needed and then tweaking those requirements to retain confidentiality but not so much that they became unrealistic. We had to structure the days of the simulation with discussion times for teams to reach deals, consult with stakeholders and report back to management. We also created a virtual calendar with "news flash" items that the team had to react to – such as Obama being elected and initiating healthcare reform [in 2007!].

None of that is rocket science but if you haven't designed a game before it is useful to have expert facilitation. The detailed insights from the game are confidential to Pfizer, but it was highly successful at addressing the questions. What was particularly interesting was that the "virtual" deals were not merely paper exercises: the wargame-initiated relationships between Pfizer and some of the diagnostics companies actually led to real deals later. So it was more than a game, partly an incubator of a real relationship.

Wargames are useful when:

- You need insights into motives and behaviors to answer specific questions, the answers to which will change the actions by the game "owner"
- You can create an engaging and realistic simulation
- You know that complex motives and interpersonal behaviors are involved
- You need answers to a number of decisions with numerous alternative options
- You can't predict motives, behaviors and alternatives without a simulation

Wargames are not useful when:

- You need few answers or can't define needed insights
- You can already predict actions based on understanding of known motives and behaviors
- Your key inputs are technical or economic not human
- The resource and cost of creating a game exceeds the value of the insights

Decision Markets

We're all familiar with opinion polls, especially around election time. The trouble with polls is that people don't always tell the truth or they may not really have made up their minds, so there is some variability and sometimes bias. The University of Iowa pioneered an alternative to a simple poll, a "decision market" where people invested a stake for the privilege of "betting" the correct outcome of an election. If they are correct then they make money, and if they are incorrect they lose it. The accuracy of their market result has consistently beaten simple opinion polls. It works because it is anonymous and there is a personal incentive for contributors to do their best to forecast the correct result – loyalty and wishful thinking are probably outweighed by this. The incentive doesn't need to be large to get people to participate in a simple poll; it can be a charitable donation or even "status points". Surowiecki would call it "wisdom" of the crowd, although I prefer to think of it as a statistical analysis of the individual inputs with less bias than usual. There aren't many business situations where a simple poll would need to be maximized like this by bringing in an external vendor of decision-market services. However, some versions can be applied to more complex situations.

In one example application I helped create, a company had a portfolio of ongoing R&D projects where many of them missed their deadlines because of unforeseen issues. The usual situation was that "everything was on target" until the deadline was imminent, and then the team would admit that they were actually going to be late, too late to do anything about it. Management was frustrated because they always heard at the last minute and couldn't manage the resources very well as a result. They were convinced that there were early warning signs but that the teams were reluctant to make them public.

We therefore created a decision market where the probability of meeting a deadline for each project was the target of the poll. Each participant was given $50 to bet on projects – the winnings would go to the winners' designated charities. If project x had a deadline on June 1st then a participant could buy shares in an on-time or early delivery, or different shares in late delivery. The market price relates to the popularity of each type of share, giving management an anonymous indicator of the likelihood of meeting the deadline. For example, if the price of a share for meeting the deadline started at a nominal $10 but the current "price" is only $5 but I think the team will meet the deadline I would buy some shares in an "on time" delivery. The software will increase the price after the transaction depending on how much I buy, so the new price reflects a higher estimate. If I am right and the project is delivered on-time then I can sell my shares for the full $10 but I only paid $5 for them whereas if I am wrong I don't get paid at all and wasted my stake. The software sorts out what each person's winnings are and the ongoing probability score serves as a real-time barometer of risk for management.

That was the theory. In practice we had problems. Firstly, people were already overworked and didn't see the result as useful because it was "only an experiment". Secondly it was time consuming to go through the whole portfolio and decide whether to bet. Thirdly it was frustrating – if the current estimates in projects where you have the most knowledge already agree with your own thoughts, either you can't play or you are forced to take bets on projects that you didn't know. This is because you could only bet to change the price, you don't bet to agree with somebody. Finally, the incentives were small and they were not allowed to benefit the individuals because of corporate policies and laws about betting. As a result, people didn't participate and the experiment failed. There are a number of examples where such markets have worked, but they don't seem to have a broad and simple application, and in the US the incentives must be low or charitable because of laws against online gambling.

Decision markets are useful when:

- You need to extract hidden knowledge from a group of people but currently there are positive incentives to secrecy
- You want to overcome wishful thinking and politics
- You would be able to act on predictions
- People in the market can be rewarded for participation sufficiently to overcome competing pressures

Decision markets are not useful when:

- People can't be rewarded for participation because of corporate policy or laws against online betting
- The predictions you need are too complex to describe – not binary (early vs. late etc.)
- The results aren't perceived as impactful

Key learnings from chapter 10:

- Use Multi Criteria Decision Analysis if you have a situation where human emotional and expert preferences represent key inputs in a high blame high value situation then consider.
- Run a War Game if you have complex but high value/harm situation where you need multiple and specific insights into motives and behaviors.
- Create a decision market if you need to reveal hidden information in simple situations.

Part 3: The aftermath

Chapter 11

It isn't over yet; how to handle the after-effects of your decision

Selecting specific actions

The easiest case is when one of your decision alternatives is so specific that you don't need to add any further complexity: I'll have strawberry ice-cream with a cherry on top please. However, many decisions require new actions to be identified once the decision is taken. You will need to identify a myriad of tasks when you have made the decision to move house or fund a research project. This is easy if you intend to do them all and they are obvious, you just need to define the order, timing and accountability – and perhaps recording of their completion.

However, sometimes there are a number of actions that could be taken but some are not essential to the process of executing the decision – they are not "on the critical path". Should you do all of them, none of them or just some? I already asked this question in chapter 8 as a risk mitigation question: which actions out of the possible total should I execute? To review briefly:

1. Define a near "perfect" decision outcome for your selected alternative
2. Identify all the factors that could harm or reduce this perfect outcome using T.H.E. Decisionability triangle

3. Score each factor for seriousness and probability to get a harm score and discard any rare and trivial effects
4. For the remaining factors identify actions that might reduce the "bad" harm from [or increase "good" harm by exposing unpleasant truths] and estimate their change in harm
5. Score each action for degree of effort/resource
6. Select the actions with the greatest degree of change in risk with the lowest degree of effort
7. Separately, for rare but serious problems ["black swans" or "gray swans"] even if they don't score highly, identify any cheap actions to reduce the seriousness if they occur

If you are maximizing in a moderate to high value/harm decision and you didn't use the process in chapter 8 then it would be worth going back to the appropriate option – now you only have to do it for one alternative rather than all of them.

Herding Cats - Back to Mission Leadership

Once you have taken the decision you may need to involve new people. Hopefully you already involved relevant people in shaping the decision, but now that's done it often happens that new people will be expected to carry out some of the subsequent actions. For all decisions – even if you aren't going to do the action tradeoff – it is simply worth reviewing the original purpose statement and going through it with everyone involved in its execution. Now that you have taken your decision what is the intended effect of your actions and why is the outcome important? You might need to adjust the wording of the "what" because your mission isn't simply about selecting alternatives any more but in executing it properly, although the "why" part of your purpose is likely to remain the same. The impact of doing this is to ensure that your proposed actions are still aligned with the purpose.

For example recall the "failed" staffing computer model that was built but never implemented. The undeclared purpose of that "failed" project without a "why" was "to build a computer model of staffing and resourcing across the company". Here is a list of actions that would plausibly result from that imperfect purpose:

Actions:

- Select vendor by competitive bidding
- Acquire appropriate budget approval
- Identify representatives from each department to give inputs
- Vendor creates model
- Model is reviewed by management and adjusted by vendor
- Model is switched on and tracks resourcing by month
- Management is informed of results

However, if the purpose had been consistent with my recommendations it could have been: "To consistently adjust departmental resources across the organization to the meet predicted requirements in order to maximize operating efficiency". Then in addition to the above tasks a number of new critical actions and decisions would have been obvious and necessary:

- Create a method for error control
- Define a policy on what actions are required if the model says a department has too few or too many staff
- Create initial action thresholds and pilot them in one department or subsets

- Create a communication and education plan
- Create incentives for compliance

The important thing with mission leadership though is that the outcome, the intended effect is paramount; if the tasks initially selected turn out not to work, or not to be the right ones because they aren't achieving the purpose then the people accountable for executing the process have to try something new. For projects that require creativity or must respond to changing circumstances, don't obsess about the exact nature of tasks but do ensure that people are well aware of the mission, why it is important, the constraints and how they will be measured. This will give direction and accountability but without the rigidity and creativity-destruction of "command and control" that so failed the Prussians 150 years ago.

Monitoring decisions, risks and adapting to change

If you are maximizing in a high value/harm situation then you will need to monitor the effects of your decision using the metrics that you proposed alongside your decision purpose, or you will need to make some up now! Once again it is a good idea to seek metrics in technical, human and economic domains; there are several types of metrics:

- Actual successful outcomes – effects of the decision: life, death, moving into a new house, acceptance of a job, payments received

- Surrogates for actual outcomes – measures that are known to correlate to outcomes: improved cholesterol or blood pressure, contracts signed, job offers accepted

- Leading indicators of success – measures that are on the path to a successful outcome: job offers received, milestones passed for R&D projects, positive emotion, offers placed or received, risk resolved

- Completion of tasks or activities – actions that might lead to success: sending off CVs in response to job advertisements, doing an experiment in an R&D project

The least desirable metric is the completion of a task – it doesn't ensure that the outcome is being delivered at all and can lead to a checklist mentality. I have to admit that I keep lists of tasks and enjoy crossing them off but I am not going to pretend that is how I monitor the success of my decisions, and when I worked in a large organization I resisted the temptation to track task completion of my subordinates. The point is to keep focused on the successful decision outcome and to perform whatever tasks are necessary; if the first ones you try are not working then you will need to keep coming up with creative ideas to ensure that the intended effect of the decision is achieved.

If your decision contained uncertainty and you have used the Decisionability tradeoff method to estimate decision risk then you can simply continue to update the same calculations [but in this case is restricted simply to your chosen alternative rather than all of them] as you get new information. This will help you see the change in risk as "bad harm" is reduced or "good harm" is exposed from your actions.

The metrics and risk tracking are methods of measuring effects that are predicted and expected. Decisions should also be monitored for unexpected negative or positive consequences – the most important part of damage limitation from a wrong decision is early detection that something went wrong.

Changing your mind

If some elements of your decision contained estimates of probability, and seriousness then it is legitimate to consider changing your mind if a) something turns out to be more serious than you thought it would be and b) something is more likely than you thought it would be [a risk you estimated at significantly less than 100% actually came to pass].

If you are maximizing a high importance decision and are tracking your risks this will be obvious. There isn't a hard and fast rule for changing your "go" into a "stop" decision based on a new risk, but the key is: is there a better alternative or can you mitigate the adverse effects of the current course of action? If you have done a quantitative analysis of value discounted by risk vs. costs then it is usually worth switching or terminating action when the remaining discounted value is less than the costs because of the emergence of risk. Switching to another option with more unknown risk isn't necessarily better – you may be in the same situation as now when you have uncovered some risks, and switching sometimes carries costs too. However, as in the contact lenses vs. laser surgery example, when 2 alternatives have similar value and risks, and one has low switching costs [contact lenses] then start with that one and switch if the adverse effects are greater than expected.

The two kinds of error are: failing to switch to a better alternative when you should, and switching to an alternative that isn't legitimately better too quickly. If you can't estimate the probabilities of either then use the safe side heuristic – go for the one with the lowest adverse consequence.

Not deciding and "keeping your options open" is actually a decision. Even though it loses the benefits of deciding, those lost benefits might be forever silent; it successfully avoids the effort of deciding and it avoids the potential harm of making a wrong decision. However, not deciding should be treated like a decision option – and if the harm of indecision is potentially high, and there is no benefit to indecision, then it should be compared with other decision options using one of the methods I've described.

If the purpose of the decision contained elements of emotional wellbeing then your emotions or feedback from others will be important. Even if you didn't have explicit emotional effects as part of the desired outcome, it is still worth listening to emotional feedback – personal feelings of unease should be analyzed because the "giant computer" of your brain is sometimes right, and has analyzed complexity and identified a problem. For decisions that are made for entirely human benefits, it is often difficult to predict in advance whether those will be achieved; I have a friend who routinely buys expensive handbags and clothes, and then returns most of them because she can't predict how great the pleasure of ownership [vs. the regret of purchase] will actually be until she has purchased them. In cases such as that, when the benefits are difficult to predict and the consequences of changing your mind are trivial, then decisions can be made and unmade freely [although handbag stores might not agree].

What happens when it looks like a mistake?

When a decision fails to deliver the intended effect, there are several possible courses of action; see if you can spot the correct answer:

1. To hide the evidence and quickly distract everyone with a decoy drama: "if at first you don't succeed then bury the evidence you ever tried"
2. To blame somebody else for not doing their part, it wasn't your fault
3. To openly admit the mistake, and quickly move on to the next thing
4. To neither admit nor blame but have the decision audited in neutral fashion and determine what action should be different or the same next time. Communicate learnings to others.
5. To assert that you didn't actually make a mistake by presenting evidence to the contrary to anyone who will listen
6. To falsely admit what you don't believe to be a real mistake for the "greater good" of supporting an open culture that admits mistakes
7. To be silent on whether a mistake is made or not

Although we've all seen blame, hiding mistakes and decoy dramas I am not going to recommend any of them as legitimate responses – before taking any action you need to establish whether a mistake was actually made [i.e. #4] – and that's the purpose of the next section.

When is a mistake a mistake.... Or not?

You will need to examine your potentially mistaken decision to find out which of three scenarios is true:

a) The decision was actually successful but somebody is calling it a failure because of misunderstanding or to seek political advantage
b) The decision was unsuccessful because of one or more mistakes
c) The decision process was perfect but the intended outcome was not achieved because of random chance or a completely unforeseeable effect – the "noble failure"

In order to consider whether you have any grounds for defense under a), you will need to show that you defined a purpose in advance and that you defined and made credible measures of the intended effect, and their results support your claim that the decision was indeed successful. If you don't have measures of the effect you are going to have to fall back on a "correct process" defense. You should critically and honestly review your process: did you correctly determine your maximizing/satisficing strategy, was the choice of method aligned with the importance of the decision, did you correctly identify whether uncertainty was important and did you identify and fairly evaluate all the alternatives? In military circles this is sometimes done by means of a board of inquiry or even a court martial – which can be welcomed by the decision-maker as a means of clearing suspicion that would otherwise have lingered. If you realize that you did not after-all use the appropriate process then admit the mistake, learn and move on. However, if you remain convinced that no mistake was made, and in the absence of a board of inquiry, the course of action you take – from being silent to vociferously defending your position – should be treated as another decision: what is the current state, the desired future state, the purpose of the decision and so on? Only then should action be taken if the benefits exceed the costs and risks – or not taken if they don't. Here are some examples of failures in the decision process:

Issue	Example Mistake
Failing to correctly and explicitly identify the decision purpose	Invasion of Iraq
Use of a non-compensatory principle that harms the greater good	Pope Benedict's antipathy towards condom use: prevention of extra-marital sex trumped HIV in Africa
Failure to involve key stakeholders in decision problem/alternative assessment:	Disposal of Brent Spar oil platform – original at-sea plan torpedoed by environmentalists
Failing to use a decision method that is "good enough"	Failing to let-go of the safe-side heuristic: not vaccinating children against measles
Failing to include and evaluate fairly all the alternatives and their features	Inefficient subsidies for bio-fuel made from corn – vs. sugar-cane, nuclear etc.
Using decision methods based on certainty when the situation is uncertain	Having a investment portfolio for retirement that is entirely made up of stocks
Failure to identify predictable unintended consequences	Public anger over "retention bonuses" paid to AIG executives after its' bailout
Failure to mitigate predictable risks and costs	US auto industry

In contrast to failures of process, below I present a table of "noble failures" – where the process and actions were reasonable but the decision outcome was not achieved through unforeseeable or random issues:

Example Decision	Why This Was Not A Mistake
For first-responders to enter the burning World Trade Center when it caved-in on top of them	Building collapse was almost inconceivable; failing to act would have killed people; no time to assess risk/benefit
To launch and market drugs which were subsequently withdrawn for unforeseen safety problems e.g. Trovafloxacin, Vioxx	Clinical trials were well conceived and well executed in large numbers of people – yet cannot ever eliminate the possibility of rare but serious side effects.
"I decided to eat nutritious food, exercise regularly, have all my health screens and I took all my vitamins – so why did I get cancer?"	Taking the right actions simply changes the probability for the better but does not create certainty.
"I drove a safe car, stayed alert and kept to the speed-limit but somebody driving while texting hit me head-on."	Taking the right actions simply changes the probability for the better but does not create certainty.

The allure of blame: when to use it and when to avoid it

The key appeal of blame is that it offers a rapid and beguilingly simple route to reduction of fear:

1. Create a simple narrative of how the problem, failure or tragedy arose
2. Punish, fire or eliminate those responsible
3. Feel reduction in fear that the problem won't happen again
4. Relieve the anger because the crime has been avenged

in 1692, Betty Parris, age 9, and her cousin Abigail Williams, age 11 had fits that were described as "beyond the power of Epileptic Fits or natural disease to effect" by the local minister. The girls screamed and made strange sounds and behaved in weird ways: they threw things about the room, crawled under furniture, and contorted themselves into peculiar positions, according to the eyewitness account of a minister in the town. The girls also complained of being pinched and pricked with pins. Other young women in the village began to exhibit similar signs and symptoms. The village, of course, was Salem Massachusetts; the end result was that 150 people were accused of witchcraft with 19 of them executed.

Reflexive blame is lazy and naïve – a simpler alternative to making difficult harm-harm tradeoffs or accepting that there really are random uncontrollable events that can hurt you. It can be regarded as another inappropriate use of the "safe side" heuristic: if failing to blame somebody who really is responsible is regarded as much worse than accidentally blaming somebody who is innocent then the person driven by instinct will choose the lesser error and blame aggressively. This can be self-directed or externally-directed.

The advantages of the strategy to externalize blame are its simplicity, its immediate effect on reduction of fear or dread, the convenient provision of a target for anger when a decision didn't deliver the intended effect and the personal satisfaction that it is somebody else being blamed this time not you. The disadvantages of blame are its injustice, the destructive effect it has on innovation and risk-taking in the future and the corrupting effect it has on good decision-making practice – which subsequently becomes entirely focused on blame avoidance rather than obtaining a potentially more valuable outcome for a decision. It can become a convenient habit or it can be used as a method of control and power in an organization. Having been a recipient of the latter at one point in my career I can attest to its effectiveness for control: when I wasn't eating antacids I was entirely consumed with acquiring evidence that would prove that I was continually being unfairly and unreasonably blamed for things that were either beyond my control or were invented by my manager. Of course that reduced my effectiveness in the organization and neutralized me as a perceived threat – which was of course the intended outcome!

While such a "blame culture" is destructive, it is probably better than a culture that has no blame and no accountability, where the risk of corruption is high, mistakes are not admitted or exposed and no learning takes place. Today's media can be argued to provide a useful oversight "blame" function to political and corporate systems that are viewed by an untrusting public as fitting all of the attributes above. Unfortunately if the source of the assertion of blame is wrong then the cost of blame can be higher than its benefits. The ideal alternative is to have an "accountability culture" where decisions are examined faithfully and impartially. The intent is not to blame but to expose mistakes so that they can be used to teach organizations and individuals learn and improve –although individuals can be held accountable too. Mistakes are discriminated from "noble failures" and people don't get blamed for creating "good harm" through the exposure of unpleasant truths. This is much less destructive than the blame culture but only seems to appear where the organization is perceived as having reasonable levels of integrity and trust. There appears to be a requirement for a perception of "common good" or "greater good" that supports the process and which overcomes self-interest. Air-traffic controllers, airline pilots, the military and increasingly doctors and hospitals are adopting procedures like this to reduce risks without losing the benefits of talent, creativity and innovation.

Key learnings from chapter 11:

- After you have made a decision, firstly identify and execute actions that are essential – i.e. "on the critical path".
- Then identify and prioritize optional actions using their contribution to the degree of change in harm for a given effort or cost.
- Review the decision mission; now that the decision is made the purpose "what" should be reworked if necessary, the constraints and metrics created and people engaged in its execution; the "why" is likely to be unchanged.
- If you are maximizing, you will need to monitor effects of actions and progress; don't simply track tasks but follow outcomes or leading indicators of success.
- You can change your mind if something changes but before doing so calculate the costs and benefits of doing so vs. staying the course.
- Even if your decision did not turn out as expected it may not be a mistake; if an unforeseeable or random event occurred it is a "noble failure."
- Review and learn from past decisions openly without blame.
- Avoid blame and being blamed; it is convenient and lazy. While it is better than corruption or pretending mistakes don't happen it is not as good as an accountability culture.

Chapter 12

How to smell and avoid decision poop

What do you do when you are confronted with the common verbal assault to "join" "buy" "do" "believe" or "contribute"? The purveyor of the information is earnestly and compellingly presenting you with the supporting information to help you make the choice that they want you to make. The first and natural response is to reduce your need for information if trust, friendship or a positive track-record are present, and the opposite if it is absent. That approach has serious limitations; this brief review is intended to enable you to be constructively suspicious whatever the source of information.

Questions to ask about information quality – could it be poop?

Here are the key questions you should be asking when confronted with an assertion, no matter how confidently or aggressively it is delivered:

1. How would they know that?
   - What kind of information would be needed?
   - How would it be measured?
2. Is it likely that the information actually exists or is it just an unsubstantiated theory?

As an example I'm going to create a hypothetical "Eye Color Diet" as the illustrative subject of these tests of suspicion. Any resemblance to existing or future diet books is purely coincidental, this is entirely fictitious [although I must credit Laurie Beebe "The diet coach" for first having the idea of a spoof eye-color diet]. The plausible-sounding theory I am selling to you is that eye color is a genetic link to a preferred diet type based on whether your ancestors lived in bright sunshine in which case they consumed big-game, ate meat and had brown eyes or whether they lived in more cloudy and rainy shines where they could grow crops more productively and were therefore blue-eyed vegetarians. The theory says that if we "eat for our eye color" we will have an immediate feeling of improved health as well as long-term beneficial health effects. The first test of suspicion is how would this information have been acquired?

The key eye colors are blue, gray, green and brown. My diet book [watch out for it in print shortly!] makes recommendations for each of 10 components of our diet for each eye color, that's 40 components. All I needed to do to prove my theory to write my diet book was to perform some scientific research where each dietary component was tested in each eye color and to measure the responses of the people I studied.

I am hoping that you will "presume innocence" of me and my theory so you will only seek support for it. When I show in my study that I gave people the recommended diet and they felt better I know I am on to a winner. What I don't want from you is "healthy suspicion" where you would take the opposite tack: presume that the diet doesn't work – that it is no different to any other diet – and to make me disprove that assumption. This assumption, that there is no difference, is called "the null hypothesis" by statisticians and trying to disprove it (i.e. when you show as false your assumption that there is no difference that means that there is a real difference) is almost universally recognized as the standard approach to research questions like this. But of course I hope you don't take that tack because then I have to study a lot more people.

The other thing that I hope you don't question is that the people in my study felt better when on the diet I ascribed to them. I am hoping that you don't know that people who know what treatment they are on and who have been told that it will help them routinely report feeling better. That is why scientists often "blind" the recipients as to which treatment they get to protect against the placebo effect. Sometimes even the investigators might bias their responses too, so studies are run "double blind" where neither the patient nor the investigator knows. When studies are run "blind" the people who ran them are proud of the fact that they were so rigorous, and broadcast that fact loudly; so the fact that I didn't tell you my study was blinded is highly likely to signal to you that it actually wasn't. Finally I don't want you to ask if there were people who were deliberately assigned to the wrong diet or no diet for comparison with my correct-diet group. That type of study is unattractive to me because I would need to study several different groups, and it is much less likely to give me the answer I want. So I am not telling you exactly what type of study I did.

But you can work out what I should have done and maybe you can see from the scant details in my diet book whether I was on the right track. Based on what I wrote about typical rigorous statistical approaches you might come up with the following design that you'd like to see:

4 groups of people –one for each eye color – of people of similar weight, age and demographics would be recruited. These people should not be told which eye color and diet type pairings are deemed "correct" by the diet theorists. Each group would be split as follows:

- A "control" subgroup that receives a normal diet of equivalent calories to the others, but nothing to do with the diet under test
- A subgroup that receives the "correct" diet for their eye color – as per diet book recommendations
- Three other subgroups that deliberately receive the "wrong" diet for their eye color

That's six subgroups for each eye color, or 24 subgroups just to see if the complete recommendation program worked. If the "wrong" diet groups did worse than the "correct" diet", and the "correct diet" did better than the "control" groups, then the results would be considered promising. The next phase of rigorous research you'd like to see me do would be to run new studies to show the contribution of each sub-component of my diet; where each of the 10 components of each diet would be removed or added for each eye color type to see if that made a difference. That's a study of 40 subgroups. Finally, given that the claims aren't just for "feeling better" but are for improved health outcomes, you'd like to see that I followed these people for at least 2 years and looked at their health outcomes. Then you'd like to see me repeat the key studies and get the same results to "confirm" that it wasn't just chance that could account for the results. Overall that's 128 subgroups of subjects, probably of 50 patients per group that would be studied for 2 years each. And that's a minimalist program – in order to make a public health recommendation based on the work, studies in thousands of subjects would be needed. The minimalist research program would take approximately 10 years and would probably cost about $5.1M.

Even without the hassle of looking for hidden results or details of clinical trial design in my diet book [I surely do give a publication reference in a journal but you'd have to go to the trouble of getting it from the library and unfortunately it is in a very obscure journal], you can ask yourself: is it credible that I, a simple author of a diet book would fund such an expensive and complicated study? Is it in my interest to fund such a study when people buy the book without it? Your Suspicion should be high!

For the above situation it is obvious that the practical and cost limitations cast a doubt on my diet book. However, sometimes suspicion does not depend on practicality; here are questions that can be asked independent of the practicality issue:

1. Vested interests:
    a. Has the information come from a trusted and independent source - independent from the party that is going to gain from your acceptance of the information?
2. Fairness and Logic:
    a. What are the alternative explanations or hypotheses? Are they presented fairly? At all?
    b. Has the evidence been fairly evaluated for supporting and refuting positions?

There are a number of unfairly appraised assertions in decision-making books. For example in Gladwell's "Blink", the finding that physicians who were more liked by their patients were less likely to be sued was taken to support the hypothesis that patients brains' subconsciously computed when doctors were better. However it is equally likely – but not mentioned – that doctors who are better liked are simply less likely to be sued even if they have the same malpractice error rate. That doesn't support any computation hypothesis – just that when you like somebody more you don't sue them as often. Why do you think the opposing hypothesis wasn't mentioned? In Surowiecki's "Wisdom of Crowds" the assertion is that "we've been programmed to be collectively smart" – and the ability of bookmakers to set point spreads on sporting bets is taken as supportive evidence; but the failure of crowds to predict the final scores of NFL games is because they don't have a "crystal ball". The latter evidence doesn't support the hypothesis so it is dismissed as irrelevant.

So far you've potentially aroused your suspicion based on impracticality and cost, on vested interests and logic, now I introduce another way of creating a healthy skepticism is by looking for sound statistical principles. This doesn't mean you need to be a statistician but just look out for some good practices even if you don't know how to do them yourself:

Statistics:

1. Are there any formal statistical tests?
2. If they are present, are they correct?
3. If they are missing, why weren't they done?
4. What hypotheses were tested?

I've discussed my "eye color diet" above and I am disappointed that you have such a high suspicion that there is insufficient evidence for my theory to create enough confidence for you to buy the book [and subscribe to my eye color food supplement program]. But what if I tell you that on my website I can show you real feedback from dieters showing that over 70% of the people in each eye color group on my diet report that they feel better than before they started the diet – 70% is a good statistic isn't it? The first statistical question I don't want you to ask me [wearing my diet book author hat] is compared with what? The 70% isn't really a statistic, it's a proportion. Has it been compared with other diets using a named statistical test? Er, no but they don't get such high percentages. How often could chance account for the results? No tests are available because no comparisons appear to have been made. What about people who tried the diet and did not report to the website: the most likely explanation for the results is that people who liked the diet were more likely to report their progress and feelings on the website than people who didn't like it. Why is this likely? Because it is a well known phenomenon called reporting bias – favorable results are far more likely to be spontaneously reported than unfavorable ones.

I could tell you that the people responding to my website were likely to be right because crowds are wise. In "The Wisdom of Crowds" where Surowiecki asserts: "if you ask a hundred people to answer a question the average answer will often be at least as good as the answer of the smartest member.... You could say we've been programmed to be collectively smart". But this is simply a property of the statistics of averages: the inputs from the one hundred individuals contain "noise" and "signal" but when averaged together, the "noise" occurs in random directions and cancels out and the estimate of the "signal" becomes more precise – yes, more precise than the estimate of any one individual. This is simply the beauty of statistics which is completely independent of the wisdom or idiocy of the crowd.

Signs that arouse suspicion: does it smell like poop?

Here are some more signs of a bad smell:

A vivid narrative

The concern that I have with vivid narratives is that they are intended to substitute for evidence or logic, they are a bit like non-compensatory principles except more subtle. Here are a few:

- I love the idea that a simply measured biological characteristic like eye color might connect me with my caveman ancestor's diet so I will feel better and be healthy.
- I am attracted to the concept that I might be able to solve complex problems by "thinking without thinking".
- It is surely right that some corporate project of no gain to me should be stopped because it harms the habitat of red squirrels.
- It would also be very convenient if crowds were inherently wise so I just get a well composed group together and my decision problems are over.

However, I am immediately suspicious of all of these vivid, simple and attractive narratives because I feel the tug of the whirlpool sucking me into suspension of disbelief; in my stubbornness I seek the comforting presence of logic and data before I stop paddling and allow myself to be sucked in. Books like "Freakonomics" and "Predictably Irrational" achieve that balance of narrative and evidence very well, but their message isn't quite as simple and vivid as others. And by the way I only started to believe in organic food after the publication of real evidence of superior nutritional value, not because of the attractiveness of the "organic" moniker. And I'm still suspicious of "all natural".

Promise of easy gains without any risk

"Easy way to make money with no risk or commitment involved", "learn how to make money online – easy, free, no risk" "Easy Bank bonuses – virtually double your money with no risk".

These are just a few of the thousands of hits on a Google search of "easy" and "no risk"; but why do they arouse suspicion? The fundamental flaw in the logic is: what do they need you for? If what was being said was the truth, providers of business capital would be providing money or the business owners would be doing it on their own without you.

Pandering to dread, fear of the unknown or lack of trust

An article in Ethicos, in 1994 reports: In the annals of business ethics, the fall from grace of Dow Corning Corporation was particularly precipitous. Here was one of America's 100 most profitable industrial companies. Its high-level Business Conduct Committee, which dated back to the 1970s, was considered an industry model: It conducted annually some 25 face-to-face audits worldwide with employee groups. More than ninety percent of Dow Corning employees considered the company "highly ethical," according to a 1988 company survey, an exceptionally high rating.

That was all before the silicone breast implants scandal. Even though the health hazards associated with the silicone implants came to light gradually, over years, the defining moment for John E. Swanson was a June 1991 story in Business Week magazine (dated June 10, 1991). This was the first article that alleged that Dow Corning concealed documents about the product's safety. "It was the first time the company's ethics were questioned in a public way. To me, it was a shock," recalls Swanson, then manager of internal communications and the sole permanent member of the company's Business Conduct Committee. After 26 years with the company, "I thought I knew where all the skeletons were." The article alleged that silicone breast implants could deteriorate and leak, wreaking havoc upon a woman's immune system. The company had long maintained that the implants it manufactured through Dow Corning Wright, its subsidiary company, would last a woman's lifetime. At the time of the article, approximately 1.5 million to 2 million women had had silicone breast implants. It was the third largest form of cosmetic surgery after nose and liposuction operations. Nevertheless, Business Week charged that the industry had known for a decade of animal studies that linked implants to cancer and other illnesses.

By 1994, Dow Corning faced 20,000 individual lawsuits, filed for bankruptcy protection and subsequently paid $3.2Bn in a class-action settlement. Appeals against the settlement continued until 2004 when the company was finally able to end its bankruptcy.

That's a great narrative, and I do love a good corporate scandal. Unfortunately, extensive, well-conducted and independent research has shown that silicone has no effect on the immune system or on the risk of cancer. Even though the truth was unknown at the time, the dread of serious effects and sympathy for individual victims coupled with the lack of trust of a faceless corporation incorrectly biased conclusions.

Reliance on relationship or friendship rather than information

Returning a favor and voting or accepting based on a friendship is a normal part of life and politics – but you should always know what you are getting into. Particularly if the consequence of poor or biased information is serious, more serious than losing a friendship, you should acquire a full and balanced appraisal to protect your own reputation, to ensure integrity and ethics and to understand how big a favor is being asked.

Key learnings from chapter 13:

- An assertion may sound plausible but a good check is to estimate what information would be needed to make that conclusion? Is the research or information practical and is it likely to have been done?
- The information could be poop if it has not come from an independent source.
- Check the logic and the fairness of the evaluation – it could be poop if it is this simply a narrative where the owner has only sought supporting evidence and hasn't looked for alternative explanations.
- Look for statistics – the absence of any test is a whiff of poop; formal tests smell better but can be cleverly manipulated so check what was compared with what.
- Vivid narratives often conceal a lack of evidence; the more vivid and attractive the story, the more you should seek the foundation of evidence for it.
- Dread, fear of the unknown and lack of trust cause our judgment to warp – another strong smell that should lead to an increased emphasis on seeking the foundation of factual and balanced evidence.

Appendix 1

Answers to Decisionability quiz

Recall that the correct answer to every question in the quiz was "no". Now that you have finished the book, see if your score has improved! I give the rationale for the "no" answers below.

1. I always seek the best decision by carefully considering every possible alternative

This is only true if you are maximizing. You should not always be doing that.... [Page 104]

2. My life is dominated by rules and others' decisions so I have very little need to decide for myself

Rules are clearly not optimal in most situations [p32], and hopefully even if the answer to this question was previously "yes" you have some alternatives to rules or to letting others decide.

3. I often feel overwhelmed by the choices I have to make

Well I am sure that it was already obvious when you answered the quiz that the correct answer to this question had to be no. However, even if you felt it was true for you before, perhaps you can now try out some new methods of limiting the number of alternatives such as the "take the best" heuristic? [p161]

4. I feel guilty or regretful about many of my past decisions

If you answered yes, maybe some of your past guilt was misplaced – are you needlessly blaming yourself for decisions that included some uncertainty, and luck wasn't with you? If you use the Decisionability tradeoff method in future you will be able to estimate the probability of success and know that you can't get a success rate of 100% even when you do everything right [p201]. Analyzing your mistakes may show them to be "noble failures" instead [p283].

5. I put off making key decisions because the information is incomplete and I dread being wrong

If you answered this question as a "yes" then you are behaving like "cautious Dick" in chapter 4 [p101]. You need to assess the relative consequences of not deciding, deciding with incomplete information and being wrong.

6. I hate committees because their decisions are often the lowest common denominator

If you enable your future committees to escape the terror of BOGGSAT [p264] by defining a purpose statement [p59] for a decision and include the appropriate Decisionability methods [chapters 6 and 7] then there is no reason for this to continue to be true.

7. I pride myself on always being fast and decisive without the need for others' input

If you answered "yes" you are "Decisive Jane" in chapter 4 [p101]; while this is often a useful skill it is a satisficing strategy and sometimes you need to maximize.

8. I only need my brain to decide, calculations and models aren't ever necessary

If this is true for you then "Blink" must be your favorite book; unfortunately it is only sometimes true; read when heuristics reach their limits in chapter 6 [p135].

9. If things didn't turn out the way I wanted it is a clear signal to me that my decision was wrong

This self-blame may be misplaced if your process was correct but uncertainty in some of the issues was inevitable [p207] – in other words a "noble failure" [p289].

10. I don't know what a heuristic really is and I don't care

If this was you in the beginning at least you now know what one is and I hope you care a little more, as they are frugal, fast and perform quite well enough for low to modest value decisions in situations where the heuristic fits the situation [p135].

Appendix 2

References and recommended further reading

Simple Heuristics That Make Us Smart – Gerd Gigerenzer, Peter M Todd and the ABC Research Group

The Black Swan – The Impact of the Highly Improbable; Nassim Taleb

Freakonomics – A Rogue Economist Explores the Hidden Side of Everything; Steven D Levitt and Stephen J Dubner

Calculated Risks, How to Know When Numbers Deceive you; Gerd Gigerenzer

Smart Choices – A Practical Guide to Making Better Decisions; John Hammond

Predictably Irrational – The Hidden Forces That Shape Our Decisions; Dan Ariely

The Paradox of Choice – Barry Schwartz

Alemein – Stephen Bungay

Think – Why crucial decisions can't be made in the blink of an eye; Michael LeGault

Why Decisions Fail; Paul C Nutt

The “Go Point” – Knowing What to Do and When to Do it; Michael Useem

How we decide – Jonah Lehrer

The Compleat Strategyst; J D Williams

Wharton on Making Decisions; Stephen J Hock and Howard C Kunreuther

Harvard Business Review on Decision Making;
Peter Drucker et al.

Nudge – improving decisions about health wealth and happiness; Richard H Thaler and Cass R Sunstein

Blink – the power of thinking without thinking; Malcolm Gladwell

The Wisdom of Crowds – James Surowiecki

About the Author

I was born in the UK and went to college in London at Charing Cross and Westminster Medical School where I got my medical degrees and my PhD in human physiology. I trained in radiology in Newcastle upon Tyne, but decided that I liked research too much and joined the Experimental Medicine group at Pfizer in the UK. The purpose of this group was to make go/no go decisions about new drugs quickly while spending as little money as possible.

I moved to Connecticut USA in 1993, still with Pfizer and ran experimental drug programs in depression, head injury, stroke, Alzheimer's, inflammatory bowel disease and urinary incontinence. I learned a lot about the way doctors make decisions – and how companies do. I started the Clinical Technology group in 1997 which grew to about 40 people across 5 sites and I became Vice President, Worldwide Clinical Technology in 2006.

I was responsible for a number of "best practice" initiatives in project selection, biomarkers, diagnostics and drug advancement. I survived 6 reorganizations but not the 7th and I was laid-off in 2007. At that point I started Decisionability, a consulting company with my business partner Declan Doogan, and we helped a number of small and medium companies improve their decisions and developed some of the methods in this book.

I was also on the National Advisory Council for the National Institute of Biomedical Imaging and Bioengineering where I learned about how government agencies make decisions, and on the Executive Committee of the Biomarkers consortium.

About the Author (Continued)

I have published about 30 articles in peer-reviewed scientific journals on subjects ranging from technology, drug efficacy and business strategy to the development of evidentiary standards. I am also on the faculty for the UCSF-FDA American Course on Drug Development and Regulatory Science.

I am currently Chief Medical Officer for a revolutionary diagnostics company, SomaLogic, where we are developing tests based on measurement of proteins in the blood, and accompanying them with decision-support tools to help patients and doctors make the best decisions for their health. Ultimately this will lead to the "Wellness Chip", a multi-dimensional annual screening test for the early detection of all the most important diseases, along with decision-making tools and displays that help the patient and the physician take the right actions.

I live in Boulder CO with my wife Elizabeth and youngest children Mia and George, while my two older girls Jessica and Antonia live in Boston and Connecticut respectively.

www.ingramcontent.com/pod-product-compliance
Lightning Source LLC
LaVergne TN
LVHW020531100826
845148LV00010B/1419